D1569312

TRIALS
of the
SELF

TRIALS
of the
SELF

*Heroic Ordeals
in the Epic
Tradition*

George deForest Lord

ARCHON BOOKS
1983

PN
56
.E65
L67
1983

© 1983 George deForest Lord   All rights reserved
First published 1983 as an Archon Book,
an imprint of The Shoe String Press, Inc.,
Hamden, Connecticut 06514

Printed in the United States of America

*The paper in this book meets the guidelines for performance and
durability of the Committee on Production Guidelines for Book
Longevity of the Council on Library Resources.*

Library of Congress Cataloging in Publication Data

Lord, George de Forest, 1919–
   Trials of the self.
   Bibliography: p.
   Includes index.
   1. Epic literature—History and criticism. I. Title.
PN56.E65L67   1983   809.1'3   83–11727
ISBN 0–208–02013–6

DABNEY LANCASTER LIBRARY
LONGWOOD COLLEGE
FARMVILLE, VIRGINIA 23901

For Robert and Penny Fitzgerald

οὐ μὲν γὰρ τοῦ γε κρεῖσσον καὶ ἄρειον,
ἢ ὅθ' ὁμοφρονέοντε νοήμασιν οἶκον ἔχητον
ἀνὴρ ἠδὲ γυνή· πόλλ' ἄλγεα δυσμενέεσσι,
χάρματα δ' εὐμενέτῃσι· μάλιστα δέ τ' ἔκλυον αὐτοί.

Contents

Acknowledgments

Like its predecessor, *Heroic Mockery: Variations on Epic Themes from Homer to Joyce* (1975), *Trials of the Self* had its origins in English courses taught at Yale. It, too, owes a great deal to the insights of some remarkable undergraduates, of whom I will mention only two of the most recent, Joyce Davis and Anuradha Malhotra. I am also indebted to two research assistants, Susie Berger and Dan Sherer, who toiled patiently through bibliographical esoterica in pursuit of the alchemist's stone.

Among older friends and colleagues who read parts of the book at various stages I wish to acknowledge the generosity of Richard Brodhead, June Guicharnaud, Paul Fry, John Gardner, Richard Drake, Charles Feidelson, Robert Fitzgerald, and Walter Schindler with the customary *mea culpa*, here all the more deeply felt because of what may appear to be the vaulting ambition of this project.

Much of the necessary research and writing was made possible through a senior fellowship from the National Endowment for the Humanities for which I am profoundly grateful. An earlier version of chapter 4 appeared under the title "Folklore and Myth in *Paradise Regain'd*" in *Poetic Traditions of the Renaissance* (ed. Maynard Mack and George deF. Lord [New Haven, Yale University Press], 1982).

G. DEF. L.
Yale University
1 February 1983

We have in mind the problem of the self that is "no self" but on the contrary a transcendent self . . . metaphysically distinct from the Self of God and yet perfectly identified with that Self by love and freedom, so that there appears to be but one Self.

Thomas Merton

From the lyre of Herakleitos to the spectrum of Jung, the soul holds polarities in harmony. It is psychic connection. But now the ego, having replaced the soul as the center of conscious personality, cannot hold the tension. With its disjunctive rationality it makes divisions where the soul gives feeling connections and mythic unities. So the soul has become unstrung; its suffering and illness reflect the torn condition of the split archetype, which the soul by its nature has in its capacity to re-join once it is allowed to return from its exile in the unconsious to its original place at the center of polarities.

James Hillman

Introduction

The purpose of this study is to explore the ways in which the heroic ordeal of individuation and the mythic patterns that surround it relate to eight works that either belong to the genre of epic or may reasonably be construed as having central affinities with "comic" epic, comic because the narrative pattern relates both the success of the hero in search of himself and his success in restoring or preserving his culture. This central experience, as archetypal myth or "monomyth," is fundamental in many epics and illuminates, even though it does not govern, some major post-Miltonic works. In moving from epics of the heroic quest for self-discovery and cultural renewal—here the *Odyssey, Aeneid, Inferno,* and *Paradise Regain'd*—to later works in which the quest is not successfully completed, or only partially so— here *The Prelude, Don Juan, Moby-Dick,* and *Heart of Darkness*—I shall concentrate on the thematic, structural, and stylistic aspects of each work as they are influenced by the full or partial presence of the archetype or by its absence.

A point central to this study is made by Frank Lentricchia in *After the New Criticism:*

> The much-documented shift from classic to romantic is massively summed up in M. H. Abrams's *The Mirror and the Lamp,* a book whose title metaphors signal a loss of all external spiritual authority as sanction of redemption, and the concomitant rise of the self—respectively God and Satan of romantic humanism—as the naked and apparently unsupported source of the autonomous imagination . . . : all in all a dubious, because inevitably ironic, authority for redemption.[1]

Along these lines we shall trace through our exemplars the shift from "external spiritual authority" to the "rise of . . . the naked and apparently unsupported human source of the autonomous imagination." The works by Homer, Virgil, Dante, and Milton all posit a

1

truth that is objective and supernaturally authoritative, while the later works project a reality that tends to be relative, unstable, and subjective. For the objective reality that shapes these epics and the hero's quest we find instead, in the later works, versions of ordeals that tend to be subjective and fundamentally egotistical.

The familiar classic/romantic dichotomy has been fully explored and provides one entrée into the comparative study that follows, but the Jungian myth of individuation and the rites of passage of Van Gennep, Joseph Campbell, Edward Edinger, and Carl Kerényi are more comprehensive. Such a process cannot be fully expressed in discursive terms, of course, but it can be identified through some of its essential features clearly enough to prove that such a monomyth is the thematic and structural center of the "comic" epics under consideration. In the later works it may have a variety of subliminal influences, or, in some instances, it may affect the meaning of a work by its absence. My final aim, therefore, after determining the ways in which each work conforms, or fails to conform, to the archetypal myth of individuation, is to examine specifically the influence of that full or partial conformity or nonconformity with the monomyth on the structural, thematic, and stylistic properties of each work. For example, as the mythic influence diminishes, the narrative structure of the work tends to become less conclusive and reveals a high degree of indeterminacy, ambiguity, and irony. At the same time the hero's ego-centered quest necessarily falls short of his goals and may even lead to results that are the very opposite of those he sought. Such openness and indeterminacy, such ironic reversal of great expectations, as in an Ahab or a Kurtz, is obviously not limited to the nineteenth century, but characterizes a prevailing aspect of the literature of our own Age of Anxiety.

One of the most relevant brief definitions of the monomyth is Joseph Campbell's:

> It is the business of mythology proper and of the fairy tale to reveal the specific dangers and techniques of the dark interior way from tragedy to comedy. Hence the incidents are fantastic and "unreal": they represent psychological, not physical, triumphs. Even when the legend is of an actual historical personage, the deeds are rendered, not in lifelike but in dreamlike figurations; for the point is not that such-and-such was done on earth; the point is that before such-

and-such could be done on earth, this other, more important, primary thing had to be brought to pass within the
labyrinth that we all know and visit in our dreams.[2]

The quest of any heroic avatar, to succeed, must conform to the
archetype. Despite Campbell's insistence on their psychological,
rather than physical, character, we can more accurately say that the
hero achieves physical triumphs whose ultimate validity depends on
their being profoundly psychological as well. If we consider the host
of debased, doggedly imitative romances that turned the wits of Don
Quixote, we may find that, despite the role played by magic and the
supernatural in them, they tend to lack the psychological or mythological substrate Campbell speaks of. The same can be said of many
picaresque fictions, in which the hero's story merely witnesses his
luck, pluck, and cunning in achieving material success.

Tragic, as opposed to comic, epic is marked by the failure of the
hero to develop a personality that is a fully individuated self from one
that is constituted by the ego. Achilles in the *Iliad* is a prime example
of that stubbornly ego-centered personality that implicitly feels any
threat to the hegemony of the ego as death. With the exception of a
ritual reconciliation with his peers in the funeral games for Patroclus
and the anagnorisis which Priam's appeal for the release of Hector's
body helps to bring about, Achilles is a hero incapable of change or
psychic growth. His view of a short but glorious career in which he
will surpass all his peers amounts to a hubristic projection of an
insatiable ego that implicitly pursues a more than mortal goal. Like
many tragic heroes, Achilles challenges the Absolute and is inevitably
destroyed by it. His commitment to his own uniqueness makes him
obsessive and unbending, and so his feeling the death of Patroclus as
an unparalleled loss sets him on a course of berserk vengefulness that
violates all standards of behavior, human or divine. It is this uncom-
promisingly egotistical spirit of revenge that has long been recognized
as a threat to society, at least since Virgil portrayed it as such in
Turnus's character. In certain crises Aeneas himself regresses into
this psychological condition. The domination of the ego in the hero
annuls any possibility of attaining the individuated self and freezes
his personality in a condition that Homer implies is primitive,
archaic, and antisocial.

Thus the hero of comic epic must be capable of the humility,
courage, and psychological flexibility to respond to his archetypal

ordeals successfully and in a way that allows for personal development. As a palindrome of Achillean heroism, the *Odyssey* presents us
with a hero whose broad and profound vision of life enables him to
confront a variety of ordeals in an original and creative and versatile
manner. As the man who is *polutropos* (well-rounded) he attains a
capacity for psychological growth that accompanies his noted self-
control. Odysseus sets the pattern for a new kind of heroism that is
mature, creative, and social and is to be found to a significant degree
in Aeneas, Dante the pilgrim, and the Jesus of *Paradise Regain'd*. All
four exemplify the paradox of true strength: that it cannot be seized
by direct action, only by humility or patience. The self that develops
in the process establishes the objective values and points of view to be
found in each of the epics and becomes associated with the divinely
inspired wisdom of the poet. The retrospective character to be found
in Odysseus' account of his adventures, in most of the *Aeneid*, in the
poet Dante's narrative of the infernal ordeal he once experienced, and
in the emphatically teleological experience of the meditative Jesus
marks the authentic self that reflects on the creation of its own
selfhood.

Such retrospective emphasis is scarcely to be found in the later
works. In Wordsworth, the poet and his experiencing persona are not
firmly established or distinguished. Since Don Juan undergoes no
significant change, a retrospective account of his development is
impossible. Ahab's Achillean obsession with vengeance absolutely
prohibits psychological growth, despite his incidental lapses into fits
of compassion or self-pity. Kurtz perhaps exemplifies a demonic
reversal of the quest for individuation, and the only retrospective
summing-up he supplies is in his dying words, "The horror! The
horror!" The firm perspective of the established self toward which the
hero of comic epic struggles entails a centripetal journey. In the last
four works considered here, the perspective is unstable and the
movement centrifugal.

These works exemplify, intentionally or not, the traumatic
plight of the personality that cannot develop beyond the ego-state
because it is incapable of seeing, in Jung's words, "the psychological
necessity for a transcendental subject of cognition as the opposite pole
to the empirical universe."[3] Dominated by the empirical, these
ventures are aleatory wanderings rather than fulfilling quests.
Wordsworth tries to see providence in random errancy, Byron makes
a joke of it, and both Ahab and Kurtz strive to impose their egotistic
psychological projections on the empirical.

The aleatory character of these last books is evident in their styles and structures. *The Prelude* wanders from the Miltonic sublime, to low, often satirical, realism, to odelike apostrophes to Nature. *Don Juan* oscillates between the satirical Miltonic sublime or elegiac and the farcical. The prevailing grandeur of style in *Moby-Dick* is intermixed with much technical description and digressions that often seem arch or pedantic. Marlow interrupts his straightforward narrative to complain of the inadequacy of any linguistic means to convey the bizarre and horrible experiences he is trying to relate. As we shall see, the fragmentation of style is a consequence of the disappearance of the controlling and authenticating myth. Another equally significant consequence is the frequent interruptions of the narrator, speaking *in propria persona*, in contrast to his virtually anonymous role in epic proper, where he subordinates himself to the Muse or to the established truth of the heroic tale he tells.

Thus the structures and styles of the *Odyssey, Aeneid, Inferno,* and *Paradise Regain'd* are not only more formal and integrated than their successors; they are also much more impersonal. While the comments and autobiographical digressions of Byron threaten to shoulder aside the nonentity he has chosen as the hero of his *soi-disant* epic, we find at the other extreme, in the *Odyssey,* a narrator who surrenders himself so completely to the Muse for whom he is a mere voice that he allows himself not even the *I* by which the other poets briefly refer to themselves. Such anonymity and impersonality in the narrator are possible because of his commitment to the absolute truth of his tale and his confidence that his point of view is established by divine providence or by the authority of his mythic archetype.

On the other side, epic impersonality allows us to be involved more intensely and more intimately with the hero's experiences than does the intrusiveness of authorial comment. The epic narrative, virtually without authorial mediation, is much more absorbing and, in its own way, more personal than the later examples under consideration.

The Prelude, Don Juan, Moby-Dick, and *Heart of Darkness* share several essential properties with true epic. As I have said, comic epic entails on the hero a series of ordeals that determine his success or failure in achieving individuation. Normally the story begins with the hero leaving home, with its protective but unchallenging milieu, on a quest that will establish his separate identity as a person of exceptional courage and wisdom. The journey requires his entering another world, usually repellent or monstrous, with incidental encounters with hostile or apotropaic figures that Jung calls threshold guardians. The other world is typically transpersonal and supernatural and often the land of the dead. Usually he has a guide or some other source of secret knowledge that allows him to travel through an underworld normally forbidden to mortals. On this journey he acquires a mystical understanding of the past and future that will afterward guide him, as an individuated self, in his efforts to return to his society and reform or reestablish it or create a new society. The ordeal of individuation may entail the hero's encounter with and integration with his anima, the feminine shadow aspect of his personality, in what Jung calls the syzygy, derived from the adjective σύζυγος, "yoked together, paired, united, especially by marriage." This monomyth is both personal, in terms of the hero's individuation ordeal, and cosmogonic, in terms of his establishing or redeeming his community. Psychologically, the effect of the ordeal is to transform an egocentric figure into one that is identified to some extent with and by his culture. The transformation is often represented as a transition from the private to the public figure.

So much for the myth that seems to lie at the heart of comic epic. Other features include an action of universal importance; the inclusion of what might be called the genetic code of a culture; the emphasis on social and cultural values; and the continuing representation of the numinous, transpersonal, or divine as the originator and authenticator of the heroic quest. The symbolic death and rebirth of the hero is paramount evidence of supernatural influence.

Out of the mysteries of the ordeal there emerges something like a consensus as to the nature of reality, and the hero's ordeal will be a pattern for the initiatory rites of other members of his society. The periodic celebration of the ritual, as in the "Troy games" of the *Aeneid*, may serve to commemorate the hero's achievements and preserve his society. In the climax of comic epic the hero often triumphs over an enemy who exemplifies the antithesis of the values he is trying to establish, as in Odysseus' defeat of the suitors, Aeneas's victory over the Latins, Dante's triumph over a host of terrible or seductive denizens of Hell, and Jesus' total frustration of Satan's designs.

The relevance of these patterns to the first four epics is easy to see and will be developed later. What is needed here is to establish the appropriateness of the later works I have chosen.

The Prelude, by its subtitle *The Growth of a Poet's Mind*, identifies itself as what Freccero, in speaking of *The Divine Comedy*, calls "a novel of the self." Wordsworth's poem, in relating the experiences that formed his mind, has closer affinities with Dante's account of his intellectual and spiritual ordeal than with the other epics under consideration. The epic qualities of *The Prelude* are especially evident in the first book, where Wordsworth describes his departure from the city and the beginning of his journey as a climax in the recent past, when he set forth, like Adam and Eve at the end of *Paradise Lost*, in the conviction that "the world was all before me," to seek his home. The Miltonic allusion, brief but highly significant and reinforced by Miltonic blank verse, invites us to see the poem as a sequel to *Paradise Lost*. But when Adam and Eve "wander" their guide is Providence, as Milton stipulates, whereas Wordsworth's is "a wandering cloud" under the guidance of which he affirms that he "cannot miss his way." He cannot miss it, I would suggest, for two reasons: since the quest is largely defined as the growth of his mind as a poet, wherever he chances to go will contribute to this inner quest; and (an alternate possibility) his random venture, somewhat like the errant Don Quixote's, he can insist on construing as a developing experience shaped by the end of "growth."

Surely there are elements in *The Prelude* that seem to correspond to the epic hero's quest: the temptation offered by a bedevilled, inchoate metropolis, the infernal ordeal that belies the hero's expectations in crossing the Alps, the numinous encounters with Nature in her sublimest moods, alternating with discouragement, loss of power, and the concluding vision of the ascent of Snowdon.

Thus it seems reasonable to see *The Prelude* as a poem in a recognizably epic style, with the hero's individuation as its subject, and as deserving a place among works in the epic tradition, most of all, perhaps, because it is inspired and motivated by a Nature that is presented as a divine force.

Such epic qualities in *The Prelude* occasionally augment the power of the poem, but in the long run they tend to expose its failure as an epic devoted to the heroic ordeal of self-discovery. This failure, as we shall see, is due mainly to Wordsworth's inability to sustain a distinction between the growing hero and the grown poet, as Dante succeeds in doing in the *Inferno*. Where the alleged process of growth is random and the point of view from which it is related unstable, the autobiographical poem becomes incapable of true completion or closure. In other words, thematic or poetic fulfillment seems to require the authentic presence of myth to establish both the validity of the hero's development and the mature vision of the older self that records it. One might add that the poem's title seems to foreclose the conclusion that Wordsworth tries to make of the vision on Snowdon.

The failure of *The Prelude* as an epic quest can shed light on the relative failure or success of the three remaining works. In some of these, the narrator tends to encroach upon the traditional autonomy of the hero and even, in some cases, to usurp much of the hero's role. Byron is an obvious case. He flouts one epic convention after another and that of authorial anonymity in particular, but he knowingly accepts the fact that his own story is as incapable as Juan's of reaching a significant conclusion. A far more subtle case is that of Ishmael, the chief narrator of *Moby-Dick*, whose ordeal takes him far beyond the stage of development any other character can attain and who seems at the end of the book to have passed successfully the ordeal of individuation. This point may have some bearing on the character of Marlow in *Heart of Darkness*, because he, too, displaces the hero and is, like Ishmael, illuminated, though to a lesser degree, by the manifold ordeals he has undergone.

1   Homer and Home

But such desire is in him merely to see the hearthsmoke leaping
upward from his own island that he longs to die.

Odyssey

Try to imagine life in a world without written words, without signs,
records, or laws, without police or courts, a world with hundreds of
small kingdoms whose authority extends, in most cases, over only a
few square miles of territory. Imagine, furthermore, the difficulties
of traveling across lands where there are almost no roads—the only
one I can recall from Homer links Pylos and Sparta—and where the
only practical way to go is by sea, in small, square-rigged open boats,
without charts, compasses, chronometers, or even the most rudimen-
tary knowledge of meteorology. In addition to these daunting obstacles to travel, consider also that there are no inns, no commercial
vendors of food (raw or cooked) or wine (the staple drink), and no
money.

Homer's is such a world, and both the terror and delight with
which it faces the voyager find their fullest expression in the
Odyssey.

Imagine the courage—or foolhardiness—it must have taken to
leave home and set sail over hundreds of miles of what Homer
repeatedly calls "the pathless sea" in order to spend ten desperate
years of battle on a bare, windswept coastal plain in Asia Minor to
vindicate the honor of an Argive prince whose wife had run off with
an Asian nobleman.

And after the war, imagine the courage—or foolhardiness—it
must have taken to attempt the long westerly voyage home, against
prevailing winds and round tempestuous capes of the Peloponnesus
like Malia. Then add to these deterrents ten more years of wandering
through strange seas beyond the ken of the real world and inhabited

9

only by monsters, witches, and ghosts, most of them bent on one's destruction.

Faced with the journey to Troy and the war there, most of us, I suspect, would choose to stay at home, as Odysseus first did, according to legend. And, after a few encounters with man-eating Cyclopes and Lestrygonians and Scyllas and Charybdises, most of us, I'm sure, would give up with relief the effort to reach Ithaka and settle down to the comfortable routine on Calypso's island.

But Homer's heroes are obsessed with the threat of oblivion. In the *Iliad* the only distinction that survives a hero is the fame he has won, the glory that preserves his *timé* in the minds of generations to come. Governed by the need for preeminent glory, Achilles must be Number One. The enormous funeral mound that he builds over Patroclus's tomb is really intended as a mausoleum for both himself and his friend, a landmark on the eastern shore of the Aegean that future mariners will always remember. Unfortunately, unlike the shaft grave of Agamemnon at Mycenae, it is not there today.

In a world without writing and with virtually no pictorial art, any hero, however glorious his deeds, is haunted by the brevity of human memory. It is this deepseated need to be remembered beyond the ephemeral deeds of one's life that helps us to understand the unique importance of the Homeric poems, poems that are constructed with so much formal skill and organic unity that, once having achieved their final state, they could be memorized and passed on through the race unaltered from generation to generation. The *Iliad* and *Odyssey* preserve not only the history of outstanding men and women from remote times; they also incorporate the code of an entire culture. Rightly called the Bible of the Greeks, the Homeric poems have preserved inviolate the essentials of a high civilization that would otherwise have vanished from our knowledge.

But the Bible is not in all ways a useful analogue for Homer. Its genealogies are traced back laboriously through many generations, while, except in a few cases, the dynasty of a Homeric figure includes only three or four generations, and human origins are lost in the mists of time. Furthermore, the Bible traces, through prophecy and retrospection, human history from the beginning to the end of time. Not so Homer, who can peer no further into the postwar future than to trace the fortunes of the few survivors among the Greeks who made it home. The brilliant civilization he records is a brief flash of light bracketed by darkness. There is neither an overarching providence that will lead to the foundation of a new city, as in Virgil, nor a history that will guide new generations as they face the future. The *Odyssey* sees no future beyond the peaceful death prophesied for Odysseus. Nor is there any afterlife in any real sense of the word, but a shadowy existence in the undergloom of Hades.

Thus Homer's epics alone keep alive the memories of great or notorious men and women, and memory (incarnate in the Muse) is *the* great mental faculty. Both the Parrys have contributed inestimably to our understanding of this point by showing how formulaic phrases, large and small, provided essential mnemonic aids to the singer of tales. In this light the term *epea pteroenta* (winged words), which occurs fifty-seven times in the *Iliad* and sixty-six in the *Odyssey*, is crucial. When I first read Homer, *epea pteroenta* struck me as a pretty conceit, if overdone. It is only now that I feel the terror in the phrase, for, in an illiterate society, words that could fly to the ears of a listener could also fly into oblivion, unless the poet could catch and save them.

It is this terror that words, spoken words, could be the only record of one's life, that provide one powerful motive for Odysseus to persist in his efforts despite all vicissitudes, to escape from an unknown and fluid world and to return home. If he fails to reach rocky Ithaka, it will be as if he had died at Troy. The *Iliad* would record some of his actions there, but there would be no *nostos* and no *Odyssey*.

Another aspect of the oral epic narrative is that it seems to have flourished only in well-established, peacetime communities. There are no epic recitals in the *Iliad*, although Achilles, during his withdrawal from battle, is found in his hut, harping and singing of the deeds of heroes. As records of a great war and the homeward voyages of the Greek survivors, the poems are composed and performed in a peacetime society that embodies the highest culture. Hence the first such performance we hear is in the court of the cultivated Phaiacians, when Odysseus, his seaborne ordeals behind him, is on the threshold of his return home. So epic poetry develops at home, a retrospective and preserving medium that tells us about all the people who left home for Troy, what they did there, and how a few of them made it back.

In one of the most famous ordeals Odysseus undergoes, in the cave of the man-eating Polyphemus, the hero identifies himself to his monstrous host as *Outis*, Nobody. It is this ruse that saves him and his undevoured companions when the blinded Cyclops complains to his neighbors. When they ask who has injured him, he replies, "Nobody", and they tell him to shut up and go to bed.

The name is more appropriate than Odysseus perhaps realizes to his unknown condition in the decade of his wanderings outside the known world. The only way he can escape this condition is to get home, the only place where he can be fully known. He may intermittently boast of himself as sacker of cities, but his full self can be realized only when he is fully reestablished in Ithaka as king, husband, father, master, son, and—most important—as the protégé of Athena, who has finally revealed herself to him again for the first time since the sack of Troy and the destruction of the Palladium.

There are, to be sure, other aspects of identity. When Odysseus congratulates Achilles in the underworld on his privileged status among the dead, Achilles delivers a famous palinode, dismissing such glory as empty, preferring to be the lowest slave of a landless man among the living. The only news that brings him joy is Odysseus' account of the son, Neoptolemus, whom the living Achilles, strangely enough, never mentioned. One might note also by way of contrast that in his first two appearances in the *Iliad* Odysseus identifies himself as "father of Telemachus," thus pledging in his fatherhood a relationship that his long-fatherless son questions in his powerlessness and depression when we first encounter him in the *Odyssey*.

One might also add that for some characters possessions may help to establish identity. Hence the importance of prizes as marks of honor, especially in the *Iliad*, most of all the interchangeable slave girls, Chryseis and Briseis, who are the occasion of the deadly quarrel between Agamemnon and Achilles. On a more practical level, the guest-gifts so often bestowed provide the only portable capital and medium of exchange in a world without money. Sometimes possessions serve as key signs of a person's identity, as, for example, the sceptre of Agamemnon, or the huge Pelian ash spear of Achilles, or the cunningly wrought tunic and brooch which Odysseus wore when he sailed from Ithaka for Troy.

In the long run, though, the Homeric character is identified chiefly by his home. Yet, when one has been absent from home for ten or twenty years, it is easy for a plausible impostor to assume the identity of the absentee, a danger of which Penelope is fully aware.

And what is home? Primarily family relationships, most often signalized by patronymics: Odysseus Laertiades, Penelope, wise daughter of Ikarios, Agamemnon or Menelaos as son of Atreus, and so forth. At times a sense of the peculiar topological and climatic features of the home place are important identifying features. Homer devotes most of book 2 of the *Iliad* to an exhaustive catalogue of the names and home towns (with some local detail) of the Greek chieftains on the Trojan expedition. This recital puts most readers to sleep, and the fact that the poet reinvokes the Muse at the beginning has led to the widespread suspicion that he was himself asleep as he sang it. But, just as G.I. Joe at Bastogne or Inchon or Guadalcanal or on the flanks of Porkchop Hill was invariably responsive to reporters' questions about where he came from, so Homer was recording the participation of hundreds of Achaeans in this archetypal world war and, at the same time, wherever he or his counterparts traveled, satisfying local pride in brief allusions to the salient character of one place or another:

> Of the Boiotians,
> Peneleos, Leitos, Arkesilaos,
> Prothoenor, and Klonios were captains.
> Boiotians—men of Hyria and Aulis,
> the stony town, and those who lived at Skhoinos
> and Skolos and the glens of Eteonos;
> Thespeia; Graia; round the dancing grounds
> of Mykalessos; round the walls of Harma
> Eilesion, Erythrai, Eleon,
> Hyle and Peteon, and Okalea,
> and Medeon, that compact citadel,
> Korai, Eutresis, Thisbe of the doves. . . .[1]

and so on for fourteen pages—a feat of memory that belongs in the Guinness *Book of Records*.

It is the peculiar horror of Odysseus' situation when we first hear of him in the *Odyssey* that, ten years since the fall of Troy and twenty years since he left his bride and infant son in rocky Ithaka, he is virtually imprisoned on the island of the nymph Calypso (her name means Concealer), weeping for home. As Athena indignantly addresses the assembled Olympians, why should mortals abide by what is right and make proper sacrifices to the gods if, like Odysseus, they are to be abandoned on some godforsaken islet, the navel of the sea? Calypso, she continues, the daughter of Atlas "whose baleful mind knows all the depths of the sea,"

> keeps on coaxing him
> with her beguiling talk, to turn his mind
> from Ithaka.[2]

But Odysseus, she adds, has such a desire if only to see the smoke leaping upward from his home fire in his native land that he wishes to die. In the surrounding passage Homer reinforces the diphthong in *hes gaies* ("native land") with a liberal scattering of internal rhymes—*daiphroni, daietai, naiei, gaian, aiei, aimulioisi*—words which dramatize the conflict between Calypso's wish to keep Odysseus with her and his wish to return to his home.

This first impression of the island-bound hero sick for home amid immortal luxuries is a vital sign of his character. During a storm-tossed decade of wandering in an enchanted and bewitched world he has not always felt such an unqualified nostalgia. In an earlier episode, the sixth of twelve that mark his erratic progress from Troy to Ithaka, he had to be roused from a long hedonistic sojourn with another nymph, Circe, by his homesick and impatient men:

> "Captain, shake off this trance, and think of home—
> if home indeed awaits us,
>
>   if we shall ever see
> your own well-timbered hall on Ithaka."
>
>   [p. 179]

In the Greek they tell Odysseus to "remember his native land." The charms, drugs, and other seductions that efface that memory are among the chief obstacles to the return of Odysseus and his men. In response to the plea Odysseus simply answers, as he tells his Phaiacian hosts, "They made me feel a pang, and I agreed."

The Circe episode is of central importance in Odysseus' wanderings. It is divided into two parts that bracket his visit to the dead in book 2. When he and his men first land on the island, Odysseus has reached a condition of utter disorientation:

> "Shipmates, companions in a disastrous time,
> O my dear friends, where Dawn lies, and the West,
> And where the great Sun, light of men, may go
> under the earth by night, and where he rises—
> of these things we know nothing. Do we know
> any least thing to serve us now? I wonder.
> All that I saw when I went up the rock
> was one more island in the boundless main,

A low landscape, covered with woods and scrub,
and puffs of smoke ascending in mid-forest."

[pp. 170–71]

Circe's shape-changing enthrallments pose a more serious threat
to the return of Odysseus and his crew than a number of other
temptations to forget home in the episodes of the Lotus-eaters,
Sirens, and Calypso. As the disguised Hermes says to Odysseus on
his way to Circe's house,

"Why take the inland path alone,
poor seafarer, by hill and dale
upon the island all unknown?
Your friends are locked in Kirke's pale;
All are become like swine to see;
And if you go to set them free
you go to stay, and never more make sail
for your old home upon Thaki."

[p. 173]

Even when Odysseus, acting on Hermes' advice, forces Circe to
restore his men to their former shapes and persuades her to assist him
on his way home, he has to augment her sailing instructions with a
visit to the ghost of the prophet Tiresias in order to escape from her
circle.

To consider Odysseus' entire voyage from Troy to Ithaka is to see
him undergoing a twofold process of attrition and accretion. The
ships and men and treasure with which he embarked are gradually
stripped away until, in the twelfth and last of his adventures, he is
cast ashore naked and exhausted in Scheria and covers himself with
the fallen leaves of two olive trees, "just as a farmer on an outlying
farm preserves the seed of fire by covering the embers with ashes."
The other process, that of accretion, is internal, as he gradually gives
up the old, egocentric, aggressive habits of the heroic warrior and
develops, through a repertoire of new responses, a deepening awareness of the meaning of home. In his visit to the spirits of the great
dead he inherits the culture of his people. In Phaiacia he discovers a
paradigm of domestic and community values.

The double process by which Odysseus is initiated into a new
and much more complex identity can be viewed as an example of the
archetypal Jungian development of the ego into accomplished selfhood. The process culminates in an astonishing peripeteia, an implicit

transformation that marks his final evening among the civilized and
hospitable Phaiacians. The time has come for the stranger to identify
himself to his hosts. Thus far he has enjoyed the best their king has to
offer simply because he is a traveling stranger, since all strangers and
guests (the word for both is *xenos)* are sacred to Zeus. The practical
reasons for this generous rule are self-evident.

As a prelude to the disclosure of his identity Odysseus asks
Demodocus, the blind harper, to sing the tale of the wooden horse
that he devised for the destruction of Troy. The harper obliges by
reciting the tale of Odysseus' master stroke as warrior and tactician.
But the expected moment of triumphant self-assertion for the sacker
of cities is suddenly transformed into an extraordinary identification
of victor and victim through a poignant simile:

> The splendid minstrel sang it.
>   And Odysseus
> let the bright molten tears run down his cheeks,
> weeping the way a wife mourns for her lord
> on the lost field where he goes down fighting
> the day of wrath that came upon his children.
> At sight of the man panting and dying there,
> she slips to enfold him, crying out;
> then feels the spears, prodding her back and shoulders,
> and goes bound into slavery and grief.
>
> [pp. 140–41]

This moment is an epiphany. It is as if, in a crisis of self-knowledge,
Odysseus were sharing in that tragic vision of the future that
Andromache, in the *Iliad*, foresees in her last words to Hector:

> "Oh my wild one, your bravery will be
> your own undoing! No pity for our child,
> poor little one, or me in my sad lot—
> soon to be deprived of you! Soon, soon
> Akhaians as one man will set upon you and cut you down!
> . . . .
> Father and mother—I have none but you,
> nor brother, Hektor; lover none but you!
> Be merciful! Stay here upon the tower!
> Do not bereave your child and widow me!"
>
> [pp. 154–55]

Homer's initial adjective for Odysseus, which resounds through the *Odyssey*, is *polutropos*, a word whose riches are barely suggested by the conventional rendering, "of many devices." Joyce's version, "allroundman,"[3] implies not only the versatility of Leopold Bloom but also his vagrant course through Dublin on June 16, 1904, and Joyce was deeply impressed by the many-sided sensibility of Homer's *aner polutropos*, including, among other qualities, his intuition of the feminine. The epithet, in the case of Odysseus, surely points to his capacity to become quintessential, prototypical, paradigmatic *man*— and thus *woman*, also. In this moment of inner illumination the sacker of cities becomes the helpless woman who tries vainly to protect her doomed husband, and Odysseus embraces, in imagination, the essential feminine component in the masculine psyche which Jung identified as the anima in the association called syzygy.[4] The nightmare world into which Odysseus was thrown ten years earlier, after his unprovoked and genocidal attack on the Cicones (cited by Grotius as the first recorded violation of international law in the Western world),[5] he has finally escaped by an act of the moral imagination. He is now ready to go home.

My interpretation of this moment gets some collateral support from a recent study[6] that demonstrates an etymological connection between *nostos*, "the return home," and *nous*, "mind, understanding," which is derived from the Homeric word *neomai*, "to know." Thus *nous* is the essential component in achieving one's *nostos*. In order to complete his voyage, Circe tells Odysseus, he must consult in Hades the seer Tiresias, "forever charged with reason even among the dead" (p. 180). *Noston dizeai meliedea, phaidim' Odusseu* ("You ask, glorious Odysseus, of your return home, sweet as honey") are the seer's opening words, and he then proceeds to inform the hero of the additional difficulties he will face once there—of the lawless and violent men who have taken over his hall and are courting his wife. Odysseus thus undertakes the second half of his adventures knowing what he must yet overcome in his own home.

Even with such painful foreknowledge, Odysseus does not hesitate to complete his journey. His reorientation accomplished, after a single night's passage on one of the Phaiacians' swift ships, he is left, still sleeping, on his native shore.

The second half of the *Odyssey*, located almost entirely in Ithaka, presents Odysseus as the obverse of the aggressive rover of the first half. By his recital of his ordeals to the spellbound Phaiacians, he has assimilated them into an epic of his own. His identity now fully achieved, his task in Ithaka is to realize it; yet, paradoxically, he can do this only by concealing that identity until the critical moment.

The physical disguises and the fictitious autobiographies he uses to protect himself mark a new phase in Odysseus' ordeal, although it is anticipated in his earlier use of the pseudonym Nobody. In his own country he must again become Nobody in the guise of a ragged old vagabond. Aided by Athena, who, significantly, now makes herself known to him for the first time since Troy, he uses a repertoire of counterfeit personalities not only in self-defense but as stalking-horses for testing the people he encounters. His various fictional accounts of himself—as a fugitive killer, a prince down on his luck, a rich youth sold into slavery by his protectors, a beggar whose former prosperity has schooled him in the vicissitudes of fortune—have nonetheless the quality of essential truth. His polytropic self, in such fictions, includes all sorts of needy, homeless, dispossessed victims who wander through the chaotic aftermath of a great war, driven, as he repeatedly tells his listeners, by "the hungry belly," an organ barely mentioned in the aristocratic *Iliad*. Man as sufferer becomes the burden of these later tales, in which Odysseus implicitly lays claim to the identity of Everyman.

As the unknown knower his existential role in the second half of the poem is the opposite of that of the roving, inquisitive, and developing character tested by so many strange, half-human creatures in the first half. At the same time, the process of attrition of comrades and physical means that occurs in the earlier experiences is now reversed as Odysseus accumulates a small band of allies to help him against the overwhelming odds posed by the 108 suitors. Proofs of fidelity are followed by recognitions. The first involves Telemachus. Then the old hound Argos lifts his head from the dunghill where he lies neglected, wags his tail, and expires, a touching emblem of unshakable fidelity and a tribute to the instinctual element in memory. Next, Odysseus' old nurse Eurykleia recognizes him by the scar left by the tusk of a wild boar on his thigh, and comes close to revealing his identity. The tiny band is complete with the addition of the swineherd Eumaios, the cowherd Philoitios, and, of course, Pallas Athena.

There are indications that Penelope, too, may be playing the game of the unknown knower. In the interview with Odysseus disguised as an old beggar, she makes a Freudian slip; she puts on her most seductive manner to solicit a shower of expensive gifts from her wooers; and she expresses her readiness to commit her future to the test of the bow.

The full realization of Odysseus' identity depends, in any event, on three trials initiated by the "wise daughter of Ikarios." That the initiative in the climax of this drama of concealed recognitions should pass from husband to wife is a triumph of Homer's imaginative sympathy for a woman whose only actions in the absence of her glamorous husband have been to abstain from action.

At the same time, Odysseus must adapt himself more and more to her role of quiet endurance in the face of threats and insults. The drunken suitors respond to his begging by flinging stools and cow hooves, while their pert mistresses, the housemaids, break scurrile jests on his old bald head. He represses his anger, but tosses (like Penelope) on his sleepless bed, as a remarkably unheroic simile puts it,

> he himself rocked, rolling from side to side,
> as a cook turns a sausage, big with blood
> and fat, at a scorching blaze, without a pause,
> to broil it quick. . . .
>
> [p. 376]

It is one sign of the comprehensiveness of the *Odyssey* that it can include such a homely detail in its repertory of human experiences, thus saluting the new heroism of endurance in terms of grilling sausages.

As a preface to the test of the bow, Penelope sets her ragged guest one other problem of identification. When he claims to have seen Odysseus about twenty years ago, she casually asks what her husband was wearing. "It's been a long time, lady," he replies,

> "But I shall tell what memory calls to mind.
> A purple cloak, and fleecy, he had on—
> a double thick one. Then he wore a brooch
> made of pure gold with twin tubes for the prongs,
> and on the face a work of art: a hunting dog
> pinning a spotted fawn in agony
> between his forepaws—wonderful to see
> how being gold, and nothing more, he bit

the golden deer convulsed, with wild hooves flying.
Odysseus' shirt I noticed, too—a fine
closefitting tunic like dry onion skin,
so soft it was, and shiny."

[pp. 360–61]

At these details—"minutely true"—Penelope weeps, for she had
dressed her husband with her own hands, and the fine tunic was
doubtless the work of those hands. Her tattered guest tries to assure
her that he has heard lately from King Phaidon of Thesprotia that
Odysseus is on his way home. This fiction, unlike the other false tales
Odysseus has told, includes much material that is factually true: the
shipwreck and death that his last surviving comrades suffered for
eating the cattle of the Sun, and his own shipwreck and arrival as a
castaway among the Phaiacians. Thus, in the tense process of approaching mutual recognition with Penelope, Odysseus' fictional
accounts and assumed identities are coming closer and closer to the
actual truth.

Penelope, in this strangely intimate interview with the ragged
wanderer late at night in the firelit hall, maintains that "Odysseus
will not come to me." And yet, a moment later, when she bids
Eurykleia wash her guest's feet, she makes a notable slip:

"Come here, stand by me, faithful Eurykleia,
and bathe—bathe your master, I almost said,
for they are of an age, and now Odysseus'
feet and hands would be enseamed like his.
Men grow old soon in hardship."

[p. 364]

Is it a Freudian slip? Or could it be a calculated gambit to convey her
secret knowledge of his identity? If one can assume that Penelope
knows exactly what she is saying, the strategy of concealed recognition has become a mutual one. When Eurykleia, at the sight of the
unmistakable scar on her master's thigh, lets his massive leg fall into
the basin of water, how could Penelope fail to notice all this crashing
and splashing or Eurykleia's tense whisper, *"You are Odysseus!"*? Or
the mute appeal of Eurykleia's look, as she turns her eyes toward
Penelope? Homer somewhat lamely tells us that "Athena had bemused the queen." Is it not more likely that Penelope employed her
goddess-given wit in an elaborate pantomime of not noticing?

However we read this scene, the fact remains that Penelope, while denying the possibility that Odysseus will return, declares her intention to marry on the morrow the man who can string the great compound bow Odysseus left behind in his storehouse—a keepsake he once received in Sparta as a gift from Iphitos. The test will be a double one, she says: to string the mighty bow and to drive an arrow through twelve pierced axeheads set in a row.

As Penelope fetches the weapons on the fatal morning, Homer evokes the mood of the moment with a variety of significant details. Penelope goes to the locked storeroom whose oaken sill, "cut long ago," was "sanded clean and bedded true." She unties the strap around the curving handle, pushes her key into the slot and shoots back the bolts:

> Then came a rasping sound
> as those bright doors the key had sprung gave way—
> a bellow like a bull's vaunt in a meadow—
> followed by her light footfall entering
> over the plank floor.
>
> [p. 392]

She sinks down, with the bow on her knees, and bites her lip to hold back her tears. Penelope's ritualistic unlocking of the long-closed storeroom and lifting down and bringing out the instrument that will enthrall or free her is a sort of epiphany accompanied by the clinking of keys, the shrieking of rusty hinges, the sudden fragrance of herb-scented robes, the movements of her milk-white arms, and the gleam of the bow's polished case. The sensuous and tactile details combine to retard the action (and thus underline its portentousness) and to endow it with a dreamlike quality.

And then she turns toward the hall where the suitors are at their usual feast. At the threshold she pauses by a pillar, "her shining veil across her cheeks," and addresses them for the last time:

> "My lords, hear me:
> suitors indeed, you commandeered this house
> to feast and drink in, day and night, my husband
> being long gone, long out of mind. You found
> no justification for yourselves—none
> except your lust to marry me. Stand up, then:
> we now declare a contest for that prize.

> Here is my lord Odysseus' hunting bow.
> Bend and string it if you can. Who sends an arrow
> through iron axe-helve sockets, twelve in line?
> I join my life with his, and leave this place, my home,
> my rich and beautiful bridal house, forever
> to be remembered, though I dream it only."
>
> [p. 393]

We need not linger over the incidents that follow in this familiar episode—on the anger and arrogance of the suitors' ringleader named, significantly, Antinoos, or the successive vain attempts by him and other suitors to string the mighty bow, the equally vain attempt to make it more malleable by rubbing it with warm grease, Telemachus' near success in stringing it interrupted by a look from his father, or the uproar that threatens to break off the contest when the beggar asks to have his turn—an uproar that Penelope quiets with her ingenious but disingenuous assurance to the suitors that she would never marry him if he did win.

So the beggar finally gets his chance at the bow. He inspects it carefully as he sits on his stool at the end of the hall. The suitors find the spectacle ludicrous and shout insults.

> But the man skilled in all ways of contending,
> satisfied by the bow's look and heft,
> like a musician, like a harper, when
> with quiet hand upon his instrument
> he draws between his thumb and forefinger
> a sweet new string upon a peg: so effortlessly
> Odysseus in one motion strung the bow.
> Then slid his right hand down the cord and plucked it,
> so the taut gut vibrating hummed and sang
> a swallow's note.
>   In the hushed hall it smote the suitors
> and all their faces changed.
>
> [p. 404]

In the hushed hall the only sound comes from that single, taut, plucked string. Then Odysseus nocks an arrow, lets it rest across the handgrip, draws it, still sitting, and sends the arrow cleanly through the twelve axeheads to thud beyond them in the Ithakan soil. And so he has come home.

This feat of arms enacts the last decade of Odysseus's life in a symbolic mode. The compound curves of the bow suggest both his flexibility and his resilience. In stringing and plucking the bow "like a harper" we may be reminded that, symbolically, at least, he is master of both instruments, since he himself was the singer in Phaiacia of his ten years' wanderings outside the known world. As it flies through the twelve axeheads his arrow cleanly recapitulates the twelve trials he underwent on the long way home from Troy to Ithaka.

There are critics I greatly respect who cannot accept my claim that Odysseus evolves from the heroic warrior's egotism to a fully developed culture hero, because of his bloody slaughter of the suitors, which they see as a brutal regression; and I concede that the punishments inflicted on some of those implicated are vile. In response I would nonetheless make two points: that he has repeatedly given the suitors the chance to mend their ways; and that, in view of the fact that his party is but four (plus Athena) against 108 men who have plotted to murder his son, he has no choice but to kill them all. They have tried in every way to destroy his home, and in destroying them he has vindicated a first principle of justice on which all the gods (except, perhaps, Poseidon) are in agreement.

The test of the bow establishes the identity of Odysseus in a public way. Any kudos he gains from it, however, is of little interest to him; when Eurykleia begins to whoop in triumph at the sight of the dead, he checks her exultation with words that have an affinity with Psalm 115, "non nobis . . . Domine":

"Rejoice inwardly. No crowing aloud, old woman.
To glory over slain men is no piety,
Destiny and the gods' will vanquished these,
and their own hardness. They respected no one,
good or bad, who came their way."

[p. 422]

And so they perished at the hand of the divine Nobody.

Now that he is again a public somebody, Odysseus has also to recover his identity in a private way. Roused from her bedchamber by Eurykleia, Penelope descends to the hall, from which all traces of the slaughter have been removed. She sits across from the bloody stranger, who never lifts his eyes. Neither speaks. When Telemachus angrily accuses his mother of being cold, she answers quietly:

> "If really he is Odysseus, truly home,
> beyond all doubt we two shall know each other
> better than you or anyone. There are
> secret signs we know, we two."

[p. 432]

Odysseus now busies himself with arrangements against expected reprisals. He takes a bath, and Athena once again transforms him from a withered old man, rejuvenating him and "lending him beauty from head to foot." He reenters the hall and takes his seat again. This time he reproaches Penelope for being aloof and orders Eurykleia to make up his bed; it has been a strenuous day and he has had enough. Resuming her role as mistress of the house, Penelope gives her own orders:

> "Make up his bed for him, Eurykleia.
> Place it outside the bedchamber my lord
> built with his own hands. Pile the big bed
> With fleeces, rugs, and sheets of purest linen."

[p. 435]

For the first time in years Odysseus' pent-up feelings erupt:

> "Woman, by heaven you've stung me now!
> Who dared to move my bed?"

[p. 435]

The bed, in its secret chamber, known only to Penelope and Odysseus, "our pact, our pledge, our secret sign," built by Odysseus upon the trunk of a living olive tree, a rare combination of art and nature, is, he declares, immovable. Eyes brimming with tears, Penelope runs to him, throws her arms about his neck, and kisses him. The reunited lovers retire to the olive-tree bed in its secret symbolic center of their home:

> Now from his breast into his eyes the ache
> of longing mounted, and he wept at last,
> his dear wife, clear and faithful, in his arms,
> longed for as the sunwarmed earth is longed for by a
>   swimmer
> spent in rough water where his ship went down
> under Poseidon's blows, gale winds and tons of sea.
> Few men can keep alive through a big surf

to crawl, clotted with brine, on kindly beaches
in joy, in joy, knowing the abyss behind:
and so she too rejoiced, her gaze upon her husband,
her white arms round him pressed as though forever.

[p. 436]

The final ordeal of his ten years' voyage from Troy to Phaiacia, when shipwrecked and half-dead he collapses on the shore, is recapitulated in this climactic simile.

The last book of the *Odyssey* is devoted largely to reestablishing Odysseus in his family, in his extended family of servants, and in his city. The last scene rejoining Odysseus with his home takes place with old Laertes, his father, wearing a tattered tunic and goatskin hat, hoeing alone in a briar patch: Saturn, the gardener, squalid and in mourning. Until now, Odysseus had always been father, and Telemachus the son, in search of the father. But now at the end, facing Laertes so perfectly sketched in his senex condition, Odysseus is his son, remembering the wound, the hunt, and the garden of his youth. And by these signs he is known (*Od.* 24: 327ff). As senex-et-puer Odysseus comes home, and his odyssey tells the tale of the diversified, polytropic process of homecoming.[7] The retributive efforts of the dead suitors' families and the spirited defense intended by Odysseus, his son, his father, and the little band of faithful servants are blocked by Zeus's emphatic intervention, and "Both parties later swore to terms of peace / set by their arbiter, Athena" (p. 462). The concluding lines of the *Odyssey* thus fulfill the vital image on the shield of Achilles in which arbitration of disputes takes the place of the vendettas that had hitherto undermined the possibility of an ordered society. We have at this point made the transition from the archaic world of unlimited, egocentric pursuit of heroic glory, characteristic of the chief warriors of the *Iliad*, to a society in which each person's worth is not gained at the expense of another's loss, a society where mutual recognition of essential human rights produces a surplus of value instead of the zero-sum game of the archaic heroic *agon*. That Athena should be the guarantor of this arbitrated compact between the Ithakan factions anticipates the similar and essential role she is to play in Aeschylus's *Eumenides,* where, in the climactic judicial hearing on the Areopagus, the obsessed and single-minded Furies are endowed with a wider vision that empowers them to move beyond the bloody and endless conflict between rights too narrowly conceived. In short, what Homer gives us so modestly in the last lines of his epic vision is the vital underlying principle of Western civilization. Odysseus and Athena catalyze a development in the conduct of human affairs that can scarcely be overrated. In Campbell's challenging conception of the epic as essentially a divine comedy with tragic beginnings, Odysseus is par excellence the first epic culture hero, in accomplishing the transition from sacker of cities to restorer of a kingdom in which the assertion of the aggressive and regressive ego gives place to the individuated and socially responsive and responsible self. In this extraordinarily promising development, achievable only by someone with polytropic capacities and authenticated by the most civilized of the Olympian goddesses, we move from a Hobbesian nightmare of contending egos to a shared commitment to Themis.

That the fulfillment of Odysseus' rite of passage should center on Penelope and be guaranteed by Athena leads to a point of ultimate importance: the hero's cleverness, endurance, and adaptability could never have delivered him from the labyrinthine entanglements of his ego nor made possible his ultimate victory—which is not simply to destroy the suitors but to establish a new society—without the active participation of the feminine principle. Odysseus' final conjunction with Penelope not only marks a center he pursues in his peripheral journey, but shows that her role, in Jung's idea of the anima—the feminine and reciprocal element in the achieved masculine self—is clearly essential.

In none of the works in the epic tradition that succeed the *Odyssey* will we find as full and excitingly delineated a version of the completed heroic quest and the concomitant establishment of a true city. Years ago, T. S. Eliot made a similar claim for the *Aeneid* in "Virgil and the Western World," but he later acknowledged the persuasiveness of the case I have tried to make here.[8] True, the political and social scope of Ithaka is diminutive, but the cultural transformation enacted there can be a guide to vaster and more complex civilizations. In Virgil's first eclogue, Tityrus has succumbed to awe at the incomparable grandeur of Rome, which he once thought was like his village: "I used to compare great things with small" (*sic parvis componere magna solebam;* line 23). Although Tityrus dismisses this view as naive, Virgil returns to it frequently as a valid principle of comparison. I see no reason, in respect to essential mythic implications, to dismiss the idea that Ithaka is the model of the true city or that it amends our vision of the only grand city Homer knew—Troy. That the new Ithaka, founded upon a divinely ordained principle of *themis* institutionalized in the arbitrations of assemblies, the precursors of Athenian democracy, and confirmed also by the vision Odysseus achieves of inalienable human rights, irrespective of power, status, or social class, should become a model for Western culture is only implied. Virgil's re-creation of the *Odyssey* is no more explicit on this point. Nevertheless, in the inconclusive assembly of book 24, where the issue under consideration is whether or not the relatives of the dead suitors should be avenged, Homer has Halitherses state the facts.

> Alone
> he saw the field of time, past and to come.
> In his anxiety for them he said:
> "Ithakans, now listen to what I say.
> Friends, by your own fault these deaths came to pass.
> You would not heed me nor the captain, Mentor;
> would not put down the riot of your sons.
> Heroic feats they did!—all wantonly
> raiding a great man's flocks, dishonoring
> his queen, because they thought he'd come no more.
> Let matters rest; do as I urge; no chase,
> or he who wants a bloody end will find it."
>
> [pp. 458–59]

Halitherses' wisdom has to be enforced by the actions of Zeus and Athena, as we shall soon see. It is a humane and moral vision like his that lies behind the ideals of the *Aeneid* as vouchsafed to Aeneas by his father's spirit: *tu regere imperio populos, Romane, memento/ (haec tibi erunt artes) pacique imponere morem,/parcere subiectis et debellare superbos* ("Remember thou, O Roman, to rule the nations with thy sway—these shall be thy arts—to crown Peace with Law, to spare the humbled, and to tame in war the proud!").[9]

The establishment of justice at the end of the *Odyssey* lays the essential foundation for a viable society. Its quietly transfiguring image of the genesis of the just city provides a touchstone by which all subsequent epic civilizations will be evaluated, from Virgil's Rome to Eliot's London and Joyce's Dublin.

Were one to attempt to reduce the vision of the *Odyssey* to one central theme, that might well be the way in which it mediates

between a past that is Hell on earth to a future that can accommodate
vital human needs for self-discovery, relatedness, *eros*, and *agape*. In
his comprehensive ordeals between Troy and home, Odysseus undergoes a transformation from sacker of cities to founder of cities. The
Odyssey, based on the perennially vital myth of the dark journey and
the transformative rite of passage, on the syzygistic encounter with
the anima figure and the transpersonal power of the gods, represented
by their consensus on the critical importance of *themis* and the
mutual obligations and privileges of *xenia*, fulfills the interdependent
personal and social functions of the monomyth.

   That the Homeric poems combine to produce a divine comedy is
clear. That the archaic, egocentric, fixated, backward-looking hero of
the *Iliad* should give place to a future-oriented, flexible, and increasingly human and social hero in the *Odyssey* is a giant step in the
growth of epic vision. In its successors there will obviously be gains
and losses. Despite his rejection of the heroic code in book 11 of the
Odyssey, the atavistic Achilles will reappear, especially in Turnus and
Aeneas. Hera, obsessed with her loss of the beauty contest in the
Iliad, though giving place to Athena in the *Odyssey*, will renew her
obsessive malignity in the *Aeneid*, where we shall also find at times a
terrible regression to the archaic preoccupation of the heroes of the
Iliad with status and personal ambition.

   Odysseus, the centripetal hero par excellence, reappears in
Dante's version and Tennyson's poem as the victim of a passion for the
eternal or interminable voyage directed to no goal. In Dante, to
whom Homer was unavailable, this radical difference is excusable. In
Tennyson, who violates the soul of the *Odyssey* and transforms
Odysseus into the image of Dante's false counselor, an irresponsible
and restless old man conning his aged fellows away from their
firesides to undertake an unfocused and disastrous journey, it is not.
His Ulysses is like an Ahab without a Moby Dick.

2 The Ambivalent Ordeal of Aeneas

If it is common today to fantasy our culture against that of old Rome, it is partly because our psyche has undergone a long Pax Romana. The gradual extension and civilization of outlying barbarous hinterlands is nothing else than ego-development. The classical description of this romanizing process in the psyche is that of Freud: "To strengthen the ego, to make it more independent of the super ego, to widen the field of perception and enlarge its organization so that it can appropriate fresh portions of the id, where id was there ego shall be. It is a work of culture."

James Hillman

In placing the *Aeneid* in the context of this study it is helpful to begin with the familiar observation that Virgil's epic is a reenactment and revision of the *Iliad* and *Odyssey*. Where Homer's ahistorical treatment of the major events in the Greek heroic past permitted a limited optimism in acts of reconciliation at the end of the *Iliad* and an almost unqualified optimism in Odysseus' triumphant restoration to his marriage, home, and country in the final books of the *Odyssey*, Aeneas's entire career, while succeeding in its fated goal of founding a new Troy in Italy, is beset at almost every step by a melancholic recognition that each apparent gain is accompanied by a loss, a loss so bitter and so contrary to expectations as virtually to cancel out the gain.

Virgil's cosmos is in some ways more dark and primitive than Homer's. The major divinities in the *Aeneid* participate in the affairs of blind mortals with the same ruthless disregard for the human agony they cause that we find in the amoral rivalries of Aphrodite, Ares, and Hera in the *Iliad*. The reconciliation of the grieving Achilles and Priam in book 24 and their joint recognition of the tragic fate that entangles victor and victim alike in the toils of war is endorsed by a unanimous synod of the gods, and Homer seems to have envisioned a

29

new Olympian commitment to *themis* that provides the vital opening keynote to the *Odyssey*. The end of the feud between Juno and Venus in book 12 of the *Aeneid* is not a true reconciliation but a political deal. Juno stands to gain nothing by continuing her savage harassment of the Trojans, and so, in the spirit of *realpolitik*, she decides to accept half the cake rather than none:

"et nunc cedo equidem pugnasque exosa relinquo.
illud te, nulla fati quod lege tenetur,
pro Latio obtestor, pro maiestate tuorum:
cum iam conubiis pacem felicibus, esto,
component, cum iam leges et foedera iungent,
ne vetus indigenas nomen mutare Latinos
neu Troas fieri iubeas Teucrosque vocari
aut vocem mutare viros aut vertere vestem,
sit Latium, sint Albani per saecula reges,
sit Romana potens Itala virtute propago;
occidit, occideritque sinas cum nomine Troia."
    Olli subridens hominum rerumque repertor:
"es germana Iovis Saturnique altera proles:
irarum tantos volvis sub pectore fluctus.
verum age, et inceptum frustra submitte furorem:
do quod vis, et me victusque volensque remitto."

"And now I yield, yea, yield, and quit the strife in loathing. This boon, banned by no law of fate, for Latium's sake, for thine own kin's greatness, I entreat from thee: when anon with happy bridal rites—so be it!—they plight peace, when anon they join in laws and treaties, command not native Latins to change their ancient name, nor to become Trojans and be called Teucrians, nor to change their tongue and alter their attire: let Latium be, let Alban kings endure through ages, let be a Roman stock, strong in Italian valour: fallen is Troy, and fallen let her be, together with her name!"
    Smiling on her, the creator of men and things replied: "True sister of Jove art thou, and Saturn's other child, such waves of wrath surge deep within they breast! But come, allay the rage thus vainly stirred: I grant thy wish, and yield me, conquered and content."

[12.818–33]

There is here, as Quinn notes, "a gently mischievous note," something like the note of bourgeois domestic comedy that Homer strikes in *Iliad* 14. Here, any delight we might take in the maneuvers and countermaneuvers of a strong-willed wife married to a very discerning husband is offset by the cruel consequence of their agreement: the betrayal and death of Turnus, a death inflicted with Achillean rigor by the pious hero who, from his own experience, has every reason to understand and admire the courage of another Hector defending his city and his wife against the invaders. Even in her submission, Juno's obsessive hatred of the Trojans, aroused long ago by a slight to her vanity, is vividly expressed in her insistence on obliterating the name of this hated people.

If we compare Virgil's treatment of the theme of anger with Homer's, a major and telling difference appears. *Menis*, the first word of the *Iliad*, refers to the anger of Achilles, but its origins, like its consequences, are extremely complex, entailing the anger of Agamemnon at the priest of Apollo, Chryses, the anger of Agamemnon at the seer Calchas, and the mutual anger of Achilles and Agamemnon, gradually spreading to include most of the major divinities and mortals participating in the war for Troy. Equally important are the key moral issues at stake in the rape of Helen as reenacted in Agamemnon's arbitrary appropriation of Achilles' prize girl, Briseis, not to mention Achilles' grief and anger over the death of Patroclus and his furious hatred of Hector. Not until all these linked *menes* are assuaged can the central conflicts of the *Iliad* find their resolution in the funeral games, in the divine council, and in the interview of Achilles and Priam and the surrender of the body of Hector.

There is no such resolution at the end of the *Aeneid*, only a truce based on the mutual self-interest of Juno and Jupiter. The double viewpoint of the *Aeneid* assures us that what has been will be again. The precarious peace imposed by Augustus at the time Virgil was writing would have brought home to him that all the horrors of internecine strife just ended might break out again at any moment. Thus when Virgil raises the problem of divine anger at the beginning of his poem, he is asking a question to which the poem has no answer:

Musa, mihi causas memora, quo numine laeso
quidve dolens regina deum tot volvere casus
insignem pietate virum, tot adire labores
impulerit. tantaene animis caelestibus irae?

> Tell me, O Muse, the cause, wherein thwarted in will or
> wherefore angered, did the Queen of heaven drive a man, so
> famous for his goodness, to traverse so many perils, to face
> so many toils. Can resentment so fierce dwell in heavenly
> breasts?
>
> [1.8–11]

Tantaene animis caelestibus irae? The words generalize, of course,
the question of Apollo's anger raised at the beginning of the *Iliad;* but
where Homer traces carefully the thoroughly understandable origins
of Apollo's wrath, Virgil raises the question of Juno's anger only to
drop it, except for a brief allusion to the judgment of Paris, an event
which does not go very far to justify or explain the fact that the only
satisfaction the queen of heaven can find for this ancient slight is to
torment some harmless and noble people who had no part in it, in the
process inflicting as much agony on those she champions—Dido and
Turnus—as she does on Aeneas. Juno does not love those she
supports; she simply detests their enemies and unhesitatingly sacrifices anyone or anything in pursuit of her obsessive vengeance.
Loyalty to her cult means nothing to her; the temple and ceremonies
Dido has dedicated to her are futile.

In all respects Juno seems to represent a primitive divine principle of irrational evil, sadism, and untempered egotism utterly opposed to the positive values which the *Aeneid* celebrates, even if it
fails to embody them except intermittently. It is as though Virgil had
gone behind his Homeric prototype to discover an ancient divinity of
satanic destructiveness whom, in the course of religious development,
a more moderate and enlightened figure would have superseded. Her
closest models seem to be the Furies of Aeschylus; and the final
settlement, when Jupiter makes concessions to her anger in order to
win her assent to a political resolution of the issues, seems like an
ironic version of the transformation of the Furies into Eumenides in
the court of the Areopagus.

Throughout Aeneas's cosmogonic struggles Juno functions as a
force of supernatural chaos. In book 1, blandly indifferent to the
territorial rights of Neptune, she bribes and browbeats Aeolus into
setting loose the storm which, for a time, apparently destroys most of
Aeneas's fleet. This is her way of seeing to it that the wandering
Trojans do not bypass her favorite town of Carthage, which, according to her plan, will hinder their pursuit of their fated goal in Italy.

Venus's subtlety in complying with the Carthaginian visit exposes
the heavyhandedness of everything Juno does. Overkill is her strategy, and overkill, reflected in her unbridled rage and purple rhetoric,
is her only mode of reflection, as seen in her response to her first sight
of the Trojan fleet sailing from Sicily:

> Vix e conspectu Siculae telluris in altum
> vela dabant laeti et spumas salis aere ruebant,
> cum Iuno, aeternum servans sub pectore volnus,
> haec secum: "mene incepto desistere victam
> nec posse Italia Teucrorum avertere regem!
> quippe vetor fatis. Pallasne exurere classem
> Argivum atque ipsos potuit submergere ponto
> unius ob noxam et furias Aiacis Oilei?
> ipsa Iovis rapidum iaculata e nubibus ignem
> disiecitque rates evertitque aequora ventis;
> illum exspirantem transfixo pectore flammas
> turbine corripuit scopuloque infixit acuto;
> ast ego, quae divum incedo regina, Iovisque
> et soror et coniunx, una cum gente tot annos
> bella gero. et quisquam numen Iunonis adorat
> praeterea aut supplex aris imponet honorem?"

Hardly out of sight of Sicilian land were they spreading
their sails seaward, and merrily ploughing the foaming
brine with brazen prow, when Juno, nursing an undying
wound deep in her heart, spoke thus to herself:
"What! I resign my purpose, baffled, and fail to turn the
Teucrian king from Italy! The fates, doubtless forbid me!
Had Pallas power to burn up the Argive fleet and sink the
sailors in the deep because of one single man's guilt, and the
frenzy of Ajax, son of Oileus? Her own hand hurled from
the clouds Jove's swift flame, scattered their ships, and
upheaved the sea in tempest; but, as he breathed forth fire
from his pierced breast, she caught and impaled him on a
crag. Yet I, who move as queen of gods, sister at once and
wife of Jove, with one people have been warring these many
years. And will any still worship Juno's godhead or humbly
lay sacrifice upon her altars?"

[1.34–49]

Rarely has a divinity identified status so baldly with arbitrary violence, while barely acknowledging that Athena's act of vengeance was a justified punishment for nefarious crimes, and never acknowledging that the queen of her favorite city, whom she will shortly destroy as an instrument of her anti-Trojan obsession, has been her most faithful and humble worshiper.

There is something grimly comic about a goddess so powerful, so unremittingly and narrowly bent on achieving her own will, and so monotonously given to lamentations over her repeated defeats. We are very close to the absurd with Juno, to a cosmos rent by purposeless violence. There is something mechanistic in her utterly predictable response to every opportunity, as when, in book 7, she decides that if heaven will not cooperate, she will try hell (*flectere si nequeo superos, Acheronta movebo:* line 312) and calls in the aid of Allecto:

> "hunc mihi da proprium, virgo sata Nocte, laborem,
> hanc operam, ne noster honos infractave cedat
> fama loco, neu conubiis ambire Latinum
> Aeneadae possint Italosve obsidere finis.
> tu potes unanimos armare in proelia fratres
> atque odiis versare domos, tu verbera tectis
> funereasque inferre faces, tibi nomina mille,
> mille nocendi artes. fecundum concute pectus,
> disice compositam pacem, sere crimina belli;
> arma velit poscatque simul rapiatque iuventus."

> "Grant me, maiden daughter of night, this service, a boon all my own, that my honor and glory not be overcome: that the sons of Aeneas not be able to cajole Latinus into wedlock or attack the borders of Italy. You can arm brothers of one soul and overturn homes with hatred; you can bring under the roof the lash and the funeral torch; you have a thousand names, a thousand means of ill. Rouse your fertile thoughts, shatter the peace pact, sow the seeds of wicked war. At once let men crave, demand, and seize the sword!"
>
> [7.331–40]

In all respects this terrible archaic goddess is the antithesis of the Roman vision, Roman virtue, Roman civilization. Mistress of the purely destructive aspects of fire, water, wind, and darkness, entrepreneur of the darkest and cruelest chthonic powers with all their

Senecan paraphernalia of venomous snakes and malign rituals, Juno embodies essentially an unqualified egotistical megalomania that is irremediably hostile to moderation. Justice, compassion, and the capacity for compromise that must provide the foundation for a new civilization reconciling the legitimate interests of Arcadians, Etruscans, Italians, and Trojans are anathema to her. In this repulsive goddess Virgil gives us the quintessence of the obsession with personal glory that had played such a disastrous part in the heroic tradition, an egotism incapable of fruitful change or development, incapable of conceiving that surrender or compromise of the claims of the ego is a precondition to the development of a true self that can participate in a goal transcending the infantile demands of the ego. Hence Juno's actions and her ideas are unrelentingly repetitive, her mind madly incapable of making discriminations, her style of speech boringly confined to hyperbole, the spuriously tragic, and the self-pitying.

As the stage manager of all the hostile efforts directed against Aeneas's mission, Juno is a uniquely difficult opponent. Alone among the gods and men and women who hinder or help his progress toward the site of Rome, Juno never appears to him, and he can know of her hostility only at second hand or through the instrumentality of her storms and fires. Part of her sadism is seen in her hiding herself from her victim and in keeping him guessing as to what he should attempt to do to mitigate her hostility. She is mystifying without being mysterious, in part because, ultimately, she does not embody any real idea or ideal. She is outside the parameters of comprehensible values and rational discourse: hence the distortions, clichés, and false histrionics that make her sound like Pope's goddess Dulness without the latter's nutty but endearing attachment to her Dunces.

Juno, however, is only one of the major factors making Aeneas's heroic ordeal one of special difficulty. Aeneas's journey has no real point of departure, and its goal is only gradually and tantalizingly disclosed after a series of false conclusions and ambiguous or misleading instructions. His journey, at the beginning, is more a flight than a quest, reluctantly undertaken at the behest of others and with the loss of most of what he holds dear, including his beloved wife and his sense of honor as a surviving defender of his wrecked city. Like Odysseus, he must undergo the rite of passage and the ordeal of individuation before he can serve as a vital link in the founding of a new Troy in an unknown part of the western world. Yet, unlike

Odysseus, his identity is so bound to his destroyed ancient mother that, at the beginning of the journey, very little of his old self survives to undertake the overwhelming difficulties of his obscure and frustrating quest. When he leaves Troy, Odysseus has a clear sense of his identity as sacker of cities, and he has a clear sense of his goal in Ithaka, from which he is kept by a series of obstacles, temptations, and trials that help him to achieve the rite of passage that will qualify him as the worthy restorer of his city. Perhaps the most important difference between the plights of the two heroes is that Aeneas must set out without his beloved wife Creusa, whose place in his future will be taken by the shadowy Lavinia, whom he never meets in the course of the poem, while Odysseus, however he may acquiesce for a time in the hospitable care of a Circe or a Calypso, is motivated by an unwavering devotion to Penelope. However bizarre or dangerous some of his experiences may be, none of them approaches the riddling obscurity that characterizes Aeneas's, and so the cleverness, resourcefulness, and virtuosity that enable Odysseus to deal successfully with a great variety of obstacles would be insufficient to Aeneas's more problematical tasks. To this we can add that the collective nature of the Trojan expedition, with all its military, navigational, sacramental, and political demands, confronts the Teucrian leader with infinitely heavier responsibilities than Odysseus' virtually unquestioned personal command over his fellows. Aeneas is conducting the remnant of an entire civilization, including women, children, gods, and domestic animals. His company is the seed corn of the new Rome, and if he loses them, the journey will fail utterly. Odysseus' men are purely ancillary to his journey, and though, regretfully, he loses all of them, the future of his restored city is not significantly impaired by the loss.

The main task of the refugee Trojan prince is to conduct his band of displaced followers safely to an unknown land and, in the process, to discover the person he is to become. Bereaved of his wife, carrying his ancient father and leading his little son by the hand, caught between a dead past and an unknown future, his first step toward the west is a submission to necessity:

> "iamque iugis summae surgebat Lucifer Idae
> ducebatque diem, Danaique obsessa tenebant
> limina portarum, nec spes opis ulla dabatur.
> cessi et sublato montis genitore petivi."

"And now above Ida's topmost ridges the day-star was
rising, ushering in the morn; and the Danaans held the
blockaded gates, nor was any hope of help offered. I gave
way and, taking up my father, sought the mountains."

[2.801–04]

Cessi: the first step in the journey that will found Rome is an act of
surrender, a letting go of a past that, at this moment, survives only in
the infirm old man he bears on his shoulders, and a simultaneous
movement toward an unknown future exemplified by the small son
he clasps by the hand. In his voyage of self-discovery, this goddess-
born prince without a country will have to discover the undisclosed
identities of his father and his son. In the process he will find,
sometimes, that the Trojan destiny can be fulfilled only through the
intertwinings of the three generations and that the future can be
gained only through a fruitful and mysterious conjunction between
them.

If the only city you know has been annihilated and your only
instructions in founding a new city are to seek out your ancient
mother, and the only ancient mother you know is irrevocably behind
you, what do you do? For six years or more Aeneas wanders from one
potential site to another, visiting or founding simulacra of the city he
has lost, most of them tiny, uninspired models of great Troy inhabited
by refugees who lead a ghostly half life. First comes Aeneadae, where
Aeneas, as part of a sacrificial act, lacerates the body of the transformed Polydorus; then Delos, where Anchises mistakenly takes the
ancient mother to be Crete. In Crete the new settlement is scourged
by pestilence, Apollo's way, perhaps, of telling the Trojans that their
choice is wrong. After an unpleasant encounter with the Harpies and
their dire predictions and a fleeting visit to Leucas, they land at
Buthrotum, ruled by Helenus, now married to Andromache, whose
miserable hours are spent in sacrifices to the memory of Hector. The
town is "a Little Troy, with a copy of great Pergamus, and a dry brook
that takes its name from Xanthus" (3.349–50), a sort of Disneyland
version of Troy. Here Aeneas learns that the part of Italy for which
he is destined is far away, on the western coast above Sicily. The
authenticating tokens, Helenus tells him, will be a white sow with a
litter of thirty pigs, the rather pedestrian allegory alluding to the
thirty years of Iulus's reign. Helenus's most important advice refers
to Juno:

"praeterea, si qua est Heleno prudentia, vati
si qua fides, animum si veris implet Apollo,
unum illud tibi, nate dea, proque omnibus unum
praedicam et repetens iterumque iterumque monebo:
Iunonis magnae primum prece numen adora,
Iunoni cane vota libens dominamque potentem
supplicibus supera donis: sic denique victor
Trinacria finis Italos mittere relicta."

"Moreover, if Helenus has any foresight, if the seer can
claim any faith, if Apollo fills his soul with truth, this one
thing, O goddess-born, this one in lieu of all I will foretell,
and again and again repeat the warning: honor mighty
Juno's power first with prayer; to Juno joyfully chant vows
and win over the mighty goddess with suppliant gifts. So at
last thou shalt leave Trinacria behind and be sped triumphantly to the bounds of Italy."

[3.433–40]

Helenus concludes with instructions about the visit to Cumae, and
the company sails for Sicily, undergoing en route somewhat perfunc-
tory encounters with Scylla and Charybdis and a refugee from
Polyphemus. The Odyssean material seems ineffective here, partly
because the encounters lack the immediacy and excitement of their
model, and partly because encounters with legendary monsters are
not appropriate to the characteristically historical trials of Aeneas.
The book ends with a visit to the gloomy shores of Drepanum, where
Aeneas's father dies, and Aeneas concludes his tale to Dido by
observing:

"hic labor extremus, longarum haec meta viarum;
hinc me digressum vestris deus appulit oris."

"This was my last trial, this the goal of my long voyaging;
departing thence, the god drove me to your shores."

[3.714–15]

Extremus means not only "the last" but "the worst." Thus briefly,
Aeneas sees himself as having suffered the worst loss that he could
imagine—all the more so since, until his death, Anchises had been the
chief guide and leader of the expedition. From now on, Aeneas
realizes wearily, the task of leadership will be fully his. Of the storm
which drove the Aeneadae to Carthage, Aeneas can say only that it

came from a god. He is unaware that it was contrived by Juno, whose sacrifices he had just performed so scrupulously on the hostile shores of Italy.

Aeneas's voyage thus far is marked by the same futility that we find in book 7 of the *Odyssey*, when Odysseus' ships come within sight of Ithaka only to be blown back by the greedy sailors' inadvertent release of the winds Aeolus has given him tied in a bag. But Aeneas's plight, at this corresponding point, seems much worse. He is now, after many years, as far from his vaguely defined goal as he was when he set out; divine powers seem inexorably opposed to his reaching it; and he has lost both his wife and the "best of fathers," who had been his chief guide and stay. Thus the Trojan hero, upon his arrival at Carthage, is at the lowest point of his fortunes, resourceless, blocked, dependent, and devoid of any convincing knowledge as to how he should proceed.

That he should snatch eagerly at what looks like the first real opportunity for personal happiness and success in Carthage should come as no surprise. The beautiful and creative widowed queen, having suffered losses like his own, offers a real opportunity to settle his weary people and share in building and ruling the new city that seems to exemplify everything a city should be. After repeated exhausting and frustrated attempts to carry out an ill-defined and obscurely communicated divine mission, both experience and reason suggest that the time has come to stop in Carthage and make the best of things. And the opportunity is heightened by the ruthless manipulations of the two most powerful goddesses in the *Aeneid*. All things considered, the behavior of the displaced Trojan widower and the refugee Tyrian widow is fair and reasonable, and there is no way for either to see, at the outset of the affair, that its consequences should bring harm to anyone, even if we take into account Dido's voluntary vows not to remarry after the death of Sychaeus. And even if, at its height, the passion of Dido for Aeneas develops explicitly into a kind of madness, an irresistible madness inflicted upon her by the trickery of Venus, Dido nonetheless refrains from trying to inflict on the Trojans a Juno-like revenge. Instead, she punishes what she considers her own dishonor by suicide. Thus whatever superficial resemblances there may be between the infatuated queen and the compulsively malignant goddess, the comparison is entirely in the mortal's favor, and we find once again that the greatest human beings in the *Iliad* and *Aeneid* are infinitely greater than the deities who dally with them.

Aeneas's conduct in the affair serves as a turning point, both

emotionally and in his public role. In the famous cavern scene during
the storm, all the associations of chthonic ritual—the ululating
nymphs, the crashing thunder, and torrents of rain—suggest that the
love match is consecrated:

> speluncam Dido dux et Troianus eandem
> deveniunt. prima et Tellus et pronuba Iuno
> dant signum; fulsere ignes et conscius Aether
> conubiis, summoque ulularunt vertice Nymphae.
> ille dies primus leti primusque malorum
> causa fuit. neque enim specie famave movetur
> nec iam furtivum Dido meditatur amorem;
> coniugium vocat; hoc praetexit nomine culpam.

> To the same cave came Dido and the Trojan chief. Primal
> Earth and nuptial Juno gave the sign; fires flashed from
> Heaven, the witness to their bridal, and on the mountain-
> top the nymphs screamed. That day was the first day of
> death, that first the cause of woe. For no more is Dido
> swayed by fair show or fair fame, no more does she dream
> of a secret love: she calls it marriage and with that name
> veils her sin!

> [4.165–72]

The second half of this passage is patent editorializing on the part of
Virgil, an attempt to associate portentously the match of Dido and
Aeneas with the bitter hostility of Rome and Carthage. Yet surely a
match contrived and celebrated by the chief deity of marriage, Juno,
with all the attendant manifestations, need not be interpreted as an
infamous fraud perpetrated by Dido. If breaking a unilateral, voluntary vow to her dead husband is a sin, surely it is a venial one, and
Dido's open recognition of her marriage is surely more honorable
than the *furtivum amorem* of which she no longer dreams.

Let us now turn to Jupiter's sudden and vehement intervention
in the affair in his message to Aeneas through Mercury:

> "vade age, nate, voca Zephyros et labere pinnis
> Dardaniumque ducem, Tyria Karthagine qui nunc
> exspectat fatisque datas non respicit urbes,
> adloquere et celeris defer mea dicta per auras.
> non illum nobis genetrix pulcherrima talem

promisit Graiumque ideo bis vindicat armis;
sed fore, qui gravidam imperiis belloque fremertem
Italiam regeret, genus alto a sanguine Teucri
proderet, ac totum sub leges mitteret orbem.
si nulla accendit tantarum gloria rerum
nec super ipse sua molitur laude laborem,
Ascanione pater Romanas invidet arces?
quid struit? aut qua spe inimica in gente moratur
nec prolem Ausoniam et Lavinia respicit arva?
naviget: haec summa est, hic nostri nuntius esto."

"Go forth, my son, call the Zephyrs, glide on thy wings, and speak to the Dardan chief, who now dallies in Tyrian Carthage and heeds not the cities granted by the Fates; so carry down my words through the swift winds. His lovely mother did not promise him such as this, nor for this twice rescue him from Grecian arms; but he was to rule over Italy, a land teeming with empire and clamorous with war, to hand on a race from Teucer's noble blood, and bring all the world beneath his laws. If the glory of such a fortune does not fire him and, for fame's sake, he does not lift the burden, does he, as father, grudge Ascanius the towers of Rome? What is his plan? In what hope does he wait among a hostile people without regard to Ausonia's race and the Lavinian fields? Let him set sail; this is all I have to say; this is my message."

[4.223–37]

Arbitrary, curt, and contemptuous, Jupiter chooses this moment to communicate Aeneas's destiny to him for the first time. *Naviget:* get going. The Tyrians are hostile. In fact they are not, but partly because of Aeneas's sudden and enforced departure they will be. Was it for this that his most beautiful mother saved him twice from the Greeks? Presumably yes, since she helped make the match. Jupiter appears not to pay much attention to what goes on among the other gods. This sudden, awful intervention has a vaguely defensive quality about it, as though the pressure brought to bear by the super-Jupiterian, Prince Iarbas, who is peeved because Dido had turned him down, had provoked this self-justifying response.

What can Aeneas do? With the message of Mercury that Jupiter is passionately interested in his fortunes, there is absolutely no way not to comply, and at once. Aeneas alternates frantically between conflicting duties and settles on a course of action that will inflict the least pain and humiliation on his lady. But his self has been shattered by the impasse so abruptly revealed to him by the awful theophany, and it is fair to say that the comparatively rich personality that we have come to know in the first third of the poem has been dealt a blow from which it will not recover. In all the remaining episodes we see little of the interior life of Aeneas, because his fated role suppresses much of his personality. From now on he acts as an instrument of a divine policy that he pursues from a sense of inescapable duty rather than from love, and often with profound distaste. What he has suffered in the Dido experience has turned out to be to some extent a setback to individuation. His compliance with the divine will requires abandonment of some of his richest feelings. More and more he becomes a figurehead whose increasing rage and frustration occasion-ally transform him, especially in the last books, into an insatiable and brutal killer. So Virgil's sombre rewriting of the *Odyssey* has the hero retrace the path of sacker of cities into restorer of cities, but the price for *imperium sine fine* begins to seem exorbitant in comparison with its Homeric precursor.

Not surprisingly, the Aeneas we see in the next episode, in book 5, is the most self-consciously public figure in the entire epic. Having returned to Drepanum on the anniversary of Anchises' death, he seizes the occasion to mark his new commitment to the public cause by holding memorial games in his father's honor. Now that he is finally en route to the destined landing in Italy the time has come to exercise his troops in preparation for war. And so, though the games are closely modeled on those of *Iliad* 23, the playing fields of Drepanum are where the battles against Turnus and his allies are to be won.

The main event of the Homeric games is the unforgettable chariot race, whose verve and individualistic spirit culminate in a quarrel between Antilochus and Menelaos. The contest is both a comic and benign recapitulation of the deadly opening quarrel be-tween Agamemnon and Achilles and an exciting discovery of the productive quality of true play, which produces a surplus of real value in contrast to the zero-sum game pursued to its logical and egotistical extremities. All this I have written about elsewhere.[1]

Virgil's main event is a ship race modeled closely on Homer's contest of chariots, but the differences are far more telling than the similarities. Unlike the charioteers, who volunteer for the race, the ships are chosen by Aeneas. The governing spirit of the chariot race is purely competitive; the ships, however, are performing maneuvers that they will act out in battle, and the contest is more a rehearsal for war, a game with an unacknowledged ulterior motive, than an *agon* undertaken in the spirit of pure play. Most important of all is the fact that Virgil's contestants are collective vessels of war in which the unseen toilers at the oar win no recognition; that is reserved for the commanders. The crucial participation of nameless, faceless, unrecognized masses of men in this contest is a clear indication of a fundamental difference between the individual who can express himself without inhibitions in Homer and the anonymous underling who must sacrifice himself to the unrelenting rhythms of the imperial ships. There are comic episodes in Virgil's ship race, as when a commander tosses his *gubernator* overboard for having steered too cautiously around a mark, but there is a collectivist quality about the laughter, as though it were officially sanctioned:

> dixit; sed caeca Menoetes
> saxa timens proram pelagi detorquet ad undas.
> "quo diversus abis?" iterum "pete saxa, Menoete!"
> cum clamore Gyas revocabat, et ecce Cloanthum
> respicit instantem tergo et propiora tenentem.
> ille inter navemque Gyae scopulosque sonantis
> radit iter laevum interior subitoque priorem
> praeterit et metis tenet aequora tuta relictis.
> tum vero exarsit iuveni dolor ossibus ingens,
> nec lacrimis caruere genae, segnemque Menoeten,
> oblitus decorisque sui sociumque salutis,
> in mare praecipitem puppi deturbat ab alta;
> ipse gubernaclo rector subit, ipse magister,
> hortaturque viros clavumque ad litora torquet.
> at gravis, ut fundo vix tandem redditus imo est,
> iam senior madidaque fluens in veste Menoetes
> summa petit scopuli siccaque in rupe resedit.
> illum et labentem Teucri et risere natantem
> et salsos rident revomentem pectore fluctus.

He spoke; but Menoetes, fearing blind
rocks, wrenches the prow aside towards the open sea.

"Whither so far off course? Make for the rocks,
Menoetes!" again shouted Gyas to call him back;
when suddenly he sees Cloanthus hard behind and
keeping the inside course. Between Gyas' ship
and the roaring rocks he grazes the leader, and
leaving the goal behind gets into the deeper water.
Then indeed the young man burned deep with anger;
he burst into tears, and, indifferent to his own
pride and his crew's safety, he throws timid Menoetes
from the high stern into the sea; steersman and
captain himself, he takes the helm, cheers his men
on, and turns the rudder shoreward. But Menoetes,
finally rising heavily from the sea, old and dripping
in his sodden clothes, makes for the dry rock. The
Teucrians laughed as he fell and swam, and they laugh
as he spews the salt water from his chest.

[5.164–82]

The foolish helmsman Menoetes is the first Trojan we have seen struggling with the ocean, and the laughter of the watchers on the shore may be construed as a collective reaction formation against their own terrors in earlier storms. Perhaps this hapless helmsman is a surrogate for their own anxieties, but, perhaps, they are unloading on him, with their contemptuous laughter, their own vicarious relief from the terrors that he has playfully undergone. In any case the episode marks the collective hardening of individual responses to real terrors, and this is part of the conditioning which the pseudo-games are designed to induce. Personal concern for a fellow in difficulty and danger is submerged in a shared and official contempt for anyone whose behavior can be regarded as weak. In the games the Trojans *en masse* have submitted to the official group psychology. Woe hereafter to anyone who seems to show too much or too little daring in coping with challenges to the imperial destiny. While Gyas loses through the excessive caution of his aged helmsman, and Sergestus through recklessly cutting the mark too close, Cloanthus wins over Menestheus by steering a judicious course and also delivering a well-timed appeal for divine help that sounds more like a promised bribe than a prayer:

"dei, quibus imperium est pelagi, quorum aequora curro,
vobis laetus ego hoc candentem in litore taurum

constituam ante aras voti reus, extaque salsos
porriciam in fluctus et vina liquentia fundam."

"Ye gods, whose kingdom is the deep, over whose waters I
run, gladly, in discharge of my vow, will I on this shore set
before your altars a snow-white bull, and fling entrails into
the salt flood and pour liquid wine!"

[5.235–38]

Considering the complex agony with which the major deities of the
Aeneid visit men and women, the easy compliance of the sea nymphs
with Cloanthus's wishes suggests a somewhat facile, institutional
piety.

The footrace that follows is won through a blatant foul by
Euryalus, when his lover, Nisus, having slipped and fallen on a pool
of sacrificial blood, trips up the leader. The fraudulent victory is
blandly confirmed by the smile of "the gracious father" to the general
applause of the crowd. Virgil's alterations of the Homeric model here
are telling. Homer's Aias Oileus also slips and falls, not on blood but
on cow dung, and he does not attempt to trip up anyone else. Achilles
confirms the right order of finishing while expressing sympathy for
Aias' mishap. The shift in details suggests a kind of cleaning up of
Homer's earthy realism in the interests of decorum and a simultaneous acceptance or affirmation of the Roman leader's right to make
arbitrary decisions, especially if they are popular, and Euryalus is a
general favorite.

In general, compared with Homer's games, Virgil's are dull and
corrupt. That the games for Patroclus are sacred rituals, in the ideal
time and space and under the rules authentic games must observe,
and that these games provide a respite from the tragic grind of war,
are ideas not really present in Virgil's official productions. Rather, the
Virgilian games are programmed activities designed to inculcate in
the mass of Trojans the virtues of moderation, pietism, and obedience
to their leader, right or wrong. Beyond this, they function, in a much
less subtle way than Homer's games, to unite the individual warriors
into a cohesive army capable of the cooperation and discipline that
will help them to achieve their destined victory. With few exceptions
the leaders singled out for special notice in these celebrations will
disappear beneath the collective juggernaut of Roman power, their
identities absorbed into the impersonal military and political struc-

ture, with its official religion, that is essential to the founding and the preservation of an *imperium sine fine.*

Against the dreary social conditioning that lies behind the first four events, the Troy game performed by Iulus and his young friends comes as a dazzling and beautiful surprise. The brilliance of these intricate cavalry maneuvers with their labyrinthine choreography is augmented by the fact that they are a true ritual reenactment of a cosmogonic archetypal myth. They are not secular contests but a sacred dance. We cannot tell the dancers from the dance, not because the individual is lost in some collectivized action but because each joyfully surrenders his ego to patterns of numinous power that will be reenacted in the consecration of the walls of Alba Longa and celebrated in Virgil's day by Augustus.

The exercise calls forth Virgil's most subtle and intricate poetry:

> postquam omnem laeti consessum oculosque suorum
> lustravere in equis, signum clamore paratis
> Epytides longe dedit insonuitque flagello.
> olli discurrere pares atque agmina terni
> diductis solvere choris rursusque vocati
> convertere vias infestaque tela tulere.
> inde alios ineunt cursus aliosque recursus
> adversi spatiis, alternosque orbibus orbis
> impediunt, pugnaeque cient simulacra sub armis;
> et nunc terga fuga nudant, nunc spicula vertunt
> infensi, facta pariter nunc pace feruntur.
> ut quondam Creta fertur Labyrinthus in alta
> parietibus textum caecis iter ancipitemque
> mille viis habuisse dolum, qua signa sequendi
> falleret indeprensus et inremeabilis error:
> haud alio Teucrum nati vestigia cursu
> impediunt texuntque fugas et proelia ludo,
> delphinum similes, qui per maria umida nando
> Carpathium Libycumque secant luduntque per undas.
> hunc morem cursus atque haec certamina primus
> Ascanius, Longam muris cum cingeret Albam,
> rettulit et Priscos docuit celebrare Latinos.
> quo puer ipse modo, secum quo Troia pubes;
> Albani docuere suos; hinc maxima porro
> accepit Roma et patrium servavit honorem;

Troiaque nunc pueri, Troianum dicitur agmen.
hac celebrata tenus sancto certamina patri.

When the boys had ridden gaily round the whole circuit of
their gazing kinfolk, Epytides shouted from afar the expected signal and cracked his whip. They galloped apart in
equal ranks, and the three companies, parting their bands,
broke up the columns; then, recalled, they wheeled about
and charged with levelled lances. Next they enter on other
marches and other countermarches in opposing groups,
interweaving circle with alternate circle, and waking an
armed mimicry of battle. And now they bare their backs in
flight, now turn their spears in charge, now make peace and
ride on side by side. As of old in high Crete it is said the
Labyrinth held a path woven with blind walls, and a bewildering work of craft with a thousand ways, where the
tokens of the course were confused by the indiscoverable
and irretraceable maze: even in such a course do the Trojan
youths entangle their steps, weaving in sport their flight
and conflict, like dolphins that, swimming through the wet
main, cleave the Carpathian or Libyan seas and play amid
the waves. This manner of horsemanship, these contests
Ascanius first revived when he girt Alba Longa with walls,
and taught the Early Latins, even as he himself solemnized
them in boyhood, and with him the Trojan youth. The
Albans taught their children; from them in turn mighty
Rome received them and kept as an ancestral observance;
and today the boys are called Troy and the troop Trojan.
Thus far were celebrated the sports in honor of the holy
sire.

[5.577–603]

The Troy game, whose etymology may include both the city and
the *turns* (as in the verb *troare*) of its evolving movement, mobilizes
many opposites in a rich symbolic complex: aggression and flight,
forward and backward movement, transformation of the whole troop
into two troops and three troops, war and truce, inextricable alienation and loss versus deliverance, implication as against the releasing
power of the dance pattern, youth and age, sons and fathers, center
and circumference, weaving and unweaving, the disciplined coordina-
tion of the military evolutions versus the exuberant but equally

harmonious pattern of the dolphins' leaps, and so on. Michael Putnam's comment is penetrating:

> This *lusus Troiae*, performed by Iulus, is an example of the order and perfection of game as seen in the grace and exactitude of a set piece which cannot be broken without spoiling the mood entirely. This very perfection, however, focuses our attention once more on one of the tensions developed within the sphere of game, namely, that it is beyond what is regularly human because death is avoided. The meaning of the *lusus Troiae* hovers between the two poles of complete escape and complete involvement with real life. It is like most games because it admits of no destruction or violence to its participants. And, after all, only children are performing it under the watchful eyes of their teachers and within limitations which demand precise order for their fulfillment. But even here there remains in the background the potentiality of war as fought by men whose goal is death, not stage play. The images never get beyond the labyrinth and the dolphins, but each looks potentially further ahead to future hazard. . . .[2]

I would modify this observation in several ways. The *lusus Troiae* obviously does anticipate war, but the war will end in reconciliation and integration of the various nations involved, and the peace will be followed by the founding and ritual consecration, by another performance of the *lusus Troiae*, of a city destined to live forever. The ritual, as W. F. Jackson Knight has shown, is ultimately apotropaic in purpose: to preserve the safety and sanctity of the city walls. But the city will itself be a Troy town, with the profound inner power and complexity of the game. Even more important is the *coincidentia oppositorum* that the ritual performs: war will be transformed into peace, the egoism of heroic individualism will yield to a surplus of value in the participation of formerly contending individuals in a divine and suprapersonal myth, and the centrifugal and centripetal drives which have torn the Trojans between extremes will be harmonized, as the ancient mother is rediscovered in a new/old world. The function, then, of the *lusus Troiae*, even though it is interrupted by the firing of the ships, is positive and conciliatory, and the performance here carries a promise for the future that the simple rivalries of the first four games are incapable of, just as the actual founding of the city will be beyond the capacity of Aeneas, with his conventionally dualistic thinking, and will be left to Iulus to accomplish. An important final point is made by Knight: "Homer's Troy and Virgil's was a 'labyrinthine' city. I take it that a labyrinthine city fulfills some or all of the following conditions. It must be supposed to depend on supernatural defence, inaugurated and sustained by magical or religious ceremonies, which are meant, either always or at least often, to create or strengthen the ring magic of the wall, particularly by means of 'labyrinthine' movements."[3] If labyrinthine Troy is to be founded anew, the new city, for all these reasons, must be a labyrinthine "Troy," and the sacrificial performance of the initiatory ritual will be one of the most important services that Iulus can render.

If the labyrinthine consecration of Rome by the ritual *lusus Troiae* will be left for Iulus to perform, a labyrinthine journey to the underworld, which serves both as a rite of passage and an initiation into the future of Rome, must be undertaken by his father. The sixth book of the *Aeneid* carries us deep into a world of death and rebirth, a heart of darkness that is the symbolic expression of the values hidden at the center of the poem. This journey transcends any purely Roman interests and founds the epic squarely upon an archetypal myth both fundamental and universal. Aeneas is faced with a mystical journey that will endow him with the power and the vision to complete his mission as founder of New Troy.

Aeneas's visit to the other world, like Odysseus', is prefaced by the death of a companion. Whereas Odysseus loses Elpenor, an amiable minor figure done in by a drunken accident, Aeneas loses Palinurus, who has navigated the Trojan fleet through all its seven years of vicissitudes since the departure from Troy. The loss of Palinurus, with the mysterious and conflicting circumstances surrounding it, marks a major stage in the journey and the conclusion of the maritime portion of the quest. From this point forward Aeneas's voyage will entail the penetration of the new land by riverine passages of the Tiber and by the culminating encounters on land. The loss of Palinurus is offset by the new orientation to the future that Aeneas acquires in the underworld, with the implication that finally, at the midpoint of the poem, he has become the sole leader of the Trojan expedition, no longer dependent on his father or on his navigator, the chief on whom its future fortunes entirely depend.

The entrance to the cavern at Cumae is marked by a temple dedicated to Apollo by Daedalus at the conclusion of his flight from

Crete. On its doors are depicted, among other scenes, the Knossian labyrinth with the Minotaur and the clue by which Ariadne enabled Theseus to "unwind the deceptive tangle of the palace, a maze inextricable, guiding blind feet with a thread" (6.27–30). The maze, corresponding to many found by anthropologists in remote parts of the world, represents the intricate and complex path from the land of the living to the abode of the spirits of the past and the future. Beyond the entrance the orientations of the familiar world do not apply. The Sibyl, his new guide, announces to Aeneas that what he will encounter in Italy is a repetition of the circumstances that beset fallen Troy. Thus, Aeneas learns he is to confront again, in the new *antiqua mater*, the problems that dogged his former city; the future and the past mirror each other:

> "o tandem magnis pelagi defuncte periclis
> (sed terrae graviora manent), in regna Lavini
> Dardanidae venient (mitte hanc de pectore curam);
> sed non et venisse volent. bella, horrida bella
> et Thybrim multo spumantem sanguine cerno.
> non Simois tibi nec Xanthus nec Dorica castra
> defuerint; alius Latio iam partus Achilles,
> natus et ipse dea; nec Teucris addita Iuno
> usquam aberit, cum tu supplex in rebus egenis
> quas gentis Italum aut quas non oraveris urbes!
> causa mali tanti coniunx iterum hospita Teucris
> externique iterum thalami."

> "O thou that hast at last fulfilled the great perils of the sea—yet by land more grievous woes await thee—into the realm of Lavinium the sons of Dardanus shall come— relieve thy heart of this care—yet they shall not also joy in their coming. Wars, grim wars I see, and Tiber foaming with streams of blood. Thou shalt not lack a Simois, nor a Xanthus, nor a Doric camp. Even now another Achilles is raised up in Latium, he, too, goddess-born; nor shall Juno anywhere fail to dog the Trojans, while thou, a suppliant in need, what races, what cities shall thou not implore! The cause of all this Trojan woe is again an alien bride, again a foreign marriage!"

> [6.83–94]

Thus the peculiar anguish of his ordeal is that the achievement of his future goal is, ineluctably, a detailed reenactment of the ordeals he has already endured and, until this awful revelation, believed he had left behind in Troy. That the horrors he is to face in Latium should mirror so closely the horrors of Troy means that, wherever Fate may take him, it will never deliver him from the nightmare of the past. Through the concluding half of his ordeal Aeneas will carry the terrible burden of knowledge that the future he seeks will be all of a piece with the past he has struggled to escape. This extraordinary condition goes a long way to account for the sombre mood which dominates him in the last half of the poem: the inferno he has fled will be replicated in the new inferno he is doomed to experience, with the added horror that, in the new inferno, he must also enact the role of the Greek aggressor from whom he once fled. In a sense, then, Aeneas's final actions require him to assume the guilt of aggression against a largely innocent people fighting, as he had fought, in defense of their city. This may be the bitterest aspect of Virgil's irony.

It is no wonder that when Anchises' ghost shows his son the spirits awaiting rebirth, Aeneas responds with amazement at "their mad longing for the light" (6.721). One life, he clearly feels, is more than enough, and his response to his father's display of glorious generations of future Romans is less than enthusiastic. The only hero Aeneas asks specifically about is the glorious Marcellus whose career was cut short by an untimely death, and the most powerful note struck in this preview of great Romans is elegiac: *heu pietas, heu prisca fides, invictaque bello/dextera* (7.878–79). With parting instructions from his father as to the strategies he should pursue in Latium, Aeneas returns from the underworld through the ivory gate of false dreams, a circumstance that perhaps suggests that the hero can endure facing the future only by forgetting most of what he has learned about it. Gates, after all, face two ways.

Whatever else the journey to the underworld means to Aeneas, it has involved his complete initiation into the labyrinthine mysteries of life and death, of fate and history. In contrast to the largely retrospective nature of Odysseus' *nekuia*, Aeneas's indoctrination is focused on the future, which from Virgil's perspective is the Roman past. And so, for the Roman hero as for Stephen Dedalus, history is a nightmare from which there can be no awakening, a nightmare in which he is destined, much against his will, to play the leading role.

The net effect of these revelations has been not to enfranchise his spirit through a conspectus of the Roman future but to bind it implacably to a course of action he sometimes detests.

❧

If the first, "Odyssean" half of the *Aeneid* is dominated by the account of Aeneas's gradual informed acceptance of his mission as a leader and founder, the second, "Iliadic" half complicates the pattern of the Greeks' siege of Troy by establishing troubling similarities between the colonizing Trojans and the Latins who, as the Trojans formerly did, are fighting in defense of their city. To be sure, the gods have divulged to old Latinus the fact that the future of his people depends on Lavinia's marriage to a man of another race, but Turnus, engaged to Lavinia, under the influence of Juno, defies prophecy and, in the Trojans' attack on Latium, dies with heavy losses to his cohorts and allies. Yet the moral position of Turnus in defending Latium in defiance of divine prediction is not very different from that of Hector, who brings ruin on his city by persisting in fighting in a lost cause— the retention of Helen—even though he cannot defend the issue. To Helen he generously admits that his brother Paris is to blame, but, after the issue has been put to the test of single combat between Menelaos and Paris, and the truce has been broken by the Trojan Pandarus, Hector does not use his power and influence as chief of the Trojans to insist that his people honor the solemn agreement they have sworn to. Whenever, after the aborted duel, he has intimations of disaster, Hector sees behind his continuing persistence in a bad cause the motive that, in yielding to what is right, he would feel shame before the Trojan women he promised to defend. The conditioning influence of a shame culture, which David Riesman calls other-directed,[4] allows him to repress or ignore his personal responsibility for the inevitable disaster.

The analogy also holds, to an extent, between Aeneas's Trojans and the Achaeans, especially Achilles. As the agent of a restored civilization and the founder of a rich culture, and as custodian of the future, Aeneas, under stress, often regresses into orgies of savagery that are much like those of Achilles when he runs berserk with grief and rage after he loses Patroclus. As we shall see, Aeneas's disciplined role as a just and restrained leader is shattered by his regression into purely personal and egoistic acts of murderous hatred. His final military triumph is achieved at a terrible cost and raises the disturbing question whether even the greatest culture hero can preserve his true values under the onslaught of violent and frustrating opposition. The Trojan right to settle in Latium is governed by the tacit condition that they act with justice and moderation, as his father's ghost suggest to him:

> "tu regere imperio populos, Romane, memento
> (haec tibi erunt artes) pacique imponere morem,
> parcere subiectis et debellare superbos."

> "Remember thou, O Roman, to rule the nations with thy sway—these shall be thy arts—to crown Peace with Law, to spare the humbled and to tame in war the proud."
>
> [6.851–53]

These solemn words indicate a way in which Aeneas can lead his nation out of the errors of the past, which arose from flagrant violation of law, and build a new society in which all men of good will can participate equally. It is, in fact, the central idea of Roman culture. To violate it is to jeopardize the foundations of future civilization. We shall explore the implications of this idea further on.

Book 7 opens with a brief and curious account of the death of Aeneas's old nurse, Caieta, which may be taken as the breaking of his last tie with his past. After the funeral Aeneas leads his fleet into the mouth of the shady Tiber.

The scene changes to Latium, where Latinus consults the oracle of Faunus, his father, and learns that Lavinia must marry a stranger. Meanwhile, the Trojans, through a chance remark of Iulus, discover that they are at the site of their new city, and Aeneas marks out the walls with a shallow trench. A Trojan embassy reaches the neighboring palace of Latinus, and after a warm welcome is sent back to Aeneas with the king's message that he is the destined husband of Lavinia. At this peaceful prospect Juno arouses the fury Allecto to stir up wrathful opposition to the match in the queen, and to transform Turnus from a level-headed young man into the incarnation of furious resentment. Turnus mobilizes the Rutulians, while the tense situation is exacerbated by Iulus's unfortunate slaying of a pet deer belonging to a little girl named Sylvia. As Allecto's poison spreads, Turnus's numerous allies are listed in an uninspired imitation of the catalogue of ships in *Iliad* 2, with which the book ends.

The movement of the first half of the *Aeneid* was toward a closer and closer focus on Aeneas, as, evading one obstacle after another, he achieved Italy and was initiated into the ultimate mysteries at Cumae. In contrast, the second half begins, after a moment of calm, with an explosion of contagious violence, and the focus widens to include the manifold and frenzied activities that follow the intervention of Aeneas's principal enemy, Juno.

Book 8 counterbalances the frenzied activity of Turnus and his allies with Aeneas's expedition up the Tiber to Evander in quest of allies. Unlike the purely reflexive Turnus, Aeneas meditates over the Trojans' plight:

> Talia per Latium. quae Laomedontius heros
> cuncta videns magno curarum fluctuat aestu
> atque animum nunc huc celerem, nunc dividit illuc
> in partisque rapit varias perque omnia versat:
> sicut aquae tremulum labris ubi lumen aënis
> sole repercussum aut radiantis imagine lunae
> omnia pervolitat late loca iamque sub auras
> erigitur summique ferit laquearia tecti.

> Thus is was throughout Latium. And the hero of Laomedon's line, seeing it all, tosses on a mighty sea of troubles; and now hither, now thither he swiftly throws his mind, casting it in diverse ways, and turning it to every shift; as when in brazen bowls a flickering light from the water, flung back by the sun or the moon's glittering form, flits far and wide o'er all things, and now mounts high and strikes the fretted ceiling of the roof above.
> [8.18–25]

This simile has interesting correspondences with the one in the preceding book that refers to Turnus's sudden lust for war:

> saevit amor ferri et scelerata insania belli,
> ira super: magno veluti cum flamma sonore
> virgea suggeritur costis undantis aëni
> exsultantque aestu latices, furit intus aquai
> fumidus atque alte spumis exuberat amnis,
> nec iam se capit unda, volat vapor ater ad auras.

> Lust of the sword rages in him, the accursed frenzy of war, and resentment crowning all: even as when flaming sticks,

loud crackling, are heaped under the ribs of a billowing
cauldron, and the waters dance with the heat; within
seethes the liquid flood, steaming and bubbling up high
with foam; and now the wave contains itself no longer, and
the black smoke soars aloft.

[7.461–66]

The gentle turbulence of the water in the first simile quoted is not
derived from fire; and its random motion, lit by moon or sun, is
reflected on the ceiling. In the second one the water billows, dances,
seethes, bubbles, and foams in a sharply recorded account of the
stages by which water becomes steam. The water then overflows its
brazen vessel and helps form the black smoke that soars upward
without limit. The effect is to emphasize the reflexive nature of
Turnus's response: even at this decisive moment he does not decide
but simply suffers the equivalent of a familiar thermo-physical
reaction, a reaction that darkens his perceptions with smoke. In the
Aeneas simile, on the other hand, fire, so often in the *Aeneid* a
symbol for the irrational, is lacking. The water, reflecting alternative
sources of light, the sun and the moon, may suggest that Aeneas is in
touch with both sides of his personality, the unconscious and the
conscious, or the modes of contemplation and action. That the light is
confined to a room instead of streaming up like smoke has various
implications: Aeneas is aware that his choices are limited; he is also
aware that he must avoid all-out war with future allies; he is also a
hero who sets great store by the Roman emphasis on limit and
measure, unlike Shakespeare's Antony. The Achaians, Dido, the
disgruntled old women who set fire to the ships in Sicily, Juno,
Allecto, Amata, and Turnus are all, psychologically, pyromaniacs,
given to the reckless use of what may well be the most dangerous of
the four elements. Aeneas, on the other hand, for the time at least, is
given to the reflecting and reflective properties of water and moonlight and to the rational associations of the sun.

In Juno's easy conquest of Turnus's will must we not conclude that
Virgil is allowing the crucial conduct of a major character of his poem
to be utterly controlled by malign divine egotism; that in influencing
Turnus, Juno's offended vanity will destroy an admirable young
prince in what she knows is a futile attempt to destroy the Trojans?
We may also suppose that Turnus has a predilection for unconsidered
violence; that his personality is in key ways savage and undeveloped;

that experience has never laid the kind of demands on him that would expose him to the opportunities and terrors of the rite of passage. Like other failed heroes we shall meet, Turnus has no interest in reflecting on the past or the future except as it affects him personally. He can expand his painful case into a persuasive but specious cause in which thousands of others will come under his spell, as Ahab mesmerizes his crew; but, for all his courage, he is a disastrous leader. With a facile political motto, "Defend Italy, drive the foe from our bounds," he magnetizes his followers, moved variously "by the peerless beauty of his form and youth, by his royal ancestry, or by the glorious deeds of his hand" (7.472–73).

Aeneas does not resort to such charismatic or hypnotizing techniques as a leader. Before he can act, he must learn. Tiberinus reassures him that "here thy home is sure—draw not back—and sure are the gods" (8.39). As a guarantee of the authenticity of his prophecy, the Tiber tells Aeneas, as we have seen, to look for a white sow just delivered of thirty young and lying under an ilex (8.43–45) as a pledge that Rome will be founded in thirty years by Ascanius. The prophecy further distances Aeneas from any compulsion he may feel toward immediate action. The prophetic river directs him toward his immediate need, to visit *regem Euandrum comites, qui signa secuti, / delegere locum et passere in montibus urbem*—the site chosen by the companions of King Evander—where he will find help, since they war with the Latin race ceaselessly. The premature vision of a peaceful cooperation between Trojans and Latins that Aeneas had entertained is dashed; nevertheless, he has the guarantees from the god of the Tiber that his mission is destined to succeed.

Far up this river, unknown to Aeneas, is the ancient, pristine city of Evander, the center of his quest. On the way he encounters the white sow with thirty piglets and sacrifices them to Juno. This theme of white sacrificial animals—like the sow in Golding's *Lord of the Flies*, like Moby Dick, like the white animals sacrificed on important occasions in Homer—marks the threshold to a new perception of reality. As part of a divine plan, this sacrifice of a white sow and her enormous brood marks a new stage in Aeneas's voyage. In contrast to the pyromaniacal suggestions of Allecto to Turnus, this portent leads to a brief idyllic voyage up the virgin Tiber to the city of the Arcadian king. Like Nestor, on Telemachus's visit to Pylos, the Arcadians are involved in a ritual celebration of their divine patron. Evander's son, Pallas, receives the strangers with Homeric hospitality. The atmosphere is Odyssean, especially in Evander's recollections of the hospitality of Laomedon. For a moment we are back in the world of the *Odyssey* with its frequent examples of *xenia*, endorsed by *themis*, between hosts and strangers. The Homeric ritual feast over, Evander provides the expected entertainment with his account of Hercules' triumph over Cacus, the fire-breathing monster, devourer of men, who lived in a cave. This is clearly a simplified version of the myth of the Cretan labyrinth, but complicated by the fact that Cacus, more inventive than the Minotaur, has escaped the cavern where the hero is seeking him, leaving trails that indicate an entrance *into* the cave, while they were, in fact, ingeniously contrived by the monster as he was taking the cattle *out* of it.

In contrast to the Latins and their allies, the Arcadians have a founding cultural hero and a living ritual by which they commemorate him. In Latium we find an early instance of a culture in which cosmogonic myth and ritual play relatively minor parts. Latinus is right-thinking but weak, and his dreadful wife imitates Juno in her behavior. Latium, for all its virtues, is an unregenerate and futureless society, one that, without some renewing intervention from without, might dwindle into a shadowy Yoknapatawpha. While Latium does have a nominal founder, Picus, he is so remote that only the impotent old king consults him. He happens to be right on the question of Lavinia's marriage, but nobody except Latinus believes him.

Aeneas's visit with Evander introduces him to a pastoral, richly mythic society. Pallanteum is, figuratively, near to heaven, and one of its great virtues, as Anchises' ghost has implied to Aeneas, is humility—not practiced for itself but for its fundamental social virtue. Thus Evander to Aeneas:

> ut ventum ad sedes, "haec," inquit, "limina victor
> Alcides subiit, haec illum regia cepit.
> aude, hospes, contemnere opes et te quoque dignum
> finge deo, rebusque veni non asper egenis."

> When they reached his dwellings: "These portals," he cries, "victorious Alcides stooped to enter; this mansion welcomed him. Dare, my guest, to scorn riches; fashion thyself also to be worthy of deity, and come not disdainful of our poverty."

> [8.362–65]

The voyage to Pallanteum is a further initiation into the mythic past that Aeneas must try to forge into unity. The Arcadian perspective on life will contribute stability to the amalgamation of these three peoples in the establishment of Rome. Evander's main contribution to the Roman future is to reinforce the implications of Anchises' message to his son in the underworld: nothing of value can be achieved by unbridled force. Cacus, as an incendiary monster, met his match in Hercules, just as the Minotaur was overcome by the combined strengths of Theseus and Ariadne. Turnus, as an attractive human version of the incendiary Cacus, like Cacus will drag his people into the cave of the past, while appearing to lead them to a real future. But the cave, rightly comprehended, is a stage in man's development into potency and identity, and the destruction of Cacus by the patron of the outcast Arcadians marks a major victory of civilization over *furor*. Significantly, Evander's tributes to Hercules are not paid in burnt offerings but in libations. Michael Putnam sensitively interprets the episode:

> Thus the river bears Aeneas into a realm where, even in the past, all has not been serene, and the grove, crucial always in Virgil at moments of change, offers initiation into a pattern which demands heroism in the face of violent opposition but yet postulates that this very heroism adapt itself closely to the spirit of Evander's pastoral realm.[5]

Throughout books 7 and 8 we can observe a pattern of contrasting values, moods, and tones: the frenzied, unthinking animation in Latium with its dominant motif of raging fire versus the serenity of the Tiber and of Evander's city, marked by sacred groves and water imagery; Evander's pious submission to destiny versus old Latinus's feckless submission to his maddened wife, Amata; and, finally, the Arcadian reverence for a rich mythic and historical past versus the Latins' relative indifference to the past and blindness to the future consequences of their impulsive commitment to war.

The contrast extends to the next scene in book 8, in which Venus seductively persuades Vulcan to design immortal arms for Aeneas. Venus

> niveis hinc atque hinc diva lacertis
> cunctantem amplexu molli fovet. ille repente

accepit solitam flammam, notusque medullas
intravit calor et labefacta per ossa cucurrit. . . .

> throws her snowy arms round about him and fondles
> him in soft embrace. At once he caught the wonted flame;
> the familiar warmth passed into his marrow and ran
> through his melting frame. . . .

[8.387–90]

The accustomed flame of sexual desire is quite distinct from the fiery
rage of Amata or Turnus, and it produces a generative warmth *(calor)*
that underlies Vulcan's creative artistry. Even the tremendous fires of
the Cyclopean forges are directed to the great creative task. This
intimate, warmly comic scene stands in contrast to Juno's act of
malice in book 7, discussed earlier. As she spies the Trojans at the site
of Rome, she soliloquizes:

"ast ego, magna Iovis coniunx, nil linquere inausum
quae potui infelix, quae memet in omnia verti,
vincor ab Aenea. quod si mea numina non sunt
magna satis, dubitem haud equidem implorare quod
    usquam est.
flectere si nequeo superos, Acheronta movebo."

"But I, Jove's mighty consort, who have endured, alas! to
leave naught undared, who have turned myself to every
shift, I am overcome by Aeneas! But if my powers are not
strong enough, surely I need not be slow to seek help
wherever it may be; if I cannot bend Heaven, then I will
rouse up Hell!"

[7.308–13]

Juno sees her marriage to Jove only in terms of the power and
privilege it should confer on her, but she feels cheated. If she cannot
bend the Olympians to her will, she can rouse up the spirits of Hell.
The *flammae* brought by Allecto have none of the creative power of
Vulcan's flames; they are like the flames that destroyed Troy. Repeated failure of her single-minded attempts to annihilate the Trojans
never leads Juno to reflect on the motives for her actions. While
knowing her efforts are doomed, she repeats them compulsively. A
divinity without wisdom, incapable of compassion or any but a
monomaniacal need to subjugate others, she is the opposite of Venus,

who knows how to put her sexual attractions, her wit, and her affection to productive uses. Aeneas incorporates to a large degree a feminine component in his psyche, from which stems his compassion and capacity for friendship and knack for cooperative action with others. Turnus may be seeking such an anima component in Lavinia, but he is incapable of achieving it because of his Achillean fixation on an archaic concept of honor.

Heavenly portents now signal the completion of the arms promised by Venus. As she presents them to Aeneas in a secluded vale by a cold stream, she embraces him, an indication of maternal affection that reminds us of her earlier aloofness in 1.305–417, when she refused his embrace.

Like Homer, Virgil concentrates on the details of the hero's shield. Unlike Homer, who depicts universal aspects of the human condition on his shield, Virgil confines himself to major events in the Roman future, ending with praise of Augustus for his victory at Actium. The implicit claim of Virgil's shield is that it represents all that is fundamentally important in the historical growth of Western civilization, while Homer's unhistorical but more inclusive vision is concentrated on the bases of culture in agriculture, song and dance, myth, and social institutions, intermixed, to be sure, with instances of violence. The effect of Virgil's design, by comparison with Homer's, is parochial. It is a series of tableaux that inevitably lacks the interwrought completeness of Homer's masterwork. It includes the mother wolf and Romulus and Remus; the rape of the Sabines; the founding of the circus games; war between the sons of Romulus and aged Tatius; a truce; the terrible execution of the traitor Mettus; Porsenna's siege; Cocles at the river; Catiline in hell; Cato giving laws; and, finally, Augustus at Actium and the victory of the Roman gods over the Egyptian. Except for an alternating pattern of disasters and triumphs, the future history of Rome seems strangely un-unified and incoherent; the historical figures involved have not survived with nearly as much vitality as the nameless people on the shield of Achilles, whose varied activities are centered on the labyrinthine dance of Ariadne and her companions to celebrate Theseus' victory over the Minotaur and deliverance from the maze. Perhaps the absence of any such unifying mythic motif accounts for my impression that the history of Rome on the shield of Aeneas is a random chronicle of the experiences of political figures who are no longer of much interest. Is an inevitable weakness in the historical perspective to be seen in the waning power of individuals once regarded as heroic?

This brings us to consider the peculiar difficulties facing the epic poet who devotes his poem to historical as well as legendary or mythical figures. In dealing with purely human agents he is bound by a higher standard of probability and plausibility than he is in dealing with figures distanced from mundane reality by their legendary, mythic, or fictional status; if the human agents are influenced by or related to divinities, the difficulties increase. For Homer, the problem of integrating the activities of mortals and immortals is relatively simple. Odysseus, Penelope, Telemachus are all *brotoi,* those who die, occasionally helped or hindered by *ambrotoi,* the everliving gods. Between the two orders there are various kinds of relationships, benevolent and malevolent. In the *Iliad* the influence on Achilles of his divine mother and his counterinfluence on her lead to partial disaster for his companions and a tragic end for himself. Odysseus, born of two human parents, must depend on purely human capabilities to see him through a dozen encounters with largely supernatural forces. When Athena intervenes to influence him, the intervention is the objective correlative to his own decision. Even in the *Iliad* divine forces do not usurp or encroach upon the free will of the mortal agents, although the latter may, like Agamemnon, blame their folly on the influence of malignant powers.

If we see the *Aeneid* as mediating between a mythic past dominated by gods and their chosen heroes and heroines, and a future that is actually the historical past, as seen from the age of Augustus, the poem undergoes a transformation from a predominantly mythic chronicle to an almost entirely historical one. To make the actual history of Rome part of a continuum from the mythical origins of Troy and its collapse requires a genius that can provide a convincing transition between two modes. The mythic view of the past sees, mostly, a repetition of primordial events. The world is complete, and any temporal experience or significance has its archetypal form and constitutes a reenactment of the archetype. From the historical point of view, the archetypes do not, necessarily, govern a future, which is subject to vicissitudes. The vision of a Rome *sine fine* was demolished in the fifth century and could only be sustained by new fictions accommodating the disaster as a prelude to the Holy Roman Empire. But the inexorable judgment of history is that the Rome Virgil celebrates had died, whereas Homer's world never died because it was never governed by a historical point of view.

Of all the epic and quasi-epic works under consideration in this study, Virgil's is the only one that attempts the transition from myth or legend to history. Camoens's disastrous *Lusiads* is so narrowly and obsessively nationalistic and Catholic in its values that it is not worth consideration, and Tasso's mélange of history, magic, and providential interventions in human affairs utterly fails to achieve the broad cultural vision that marks epic. Thus *Gerusalemme liberata*, whatever its scholarly interest may be, does not qualify for consideration in this study. We are left with the *Aeneid* as the only Western epic that combines the legendary and mythic genesis of a great civilization with its development toward a largely secular modern culture. Despite the persisting influence of the old Olympian gods, modified by the social and political values of Augustan Rome, the *Aeneid* starts from a mythic, Homeric past to transform itself into an essentially agnostic view of human destiny, however that view may, occasionally, be qualified by ritual celebrations.

To be bold, and possibly reckless, my contention is that Aeneas's emergence from his underworld visions through the ivory gates at the midpoint of the poem marks the shift from a primarily archetypal vision to a historical and dynastic one. Having been exposed, like Adam in the final books of *Paradise Lost*, to a historical account of the future of the race, Acneas, unlike Adam, emerges with a Pisgah sight of a thrivingly materialistic civilization whose final establishment he will not live to realize. Thus the psychic or spiritual death that is part of the ordeal in the underworld is not, for Aeneas, merely a prelude to rebirth but a significant farewell to the old mythic order in preparation for the pursuit of a new, essentially temporal one. In the process he is reoriented from his divine origins toward a more purely mortal role. Despite the interventions and portents that encourage him in his destined historical role, Aeneas, after book 6, is essentially a secular political and military leader whose final success is due mainly to his competence and commitment as a man of unusual mental and physical powers.

If we feel that the second half of the *Aeneid* falls short of the first in interest, it may be due to the gradual occlusion of those vital mythic visions and archetypes that pervade the first half of the poem. For some of us, the new Aeneas is all too familiar as an exemplar of modern man. The divine machinery which impinges on him without interfering with the practical fulfillment of his military and political triumph begins to seem outdated, a relic of a once vital, numinous power. As the destined process moves along, Aeneas becomes less and less a partner in a great joint enterprise and, more and more, the

lonely agent of a future in which his emotional involvement diminishes. Once he has found his ancient mother in Italy, his role shrinks
as he becomes less a leader than an instrument of its accomplishment.
No doubt this is a realistic accommodation to military and political
goals. It is accompanied, however, by Aeneas's sad awareness that,
despite his personal sacrifices as a restorer of Troy, his role is now
reduced to a subordinate function. As part of his heroic career,
Aeneas must accept this last negation of his personal dedication
toward the great end. His function is reduced from godlike to
strategical, and, finally from strategical to tactical. In his absence
from the embattled Trojans in book 9, his cohorts commit two drastic
errors, one defensive, one thoughtlessly aggressive. On the one hand,
the Trojans allow Turnus within their walls but lack the wit to trap
him; on the other hand, the romantic heroes, Nisus and Euryalus,
desperately weaken their imperiled salient by a sortie modeled on
book 10 of the *Iliad,* in which they slaughter the sleeping forces of the
enemy but, in their impulsive preoccupation with personal glory,
jeopardize the whole enterprise. The night raid of Odysseus and
Diomedes is recapitulated here by what appears as two junior would-
be heroes' self-indulgent jaunt. So, even as an instrument of the
future, Aeneas cannot trust his own instruments. They reenact his
own former reckless, and futile, counterattack against the triumphant
Greeks who destroyed Troy. Equally admirable and absurd, Aeneas's
foray in book 2 is based on a doomed, heroic, egoistical impulse:

> arma amens capio; nec sat rationis in armis,
> sed glomerare manum bello et concurrere in arcem
> cum sociis ardent animi; furor iraque mentem
> praecipitant, pulchrumque mori succurrit in armis.

> Frantic I seize arms; yet there is little purpose in arms, but
> my heart burns to muster a force for battle and hasten with
> my comrades to the citadel. Rage and wrath drive my soul
> headlong and I think how glorious it is to die in arms!
> [2.314–17]

This is essentially the furious pattern that Turnus pursues in a similar
situation. If such heedless aggressiveness is a phase even of this great
hero's experience, what hope is there that lesser heroes will not revert
to a facile and unreflecting violence? To this extent, at least, it appears
that Aeneas's history somberly repeats itself, for in both the begin-

ning and the end of the poem he is an instrument of unrestrained
violence, with intermissions that sometimes indicate the larger cosmogonic role he is partly to fulfill.

Book 9 relates the tragic adventure of Nisus and Euryalus and
the panic when Turnus enters the Trojan camp during Aeneas's
absence. It is besieged, like Troy, by the forces of Turnus, and, unlike
the besieged Achaians in the *Iliad*, two of the bravest of the invaders,
Nisus and Euryalus, set forth without authority on an ostensible
mission to Aeneas that is actually an opportunistic and unheroic
slaughter of some newly arrived allies of the enemy. The brutal,
unheroic night raid of Odysseus and Diomedes in *Iliad* 10, sometimes
challenged as an inauthentic addition, is here reenacted with a
difference. But the heroic ambitions of Nysus and Euryalus do not
really change their attack on the sleeping warriors from the kind of
clever, clandestine, subheroic foray of Odysseus and Diomedes, which
is, nonetheless, a vital intelligence mission. Heroic, and bemused by
their romantic heroism and by their bonds of fellowship, Nisus and
Euryalus, lacking the shrewdness of Odysseus, jeopardize the Trojan
cause.

This is Virgil's most telling attack on the archaic pursuit of
personal glory. Nisus and the dead friend for whom he died earn this
eulogy:

> Fortunati ambo! si quid mea carmina possunt,
> nulla dies umquam memori vos eximet aevo,
> dum domus Aeneae Capitoli immobile saxum
> accolet imperiumque pater Romanus habebit.

> Happy pair! If aught my verse avail, no day shall ever
> blot you from the memory of time, so long as the house of
> Aeneas shall dwell on the Capitol's unshaken rock, and the
> Father of Rome hold sovereign sway!

> [9.446–49]

An elegy, indeed, to an instance of romantic heroism, but an elegy
also to the obsolete example of romantic, heroic individualism. The
mission of Diomedes was an intelligence-gathering one; the slaughter
of the sleeping foes was incidental to it. The Virgilian version denies
the values Nisus and Euryalus celebrate. An apparent gain in human
values is offset by a loss in the necessarily more complex values that
can make the *imperium Romanum* a reality. Henceforth, any unre-

flecting act of courage on either side will be, in the long view, a failure. Little by little, the grand collective enterprise will absorb into itself, or will destroy, those brilliant, recalcitrant spirits who jeopardize the fated amalgamation. The diminution of personality Aeneas suffered in his abandonment of Dido will be the pattern to which many of the other brilliant individuals will submit; they will either submit or be destroyed by what are now established as suprapersonal social values: Mezentius, Camilla, Turnus will all die, vainly affirming their individuality.

The crisis of the last half of the *Aeneid* occurs in book 10, which opens with the only full debate among the gods principally concerned in the epic. Jupiter, in an attempt to stop further intervention, reminds the conclave that there will come a time, in the Roman war with Carthage, when they can intervene at their pleasure. Now, let them abide by the covenant he ordains. Venus then makes her longest speech in the poem, gracefully and persuasively mentioning the manifold persecutions Aeneas has suffered from Juno, whom she tactfully refrains from naming. Juno, though "spurred by fierce frenzy" (*acta furore gravi*), observes the decorum of this plenary session of the Olympians in a speech that is persuasive and rhetorically pitched to gain support from her audience. The discussion amounts to a real, conjoint inquiry of the gods into the tangled rights and duties of Turnus and Aeneas and their divine protagonists. The meeting ends in a deadlock, with Jupiter, as "king over all alike," leaving the adjudication of the issues to the war.

The whole scene is a weighing of all the relevant historical events that have led to the present impasse, and if the impasse is not yet solved, the debate puts the entire Trojan past, both Homeric and Virgilian, in a wider and more coherent perspective than we have had heretofore. The perspective does not last long, for we are thrust into the midst of the action as Aeneas returns and, after a struggle at the salient, enters his camp. In the ensuing battle Pallas, the beloved son of Evander and the closest friend that Aeneas has in Italy, is slain by Turnus, who takes Pallas's notable bronze belt as spoils. Like Achilles, inflamed with wrath and grief by the death of Patroclus, Aeneas runs amok. The following lines from Virgil's long account of Aeneas's maddened *aristeia* are representative:

> proxima quaeque metit gladio latumque per agmen
> ardens limitem agit ferro, te, Turne, superbum

caede nova quaerens. Pallas, Euander, in ipsis
omnia sunt oculis, mensae, quas advena primas
tunc adiit, dextraeque datae. Sulmone creatos
quattuor hic iuvenes, totidem quos educat Ufens,
viventis rapit, inferias quos immolet umbris
captivoque rogi perfundat sanguine flammas.
inde Mago procul infensam contenderat hastam.
ille astu subit—at tremibunda supervolat hasta—
et genua amplectens effatur talia supplex. . . .

With the sword he mows down all the nearest ranks, and
fiercely drives with the steel a broad path, seeking thee,
Turnus, still flushed with new-wrought slaughter. Pallas,
Evander, all stand before his eyes—the board whereto he
came first, a stranger, and the right hands pledged. Then,
four youths of Sulmo, and as many reared by Ufens, he
takes alive, to offer as victims to the dead and to sprinkle the
flame with captive blood. Next at Magus he had aimed the
hostile lance. Deftly he cowers—the lance flies quivering
over him—and, clasping the hero's knees, he speaks thus in
suppliance. . . .

[10.513–23]

Aeneas is compared in his rage to Aegaeon, who,

centum cui bracchia dicunt
centenasque manus, quinquaginta oribus ignem
pectoribusque arsisse, Iovis cum fulmina contra
tot paribus streperet clipeis, tot stringeret ensis:
sic toto Aeneas desaevit in aequore victor,
ut semel intepuit mucro.

men say, had a hundred arms and a hundred hands, and
flashed fire from fifty mouths and breasts when against
Jove's thunders he clanged with as many shields and bared
as many swords; so Aeneas gluts his rage over the whole
plain, when once his sword grows warm.

[10.565–70]

One wonders how Patroclus would receive the extraordinary
funeral tribute of the innocent Trojan youths Achilles sets aside for
his holocaust. Achilles understandably felt an inexhaustible grief and

guilt over the death of his old comrade. Aeneas, who likes and admires Pallas but barely knows him, acts as if the death of Pallas had released him from any restraints on his murderous rampage. Pallas entered the war knowing, as his loving father did, the risks he was freely undertaking. Aeneas allows the loss, purely due to the fortunes of war, to free him from the injunction of his father, *parcere subiectis et debellare superbos.* Instead he destroys indiscriminately anyone he can. Would Pallas feel honored by the random sacrifice of Rutulian youths? Aeneas rages like a stream in freshet or like a black tempest, having denied every impulse to compassion. The camp is freed: *tandem erumpunt et castra relinquunt / Ascanius puer et nequiquam obsessa iuventus* ("At last the boy Ascanius and the vainly beleaguered warriors burst forth and leave the camp") (10. 604–05). That Ascanius has no comment to make on his father's actions is all the comment needed here.

History requires generations, and generations, dynasties and families. Iulus, the growing son, in the vision of the *Aeneid* is to be the actual founder of Rome, whereas Telemachus' future is simply to carry out the tasks that preserve his civilization *in statu quo*—to adapt his less heroic skills to preserving what his father has won. The difference in these functions marks a distinction between an epic oriented toward the historical future and one that celebrates an archetypal reaffirmation of its formative cultural values.

Iulus, in some ways, is worse off than his father. His dynastic role, his indispensible function in the Roman future, reduces him to the nonbeing of a historical instrument. The spermatozoa of Iulus must be preserved, since he is, more than his father, the future father of Rome. But he never can escape his subordinate, instrumental role. Motherless and essentially fatherless, he is primarily a destined genetic instrument. Thus do the pressures of destiny—future national history—thwart the personalities of those whose function is instrumental. To be sure, Iulus is the custodian of the cosmogonic myth of the labyrinthine *Troia*, which will restore the mythic foundations of his new city, but, while the murderous war his father is involved in continues, he can only stand and wait. At no point in the *Aeneid* does he develop any real self. Rarely does he say anything of note or perform any significant act, and his father's love seems to be diverted to Pallas during that short-lived comradeship. Telemachus has a chance to prove himself and to learn something of the world on his journey for news of his father, and Homer makes him indispensible to the successful battle with the suitors. Surprisingly, then, despite the *Aeneid's* emphasis on the collective character of the great enterprise and the *Odyssey's* emphasis on individual prowess, the future founder of Rome is left waiting in the wings, while Telemachus is a full participant in the domestic and political life of Ithaka. Obviously, a figure so vital to the future Roman nation must be safeguarded, but the implications of Iulus's—and Lavinia's—lack of personality may reflect a theme that pervades the *Aeneid:* the cost in self-denial to the individual destined for a crucial public function.

Another important aspect of the question of individuality in Virgil is the behavior of the gods. To a far greater degree than Homer's gods their interventions override human choices and actions, and even major characters are often manipulated like puppets. As E. R. Dodds has shown, divine interventions in Homer are usually objective acts that correspond to mental processes of the human characters involved.[6] To be sure, Aphrodite can spirit Paris away from the battlefield and rescue Aeneas by hiding him in a cloud, and Hera can seduce Zeus into forgetting, for a while, to keep an eye on the course of the battle below. None of these interventions is critical, however, and the main action is unaffected by them. In the *Aeneid*, Venus's plan for Aeneas succeeds, with some concessions to Juno, but Juno manages to alter radically the behavior of Amata, Turnus, Juturna, and others. In *Iliad* 1, when Athena tugs Achilles by the hair as he is drawing his sword under the impulse to kill Agamemnon, her intervention corresponds to Achilles' indecision about acting on the impulse, and he chooses not to. Similarly, in *Odyssey* 1, when Athena in the guise of Mentor suggests to Telemachus that he might go off in search of news about his father, circumstances have already brought the young man to the point where he can make the decision without such prompting. Much more than in the *Iliad*, the gods of the *Odyssey* are in agreement about basic issues and values, and Poseidon is the only one who can harass Odysseus in revenge for his blinding of Polyphemus and hubristic taunts; but even Poseidon cannot interfere with Odysseus' mental processes.

Another restriction of free will in the *Aeneid* originates, at times, in the characters themselves, when they deceive themselves about situations or circumstances. In the middle of book 10, for example, Aeneas refuses to spare the suppliant Magus on the grounds that *belli commercia Turnus / sustulit ista prior iam tum Pallante perempto* ("Such negotiations in war Turnus put an end to when Pallas was slain") (10.532–33). But Turnus slew Pallas in a fair fight, and Aeneas's ruthlessness after the death of his young friend suggests that he is trying to distract himself from the grief and guilt he feels, very much as Achilles, after the death of Patroclus, with the same motives, spares no one, suppliant or innocent, who comes in reach of his weapons. Aeneas's brutality is less defensible because Pallas was only briefly his companion, while Patroclus was Achilles' lifelong friend. Nor does Achilles try to evade personal responsibility for his vengeful and indiscriminate killings, as Aeneas does when he tells Magus, *hoc patris Anchisae Manes, hoc sentit Iulus* ("Thus judges my father Anchises' spirit, thus Iulus") (10.534). When we remember Anchises' injunction to his son to spare the suppliant and put down the proud, this remark can only reveal ironically a profound self-ignorance at this point, nor can we accept Aeneas's bland assumption that his son would approve of this killing. The implications are driven home when Aeneas proceeds immediately to hunt down and slay a priest of Apollo wearing the consecrated fillets of the god. Only when he kills young Lausus, who is fighting in defense of his wounded father, does Aeneas's sense of compassion return:

> at vero ut voltum vidit morientis et ora,
> ora modis Anchisiades pallentia miris,
> ingemuit miserans graviter dextramque tetendit
> et mentem patriae strinxit pietatis imago.

> But when Anchises' son saw the look on that dying face—
> that face so wonderously pallid—he groaned in pity, and
> stretched forth his hand, as the likeness of his own filial
> love rose before his soul.
>
> [10.821–24]

This is a moving, richly suggestive passage. In killing young Lausus Aeneas has, in effect, duplicated Turnus's slaying of young Pallas. Virgil's identification of the two acts is intensified by the potent word *pallentia*, which encapsulates Pallas's brief career, while the use of the patronymic for Aeneas stresses the tragic losses of fathers and sons. The paternal-filial relationship is paramount in the *Aeneid*, and at this moment Aeneas sees in Lausus the image of Iulus. Such subconscious intimations mark a radical change of mood, if only for a while, in the hero, and the bloody horror of Aeneas's previous acts is

tempered by this powerful elegiac note. The habitual brutality of
Lausus's father, Mezentius, is also modified by his loss, and he
resolutely meets his own death with a heart surging with a vast tide
of shame and madness mingled with grief (870–71).

The truce, during which the funeral obsequies of Pallas take
place, is plainly modeled on the funeral of Patroclus, with the
significant omission of the funeral games in *Iliad* 23. Since the
Trojans' ordeal has not included the internecine divisions of the
Achaeans in the *Iliad*, there is clearly no need for such rituals of
reconciliation. Without them, however, the climax of the *Aeneid* is
singularly joyless, and the *Iliad's* brilliant conciliatory contests with
their profound comic vision is remote from the Trojans' obsession
with victory.

The funeral is, like Patroclus's, excessively magnificent. First,
Aeneas creates from a mighty oak a skeleton which he adorns with
the armor of Mezentius, including the *ensem eburnum* (ivory sword)
suspended from the mannequin's neck, possibly suggesting Mezentius' false dreams of victory. Then the wicker bier for the corpse is
decorated with elaborate robes "stiff with gold and purple," gifts of
Dido, followed by a procession of captured steeds and arms and the
captives to be sacrificed, and the arms of Pallas, except for the spoils
Turnus has kept. The elaborate show has some of the vulgar excess of
the funeral of Patroclus and is about as inappropriate to the deceased.

Most of the rest of book 11 is devoted to a bitter debate between
the arch-politician Drances and Turnus, which is broken up by news
of the Trojans' approach to Latium and to the inconclusive mêlée that
follows. Turnus, having for once contrived a well-prepared mountain
ambush of the main Trojan force under Aeneas, impulsively decides
to leave the pass unguarded just before Aeneas enters it. It is a fatal
move.

Turnus's impulsiveness is fed by the desperate plight of the
Latins, and in the beginning of book 12 he announces his readiness to
meet Aeneas in single combat:

> "nulla mora in Turno; nihil est, quod dicta retractent
> ignavi Aeneadae, nec quae pepigere recusent:
> congredior. fer sacra, pater, et concipe foedus.
> aut hac Dardanium dextra sub Tartara mittam,
> desertorem Asiae, (sedeant spectentque Latini)
> et solus ferro crimen commune refellam,
> aut habeat victos, cedat Lavinia coniunx."

"With Turnus lies no delay! there is no need for the coward
sons of Aeneas to renounce their words or their pact. I go to
meet him. Bring the holy rites, sire, and frame the covenant. Either with this arm will I hurl the Dardan to hell, the
Asian runaway—let the Latins sit and watch—and with my
single sword refute the nation's shame; or let him be lord of
the vanquished, let Lavinia pass to him as bride."

[12.11–17]

In the face of Latinus's objections, Turnus reiterates his purpose and
sends his herald to challenge Aeneas to a duel at dawn, but the duel is
violated by the Rutulians. Aeneas tries to stop the fray, but in vain.
Turnus slays many Trojans while Aeneas is incapacitated by an arrow
wound in the thigh, but he is miraculously healed and sets forth for
the last battle. Juturna, impersonating her brother's charioteer, seizes
the reins and undertakes a series of maneuvers that look as if she
were trying to close with Aeneas, while in fact she is avoiding him:

> iamque hic germanum iamque hic ostentat ovantem,
> nec conferre manum patitur, volat avia longe.
> haud minus Aeneas tortos legit obvius orbis
> vestigatque virum et disiecta per agmina magna
> voce vocat.

> And now here, now there, she displays her triumphant
> brother, yet doesn't allow him to close in fight, but flits far
> away. None the less Aeneas threads the winding maze to
> meet him, and tracks his steps, and amid the scattered ranks
> with loud voice calls him.

[12.479–83]

The brief image here brilliantly unites the two aspects of the mythic
labyrinth in the *Aeneid* in combining the mazelike defensive and
offensive maneuvers of Iulus's *lusus Troiae* in book 5 with his father's
labyrinthine exploration of the underworld in book 6. The initiate
Aeneas is determined to get to the center of this animated maze and
to kill his opponent, but Turnus, now gloomily aware that he cannot
win the contest, submits unprotestingly to the evasive actions of his
sister. It appears later that he recognized her from the moment she
took the reins of his chariot. As long as he can, Turnus moves around
the periphery of the decisive center, governed by terror of death. In
the general description of the battle that follows, Aeneas finally hits

on a way of bringing Turnus to face him. He sets fire to Lavinium.
Turnus's desperate mood reminds us of Mezentius's when he learns
of his son's death:

> obstipuit varia confusus imagine rerum
> Turnus et obtutu tacito stetit; aestuat ingens
> uno in corde pudor mixtoque insania luctu
> et furiis agitatus amor et conscia virtus.

> Aghast and bewildered by the changing picture of disaster,
> Turnus stood mutely gazing; within that single heart surges
> mighty shame, and madness mingled with grief, and love
> stung by fury, and the consciousness of worth.

$$[12.665\text{–}68]$$

As we have seen, a modus vivendi worked out for Trojans and
Latins by Juno and Jupiter is the prelude to Aeneas's final victory. It
is the victory of a hero who has successfully passed through his
ordeals and has achieved the wisdom and power to lead his people,
despite occasional regressions, over a young man of no transcendent
vision who has been forced to be brave. Were Aeneas to spare him,
Turnus would have no imaginable future but to live in shame. The
fact that Aeneas kills him in a spasm of anger over the belt of Pallas,
the spoils Turnus wears, as is customary in heroic warfare, indicates
the terrible strains Aeneas has suffered to bring to an end war that
was not of his seeking. Turnus is an essentially archaic figure in his
heroic egotism, and Virgil's epitaph is chillingly brief but appropriate:
vitaque cum gemitu fugit indignata sub umbras ("and with a moan
his life passed to the Shades below") (12.952). It is the line that
Milton will apply verbatim to Satan when he is defeated in the
encounter with Gabriel at the end of book 3 of *Paradise Lost*. It is also
Virgil's epitaph on the old heroic code.

3 Dante's Infernal Initiation

> These ambiguities of metaphor [as in Ulysses' quest in the
> Inferno] account for and engender the possibility of a double
> reading of the poem. The Divine Comedy overtly tells the story
> of the pilgrim's progress from the sinful state of the "selva
> oscura" to the beatific vision of Paradiso XXXIII. From this point
> of view, Dante dramatizes the spiritual conversion of the self
> and envisions the providential order of history and the cosmos
> as a significant totality. . . . It is a text, that is, which belongs to
> a redeemed order and which shifts its modes of representation,
> the visio corporalis, spiritualis and intellectualis, according to the
> order of reality it renders. But the poem undercuts, and recoils
> from, this prominent pattern of clear and distinct order. It also
> tells of the persistent ambiguity of metaphorical language in
> which everything is perpetually fragmented and irreducible to
> any unification. Alongside the presence of a representation
> adequate to its spiritual reality, the poem repeatedly dramatizes
> a world of dissemblances, empty forms and illusory appearances
> which the poet repeatedly demystifies but to which the poem is
> irrevocably bound.
>
> Mark Musa

Of all the epic journeys to the underworld from Homer to Joyce,
Dante's is the most elaborately structured. The nine circles of Hell
with their subdivisions are arranged as a downward-pointing cone
through which the pilgrim and his guide make their spiral descent. As
the circles contract they tend to become more crowded and constricting and their occupants increasingly immobilized until the bottom
point is reached where the traitors are frozen in ice.

The characters of the damned and the nature of their sins and
punishments are minutely and concretely reflected in a mass of
topographical and architectural detail. Thus each sinner's character
and the character of his sin and punishment correspond to the special

place to which he is assigned, and Dante the pilgrim's descending journey requires an increasingly sensitive and discriminating response to the many damned souls he encounters. His intellectual and spiritual ordeal resembles Adam's education into the consequences of the Fall under the tutelage of Michael in the final books of *Paradise Lost* in moving from ignorant or mistaken responses to ones that are increasingly perceptive and true, while both heroes acquire more freedom and autonomy in the process and become less dependent on their guides. But Adam's journey is a journey of the mind only, while Dante's descent is strenuously physical and involves not only his mind but all his senses. Thus the horror and pity of Adam's journey is mitigated by the mode of its presentation—historical narrative and historical vision—while Dante encounters and speaks and interacts with a vast number of individuals in various milieus that are inescapably physical and immediate. Adam cannot question the figures Michael represents to him, but Dante's education depends heavily on what he learns from his dramatic encounters with each of the damned souls he meets.

The overwhelming impression of the *Inferno* is due to its phenomenal impact on the senses, as Dante weaves into the variegated milieus of Hell: darkness, lurid flames, winds, heat, intense cold, rocks, rivers, mud, ice, and stenches. As Auerbach says, "The law of appropriate retribution governs the system of punishment in Hell, giving rise to very realistic and concrete allegorism which in turn provides suitable and varied backgrounds for the appearance of the various figures."[1] The unmatched vividness of so many shocking and contrasting impressions evokes a wide variety of responses from the initiate: dread, terror, pity, and anger. His development in this spiraling rite of passage leads gradually to more reasoned and disciplined responses and, finally, to what might be called the centered self, when he "arms himself with fortitude"[2] and looks directly on Satan before emerging from Hell.

Unlike the wanderings of many epic heroes, Dante's passage through the Inferno follows a predetermined course. As Ferguson remarks, "Dante believed that the path toward self-knowledge was as old as antiquity, and he built the ancient wisdom into the very structure of the mountain path, the route which the soul in its quest for freedom and understanding *must* take."[3] At the opposite extreme of this elaborate and highly structured itinerary with its mass of topographical details is Jesus' pursuit of self-knowledge in the wilderness, where, as we shall see, Milton makes topography, direction, place, and time matters of sublime inconsequence.

Dante's realistic and concrete allegorism reflects his belief in the basic truth of the Scriptures. As John Demaray says, "The reader is asked to regard the sojourn of a single living poet through Hell, Purgatory, and Heaven as something that actually happened," and goes on to quote Singleton's remark that "the fiction of the *Divine Comedy* is that it is not a fiction."[4] Accompanying this unquestioning belief in the literal truth of Scripture is an equally strong belief in the elaborate and detailed representation of the damned. Within the general categories of those who sinned through passion or wickedness or who employed force or fraud we find many smaller, more finely discriminated groups and, among *them*, sharply differentiated individuals, a remarkable feat in a poem which, according to Thomas Bergin, contains 164 characters, including monsters.[5]

"To give dramatic unity to the shadowed diversity of human history in the *Commedia*, to embrace the staggering variety of earthly life within some general sequence of events . . . Dante had recourse to the typology of a Great Circle pilgrimage,"[6] the major prototype of which was the exodus of the Israelites from Egypt and their journey to the promised land. "The various modes of the poet's figurism" can be understood through the threefold "typologies of biblical imitation, internal recurrence, and worldly imitation," examples of the latter being the Crusades and many privately organized pilgrimages to the Holy Land that followed the course of the Exodus.[7]

The three stages of the soul's journey, patterned on the familiar medieval "ladder of salvation," are (1) conversion, (2) reception of the benefits of Christ's redemption, and (3) entrance into spiritual glory.[8] "Dante's trip from the Egypt of this world to the Jerusalem of the Earthly Paradise culminates in the poet's figured reception of the redeeming person of Christ."[9] Egypt, Jerusalem, and Heaven are the symbolic centers of the events of the *Inferno*, *Purgatorio*, and *Paradiso*.

Finally, in respect to the structure of the *Commedia*, we should recognize the pervasive numerological symbolism of the poem. It begins on the eve of Good Friday and ends, three days later, on Easter Sunday. It was written in the year of the Great Jubilee of Rome, 1300, when there were not only innumerable pilgrimages to Rome but widespread enthusiasm for a new Crusade, the year in which Dante reached the crucial age of thirty-five, the time of the midlife crisis.

The trinitarian symbolism of the *Commedia* is everywhere: the thirty-four cantos of the *Inferno*—including, according to some interpreters, one introductory canto to the whole poem—followed by two books of thirty-three cantos each in the insistent *terza rima*. One other instance is the figure of Satan with his three heads as a perversion of the Trinity.

Enough has been said to indicate the highly integrated and structured complexity of the *Commedia* and especially of the *Inferno*. Of the latter one should add that it assimilates very subtly the models of Christ's descent into Hell, of Saint Paul's legendary visit there, and of Aeneas's *nekuia* in *Aeneid* 6, thus combining Dante's commitment to the Roman Church with a commitment to the Roman Empire.

The condition of the dead in the *Inferno* sets them apart from those in Dante's predecessors and successors. The underworlds of the *Odyssey* and the *Aeneid* are only partly inhabited by the wicked, and neither place exemplifies the elaborate structure of the *Inferno*. One is struck by the mobility of Homer's and Virgil's ghosts and the vague spaciousness of their abode in contrast to the fixity of Dante's damned and the constricting and congealing places in which they face an eternity without change. Each of Dante's sinners is caught in a single attitude that reveals the essential moral truth about him. Auerbach is revealing on this point:

> Even classical tragedy, which may be said to "omit" a great deal and yet to aim at the whole of the man, requires an event which unfolds in time; on the basis of this event, the tragic poet decides what is to be included and what omitted, and it is through the event that the hero replies, more and more clearly and in the end definitively, to the question put to him by his destiny, to the question of who he really is. But Dante records no events; he has only a moment in which everything must be revealed, a very special moment, to be sure, for it is eternity. And he gives us something which Greek tragedy scorned, namely, the individual, concrete qualities of man: through language, tone, gesture, bearing, he penetrates to the essence.[10]

The sinners of the *Inferno*, in their striking invidividuality, may thus be distinguished from the shades in most other epic underworlds who are typically mere ghostly simulacra of the living, or who are distanced from the living visitor by a mediating narrator. The leaders among Milton's fallen angels, on the other hand—Satan, Beelzebub, Belial, Moloch, and Mammon—are intensely and brilliantly individualized, and they participate vigorously in a variety of ways—in debating plans that have consequences, building Pandemonium, playing heroic games, and engaging in philosophical discussions, however vain. But Milton's devils, of course, are not dead, however diminished their original brightness may be.

In the *Inferno*, then, Dante has undertaken a creative task of unusual difficulty in attempting to differentiate and give life to such a huge cast of damned souls cut off by their sins (always perversions of love), their egotism, and their incapacity for action or development, from the future, from each other, and from hope. Limited to brief appearances in which every word and gesture must be tellingly characteristic, often reduced to nearly total immobility, sometimes entombed or frozen or transformed into shrubs or embedded in filth, tormented by sadistic monsters, and crammed into tiny spaces encroached on by their fellows, they are in every way deprived of the scope for self-revelation that is granted to the dead in Homer and Virgil.

The crucial task of Dante the pilgrim is to achieve the powers of discrimination of Dante the poet and his surrogate, Virgil. This is the ordeal that the pilgrim must complete in his quest for self-knowledge.

In the prologue to the *Commedia*, Dante relates the crisis in the middle of his life that provides the point of departure for his journey. He moves through the dark wood in which he has lost the true way, to a valley where he can glimpse the planet "that leads men straight on every road." Momentarily comforted by this sign of hope, his gaze is repeatedly drawn back to that entrance "which never yet let any go alive" (1.27). His dilemma is expressed in a compelling simile:

> Allor fu la paura un poco queta
>   che nel lago del cor m'era durata
>   la notte ch' i' passai con tanta pièta.
> E come quei che con lena affannata
>   uscito fuor del pelago alla riva
>   si volge all'acqua perigliosa e guata,
> cosi l'anìmo mio, ch'ancor fuggiva,
>   si volse a retro a rimirar lo passo
>   che non lasciò gia mai persona viva.

> Then the fear was quieted a little in the lake of my heart during the night I had spent so piteously; and as he who has escaped with labouring breath so piteously from the deep to the shore turns to the perilous waters and gazes, so my mind, which was still in flight, turned back to look again at the pass which never yet let any go alive.
>
> [1.19–27]

Dante's situation recapitulates in detail the crisis in Odysseus' career when, after the culminating shipwreck of his decade of wanderings, he reaches the shore of Phaiacia. In the context of Exodus, this passage through perilous waters also suggests the stage of conversion that led from Egypt to the transit of the Red Sea, although Dante does not specifically mention it.

He now moves across a desert slope (the wilderness of Exodus?) but is blocked by a panther, a lion, and a wolf, symbols of lust, violence, and fraud. In this dilemma Dante hails an approaching stranger, who turns out to be the shade of Virgil and undertakes to guide him through the Inferno. Yet the pilgrim suffers further misgivings, and only when Virgil has established his credentials as a guide sent by Beatrice and, incidentally, accused Dante of cowardice, do the two set off. Virgil explains to Dante that in order to reach the Mount of Purgatory, which will be the halfway point in the completed journey, they must first descend through Hell. Hence the importance of the Heraclitean motif that the way up is the way down. Only after they are halfway through their descent through the nine circles of Hell does Virgil supply his protégé with a plan of Hell. One reason for this delay may be that the journey must be an *auto da fé*, that Dante's faith must be tested without guarantees of a successful passage; such guarantees, obviously, would undermine the validity of the trial and encroach on Dante's essential freedom of will.

My hesitant reading of Dante's infernal journey emphasizes the development of his moral imagination. As Freccero has said, the *Commedia* as "a novel of the self" requires an established, centered self to authenticate a true retrospect of what Dante the pilgrim underwent in his ordeal.[11] Virgil, to some extent, represents this fully individuated point of view, but the critical process is to be traced in the development of the distressed, disoriented, angst-ridden pilgrim into an individuated self. Only an enfranchised person can record reliably, in "a novel of the self," his development through a variety of ego-threatening encounters into this condition of the centered self.

Dante's first major encounter is with Francesca di Rimini, damned for her adulterous passion for Paolo. After a succession of encounters with famous women who have been a threat to moral and social institutions—Semiramis, Dido, Cleopatra, Helen—Dante encounters a couple eternally suffering because of their devotion to *amor*. The impassioned couple approach as a pair of flying doves:

Quali colombe, dal disio chiamate,
 con l'ali alzate e ferme al dolce nido
 vegnon per l'aere dal voler portate;
cotali uscir della schiera ov' è Dido
 a noi venendo per l'aere maligno,
 si forte fu l'affettüoso grido.

As doves, summoned by desire, come with wings poised and motionless to the sweet nest, borne by their will through the air, so these left the troop where Dido is, coming to us through the malignant air; such force had my loving call.

[5.82–87]

Cotali uscir della schiera ov' è Dido, the *ipsissima verba* of Shakespeare's Antony: "Dido and her Aeneas shall want troops/And all the haunt be ours." The romantic egotism of Francesca has spellbound generations of readers of the *Inferno*. The institution of arranged, politic marriages (Antony and Octavia, Aeneas and Lavinia) gave marriage a bad name, especially when such marriages were fundamental for *ragione di stato*. Dante the pilgrim is overwhelmed with pity for this charming woman, who explains so ingenuously the beginning of the affair. She delivers the killing line that also appears with various degrees of irony in Chaucer: *Amor, ch'al cor gentil ratto s'apprende* ("Love, which is quickly kindled in the gentle heart":5.100)—"Lo pitee renneth soon in gentil herte."[12]

That Dante might be permitting a little ironic self-ignorance to peep through the romantic egotism of Francesca, as Chaucer is doing with Criseyde, is likely. That Francesca has, like Criseyde, invented her romantic self is clear:

"Amor, cha'l cor gentil ratto s'apprende,
 prese costui della bella persona
 che mi fu tolta; e 'l modo ancor m'offende.

Amor, ch'a nullo amato amar perdona,
    mi prese del costui piacer si forte,
    che, come vedi, anco non m'abbandona."

"Love, which is quickly kindled in the gentle heart, seized
this man with the fair form that was taken from me, and the
manner afflicts me still. Love, which absolves no one beloved from loving, seized me so strongly with his charm,
that, as thou seest, it does not leave me yet."

[5.100–05]

Paolo never speaks, leaving the question of the mutuality of the affair
unanswered, although throughout eternity he and she will pursue
each other like doves. It is a long way, to be sure, from this
enchanting passion of Francesca's to Paris's deflating comment on
Pandarus to Helen in *Troilus and Cressida*:

He eats nothing but doves, love; and that breeds hot blood,
and hot blood begets hot thoughts, and hot thoughts beget
hot deeds, and hot deeds is love.

[3.1.122–24]

On the other hand, the sexual passion of Paolo and Francesca,
nurtured by a book she calls a pander *(Galeotto)*, has apparently
obliterated Paolo and left Francesca, charmed by *his* passion for *her*,
caught for eternity in the pursuit of a fulfillment that will forever
evade her. Francesca is a female version of Dante's Ulysses, and Dante
the pilgrim's totally sympathetic response to her plight suggests that
he has a lot to learn. He swoons in pity and falls as if dead.

From the ethereal beauty of the Francesca episode we are
plunged, in the third circle, into a completely contrasting milieu:

Io sono al terzo cerchio, della piova
    etterna, maladetta, fredda e greve;
    regola e qualità mai non l' è nova.
Grandine grossa, acqua tinta e neve
    per l'aere tenebroso si riversa;
    pute la terra che questo riceve.

I am in the third circle, of eternal, accursed rain, cold and
heavy, never changing its measure or its kind; huge hail,
foul water and snow pour down through the gloomy air,
and the ground that receives it stinks.

[6.7–12]

This inescapable and oppressive atmosphere, engaging all of Dante's senses, weaves his multifarious impressions into a single synesthetic aura of malignity. The static character of the description intensifies its changeless horror in its relentless piling up of ugly adjectives, while the subtle interplay of alliteration and assonance and wordplay (*nova* and *neve*) contributes to the fixed and hopeless mood. Cerberus, appropriately the guardian of this threshold, challenges the wayfarers, and Virgil, like his Sibyl, immobilizes him.

The damned gluttons of this circle are embedded in cold mud. In all respects the episode contrasts with the preceding one, with the dovelike flight of the lovers and Francesca's idealistic but unexamined dedication to the romantic. The contrast shocks us because of the juxtaposition of beauty and pathos with sheer physical grossness, as Ciacco, after answering Dante's questions, falls back into the filth in which he will lie until the Last Judgment.

The increasing constriction of Hell is marked in the transition to the fourth circle, which contains the avaricious and the prodigal. They are challenged by Plutus, who, like Cerberus, exemplifies in his predatory wrath that psychic state Jung calls "inflation," but Virgil takes the wind out of his sails: *Quali dal vento le gonfiate vele / caggiono avvolte, poi che l'alber fiacca, / tal cadde a terra la fiera crudele* ("As sails swollen with the wind fall in a heap when the mast snaps, so fell the cruel beast to the ground") (7.13–15):

Così scendemmo nella quarta lacca,
   pigliando più della dolente ripa
   che 'l mal dell'universo tutto insacca.
Ahi giustizia di Dio! tante chi stipa
   nove travaglie e pene quant' io viddi?
   e perche nostra colpa sì ne scipa?

Then we descended into the fourth hollow, passing further down the dismal slope which ensacks all the evil of the universe. Ah, Justice of God, who crams together all the new toils and pains that I saw? And why does our sin so lay us waste?

[7.16–21]

In contrast to his extended single interview with Ciacco is Dante's contemplation of two huge, contending mobs of spendthrifts and misers. Their punishment is eternally to dispute the questions "Why hoard?" and "Why squander?" As Virgil explains, "There was

no measure in their spending" (7.42). The infinite repetition of their
accusations indicates, simply, that mortal excess of any sort brings
about a reaction equally excessive, the clear image of "getting and
spending" *in extremis*. The simple connection between retentiveness
and prodigality is expressed in this banal economic relationship that
has stripped all these contenders of identity, like Auden's beastly
brokers clamoring on the Bourse.[13] Dante's heart is pierced by the
spectacle until Virgil exposes "the brief mockery of the wealth
committed to fortune, for which the race of men embroil themselves"
(*la corta buffa / de' ben che son commessi alla Fortuna, / per che
l'umana gente si rabuffa*: 7.61–63). *Buffa* and *rabuffa* effectively
define these contentions as a zero-sum game which only a fool would
play. Thus the sterile economics of this contention identifies another
appropriate damnation, this one, it appears, freely chosen by the
damned as their eternal and interminable and valueless *agon*. Dante
suggests to Virgil that there must be in these mobs *someone* he
knows, but Virgil points out that their undiscerning lives made them
indistinguishable (7.53–54), an exception to the prevailing mode of
individualization. And so the pilgrim and his guide leave the realm of
Fortuna to enter the marsh of the Styx, where the violent dwell, and
come at last to the foot of a tower. Virgil easily puts down another
threshold guardian, Phlegyas, and he and Dante make their way
across the swamp. In what may be a turning point in his rite of
passage, Dante inveighs against the ghost of Filippo Argenti with
encouragement from Virgil. According to Sinclair, this "strikes modern readers with something like disgust at what is felt to be [Dante's]
monstrous inhumanity and moral indecency."[14] In any event Dante's
anger is a relief from his earlier tendency to weep too readily over the
sinners; in Dante's view, Argenti's betrayal of Florence justified this
singularly self-assertive utterance. "There is also," as Sinclair says,
"an anger that comes from above."[15] Perhaps one could claim that
Dante's will is, little by little, aligning itself with the divine wisdom
that has created Hell. At any rate, Virgil corrects the variety of
Dante's reactions to what he witnesses in somewhat the same way
that Michael, in the last two books of *Paradise Lost*, tutors Adam into
perceptions that are at the same time more discerning and more free.

There is a danger in the *Inferno* that Dante, in his loving and
respectful awe for Virgil, may be reduced to a puppet. This possibility
is aggravated by the minutely structuralized condition of Hell and
further aggravated by the abyss that separates Dante and his guide

from the damned. Dante's ultimately successful performance in the manifold ordeals of Hell requires that he achieve a balance between contempt or hatred for the sinners and a recognition that, in some cases, he might have ended among them. The desperate dilemma in which he finds himself at the outset of his journey must be reflected in a developing capacity for judicious compassion. If he fails to judge firmly, he is in danger of acquiescing in the sin. If he fails to comprehend and imaginatively share the sins of at least some of the damned, he is simply a tourist with an exceptionally able guide.

In contrast to the damned who have made, or avoided, critical choices that have led to their damnation, Dante, as one who began his journey under the imminent threat of his own damnation, must demonstrate however hesitantly or intermittently, his freedom of will. Yet, so structured is the Hell he traverses, so apparent the connection between specific sins and punishments, that there is danger that he may undergo the experience with the complacent detachment of a museum visitor, "peeping and botanizing" upon the curiously aberrant persons he encounters, much as Pope's and Swift's contemporaries visited Bedlam with a detached curiosity.

Does Dante the poet prevent his pilgrimage through Hell from being a visit to a Coney Island horror house or a sideshow of freaks? The powerful component of medieval grotesque, the quality we find in Hieronymus Bosch, threatens to produce an abyss between the eager and civilized *homme de bonne volonté* and these figures who were once, like him, human beings with the same opportunities for self-realization that he has, at the outset, failed to achieve.

Much of the dramatic tension of Dante's initiation derives from a variety of spiritual crises he undergoes in reacting to the pathos or terror or ugliness of different situations in the *Inferno*. Even more vivid are those moments of despair when he experiences what might be called apocalypses of the demonic. A crucial instance is his terror as he and Virgil approach the city of Dis, the abode of thousands of fallen angels who threaten to keep Virgil with them and dismiss Dante:

> "Vien tu solo, e quei sen vada,
> che sì ardito intrò per questo regno.
> Sol si ritorni per la folle strada:
> pruovi, se sa; chè tu qui rimarrai
> che li ha' iscorta si buia contrada."

"Come thou alone, and let him go off who has dared thus
to enter on this kingdom. Let him return alone on his mad
way and see if he knows it, for thou shalt stay here who hast
been his guide on that dark road."

[8.89–93]

Dante's thoroughly understandable dread follows his deliberate exac-
erbation of the sufferings of Filippo Argenti. Although his indignation may be divinely inspired, the horror he feels immediately after at
the prospect of his own imminent abandonment identifies him, willy-
nilly, with the lost souls.

That this crisis occurs before the gates of Dis, the boundary
between those who sinned through weakness and those who sinned
through wickedness; that even Virgil for the moment is irresolute
and perplexed before his confidence returns; and that Dante identifies
the gates of Dis with the gates of Hell in canto 3 all indicate the
importance of this moment in the journey. They enter Dis with the
aid of an angel of grace and encounter the avenging classical spirits,
chief among whom is Medusa. Virgil covers Dante's eyes to protect
him from her fatal glance. So, in rapid succession, the pilgrim feels
exultant contempt, deep despair, and equally deep relief.

The human verisimilitude of these notations of fluctuating
moods endows the pilgrim with a flexibility of response clearly vital
to spiritual growth, a flexibility which sets him off from the damned
with their fixed and unchangeable responses. Through eternity they
can only reiterate or reenact the essential causes of their perdition.
Even the colossal and heroic Farinata in canto 10 is frozen in a vain
attitude of defiance of Hell, reaffirming the heretical will for which he
and his wife were put to death by the Inquisition.

After this striking encounter, Virgil in canto 11 provides his
protégé with a plan of Hell, and especially of the lower circles where
the violent and the fraudulent abide, and reminds Dante of the
fundamental distinction God has made between the incontinent and
the wilfully wicked, which he should remember from Aristotle. On
the morning of Holy Saturday they descend to the seventh circle,
where they are challenged by the Minotaur, the epitome of brutish
violence, and helped by the centaur Chiron. Commentators have been
struck by Dante's serene detachment here, in contrast to his shocked,
sympathetic, contemptuous, or fearful reactions in other episodes.

To these emotions one must add the sheer astonishment Dante

experiences in the barren wood of the suicides in canto 13, a place that
fully illustrates a "world that desire totally rejects: the world of the
nightmare and the scapegoat, of bondage and pain and confusion.
. . ."16

> Non era ancor di là Nesso arrivato,
>   quando noi ci mettemmo per un bosco
>   che da nessun sentiero era segnato.
> Non fronda verde, ma di color fosco;
>   non rami schietti, ma nodosi e 'nvolti;
>   non pomi v'eran, ma stecchi con tosco:
> non han sì aspri sterpi nè sì folti
>   quelle fiere selvagge che in odio hanno
>   tra Cecina e Corneto i luoghi colti.
> Quivi le brutte Arpìe lor nidi fanno
>   che cacciar delle Strofade i Troiani
>   con tristo annunzio di futuro danno.
> Ali hanno late, e colli e visi umani,
>   piè con artigli, e pennuto il gran ventre;
>   fanno lamenti in su li alberi strani.

Nessus had not reached the other side again when we set
out through a wood which was not marked by any path. No
green leaves, but of dusky hue; no smooth boughs, but
knotted and warped; no fruits were there, but poisonous
thorns. No brakes so harsh and dense have these savage
beasts that hate the tilled lands between the Cecina and
Corneto. Here make their nests the loathsome Harpies that
drove the Trojans from the Strophades with dismal presage
of future ill; they have wide wings and human necks and
faces, feet clawed and their great bellies feathered, and they
make lamentations on the strange trees.

[13.1–15]

Just as Aeneas, in plucking the branch of a shrub that is the
metamorphosed Polydorus, is struck dumb with horror (*tum vero
ancipiti mentem formidine pressus / obstipui steteruntque comae et
vox faucibus haesit: 3.47–48*), Dante drops the branch of the bush
that was once Piero delle Vigne and is transfixed by astonishment and
fear (13.44–45). Then he piously restores the leaves to the plant and
moves on to the region of the violent against God, who occupy an

anti-Eden defined, like Eden, by four rivers. These descend from the Old Man of Crete—Acheron, Styx, Cocytus, and Phlegethon, a mixture of tears and blood "Shed by the whole race which is incurably afflicted by the guilt of Adam," as Sinclair observes.[17]

Dante's most poignant experience in the *Inferno* is his encounter with his revered teacher, Brunetto Latini, to whom he confides the origin and object of his journey. Latini's sympathy shines through his anguish as he encourages his former pupil, and Dante responds with a tribute to Latini for having taught him "how man makes himself immortal" (15.85). His life cut off before he could repent of his sin, Latini preserves a dignity and beauty of spirit rare among the damned and, in our parting view of him, is compared to those who race at Verona, "and he seemed not the loser among them, but the winner" (15.123–24).

Dante's imaginative virtuosity introduces another wondrous monster in Geryon, on whose back the travelers descend through the dusky air to Malebolge. Dante's terror is both convincing and comic, like Chaucer's on the eagle's back in *The Legend of Good Women*:

> Qual è colui che sì presso ha 'l riprezzo
>   della quartana c' ha già l' unghie smorte,
>   e triema tutto pur guardando il rezzo,
> tal divenn' io alle parole porte;
>   ma vergogna mi fè le sue minacce,
>   che innanzi a buon segnor fa servo forte.
> I' m'assetai in su quelle spallacce:
>   sì volli dir, ma la voce non venne
>   com' io credetti: "Fa che tu m'abbracce."

> As one so near the shivering-fit of the quartan that his nails are already blue and he trembles all over at the mere sight of shade, such I became at these words of his; but shame threatened me, which makes a servant brave before a good master, and I settled myself on those great shoulders. I wished to say, but the voice did not come as I thought, "See that thou embrace me!"

> [17.85–93]

The *buffo* grotesquerie of this flight is counterbalanced by the psychological realism of Dante's terror, which in turn is modified by an appealing self-irony he can direct from his present perspective on his former self.

Geryon, the monster of fraud, conveys Dante and Virgil to one of the climactic encounters in the *Inferno,* the celebrated meeting with Ulysses, discussed earlier in this study. Dante's flight on Geryon is in tacit contrast with the insatiable quest for novelty in Ulysses' goalless quest.

From the somewhat childish figure of Dante on Geryon we move to one clearly more self-assured in his meeting with the simoniac Boniface in canton 19:

> "Deh, or mi dì: quanto tesoro volle
> Nostro Segnore in prima da san Pietro
>   ch'ei ponesse le chiavi in sua balia?
>   Certo non chiese se non "Viemmi retro."
> Nè Pier nè li altri tolsero a Mattia
>   oro od argento, quando fu sortito
>   al luogo che perdè l'anima ria.
> Però ti sta, chè tu se' ben punito. . . ."

> "Pray tell me now, how much treasure did our Lord require
> of Saint Peter before He gave the keys into his charge?
> Surely He asked nothing but "Follow me," nor did Peter or
> the others take gold or silver from Matthias when he was
> chosen for the place lost by his guilty soul. Stay there then,
> for thou art rightly punished. . . ."

> [19.90–97]

Speaking calmly, without the indignation, sentimentality, or contempt that have colored some of his earlier reactions, Dante has shed the residual egotism evident in earlier parts of the poem, and this gain is affirmed by Virgil's pleased reaction.

In canto 26 Dante encounters the spirit of Ulysses. The tragic power of the episode is heightened by the fact that after Ulysses, with a degree of self-knowledge rare among the damned, tells of his last voyage, Dante is silent. Nothing needs to be said.

But the pilgrim's spiritual journey is not plotted steadily along a rising curve. Were it, we would inevitably lose interest in his story, and normal human psychology and human development would be misrepresented. The experiences of Dante and his reactions to them must allow for true freedom of response. He must be free to make mistakes, as he does in his fascinated attention to the lively exchanges of invective between Sinon and Master Adam. Virgil rebukes the voyeurism implicit in Dante's curiosity.

In Dante's last encounter with one of the truly great figures in the *Inferno*, the pathos and horror of Ugolino's story, offset by his unremitting vengeance on Ruggiero, maintains an extraordinarily delicate balance of feeling, and the balance is reflected in Dante's comment:

> Ahi Pisa, vituperio delle genti
>   del bel paese là dove 'l sì sona
>   poi che i vicini a te punir son lenti,
> muovasi la Capraia e la Gorgona,
>   e faccian siepe ad Arno in su la foce
>   sì ch'elli annieghi in te ogni persona!

> Ah, Pisa, shame of the peoples of the fair land where sounds the *sì*, since thy neighbours are slow to punish thee may Capraia and Gorgona shift and put a bar on Arno's mouth so that it drown every soul in thee!
>
> [33.79–84]

While acknowledging Ugolino's betrayal of the Pisan fortresses, he goes on to condemn the city for the cruel deaths of Ugolino's innocent children. My point, not a subtle one, is that Dante here shows that the forces of judgment and of sympathy must be given free and simultaneous expression.

When they clamber down the body of Satan and emerge from Hell Dante's sense of direction is reversed, and Virgil reorients him. The way down has become the way up.

What has Dante the pilgrim accomplished in this elaborate, variegated, sometimes ennui-ridden transit of the most comprehensive museum of human aberrations ever known? Far more energetic and involved than other visitants in the underworld, he has encountered representatives of all the categories of human failure, egotism, meanness, cruelty, and self-deception of which we are capable. He has also witnessed the far more elusive instances of the persistent human passion to project its egocentric desires as heroic. The critical case is that of Francesca and her speechless adulterous partner, Paolo. They enjoyed, according to René Girard, "A very special popularity at the beginning of the nineteenth century":

> The two young people defy human and divine laws and appear to bring about the triumph of passion, even in the realm of eternity. What does Hell matter to them, since

they are there together? In the minds of innumerable readers in modern times as well as in the Romantic era, the infernal setting, however artistically remarkable it may be, is no more than a deferential nod in the direction of the moral and theological conventions of the time.[18]

The pilgrim Dante responds to Francesca's account of the irresistible power of *Amor, ch'al cor gentil ratto s'apprende*, but he fails to note that the resonant term *Amor* repeatedly invoked by Francesca is never defined or illustrated. It was Paolo, she continues, who was seized by her *bella persona*. So, while tacitly disengaging herself from responsibility for her fate and attributing the initiative to Paolo, who, she concedes narcissistically, was overcome by her beauty, she fails to define the reality that she claims so pathetically for their endless pursuit of each other. It is hard to admit that Francesca is an auto-intoxicated romantic; harder still to concede that all that the lovers have in common is a joint fascination with her beauty. Most of all it is hard to admit, with Girard, that "no true union is possible between the disembodied 'doubles' that Paolo and Francesca represent for each other."[19] To take Girard's point further, for most readers it is utterly impossible to believe, as, I think, Dante implies, that Paolo exists for Francesca simply as a projection of her egotistical passion. Dante the pilgrim is incapable of such an inference and swoons out of commiseration, and readers have been swooning ever since, as they remember that gripping account she gives of how they were seduced by reading of how Guinevere and Lancelot were seduced. "The romantic and individualist reader fails to perceive the role played by bookish imitation precisely because he too believes in absolute passion."[20] Paolo and Francesca are dupes of Guinevere and Lancelot, Girard continues, and "the romantic readers are dupes of Paolo and Francesca."[21] So is Dante the pilgrim, while Dante the poet has the tact to let his readers draw their own conclusions, and so, for some, "an extremity of blindness . . . forces into the role of pander the very work that expressly denounces it."[22]

For most readers the *Inferno* is a *Galeotto* in this episode mainly because Francesca is beautiful, charming, lyrical, and the only attractive woman in Hell.

This leads us to the obvious point that a season in Hell must present both evil that is attractive and evil that is repulsive. The humanistic and religious vision of the *Inferno* should make us realize that the evils we find ourselves drawn to and the evils we find repellent are all aspects of misdirected love. Beyond the fundamental distinctions between weakness and wickedness, violence and fraud, the damned—all 164 of them—illustrate love perverted to a variety of unworthy ends. Were Dante the pilgrim not to find numerous characters among the damned that he despises and many that he admires, were he not to grow in his capacity to discriminate between those whose damnation has extenuating virtues and those who have utterly alienated themselves from the sympathy of a troubled initiate into the manifold visions that Hell provides, the ordeal would be reduced to a visit that merely regards at a distance the plight of the damned. The pilgrim Dante must therefore be capable of reacting to his observations and encounters with varying degrees of sympathy and rejection. And Hell is objectively structured to make careful discriminations between the specific instances of evil. That Dante, as pilgrim, is immune to the attractions of simony, barratry, miserliness, and wastefulness does not mean that he can be immune to what he finds to be more appealing roads to damnation. Granted that the *Inferno* distinguishes objectively between sins that are normatively repellent and sins we would gladly forgive, the discipline of its carefully graded rite of passage demands that the pilgrim develop a capacity to share a deeper imaginative response to both. The scheme of the *Inferno*, as we have seen, is objectively rigorous. The responses of the pilgrim must be increasingly full of insight. Otherwise he will respond in utterly predictable ways to every manifestation of Hell. "The genius of Dante, like that of Cervantes, is bound up with the abandonment of the preconceptions of individualism."[23] The cases Dante is faced with in his journey pose increasingly difficult problems for his feelings and judgment. As he makes his way down to the triune figure of Satan, his powers of discrimination are fully established. The quintessential antitype of the divine clearly poses no problems for him, beyond the recognition that at the bottom and center of the infernal vortex is the fundamental principle of evil and that the fundamental principle of evil has no identity of its own except its parodic, antithetical relationship to the good.

> At a lower level of "degradation" every obstacle will serve as a model. Masochism and sadism are thus forms of mediated desire. When the erotic attachment is displaced from the object onto the mediary rival, one has the type of

homosexuality demonstrated by Marcel Proust, another instance of narcissism. The divisions and agonies produced by mediation find their climax in the hallucinations of the double present in the work of numerous Romantic and modern writers but comprehended only by the greatest as a conflictual situation."[24]

Girard makes his point by concluding: "the initial captivity of the writer in illusion corresponds, in his major work, to the illusion, revealed as such, of the hero himself. The hero never frees himself until the end of the novel, through a conversion in which he rejects mediated desire, i.e., death of the romantic self, and resurrection in the true world of the novel."[25]

In his own way Girard confirms the views of Jung and Edinger, among others, that the defeat of the ego is felt as a death of the personality, but that it is a precondition to resurrection as an achieved self. Dante's full self-individuation is not complete at the end of the *Inferno*. His filial dependence on Virgil must be followed by his syzygy (or conjunction) with the anima, Beatrice. Odysseus, as we have seen, completes such a ritual passage successfully, despite the attractions of objects of mediated desire, such as Circe and Calypso. Aeneas rejects the unmediated anima of Dido to accept, as part of the pattern of destiny imposed on him, the pathetic simulacrum of the anima represented by Lavinia. In a muted way, Milton's Jesus, who at the end of the poem "Home to his mother's house private returns," has accomplished his ordeal fully in symbolic terms. The pattern is intermittent and incomplete in Wordsworth in respect to Nature maternally conceived, while in Don Juan's manifold encounters with women there is an unfulfilled possibility of a "maximal conversion" in his love affair with Haidée. Girard's authentic novel, in its final revelation, "Illuminates retrospectively, the path traversed."[26] This is true of the *Inferno* and much more evident if we follow Dante the pilgrim's course through the entire *Commedia*. The spiral descent is a necessary prelude to the spiral ascent. The way up and the way down are the same. *Il faut reculer pour mieux sauter* is a structural principle, spiritual and aesthetic, of the *Aeneid*, the *Inferno*, and *Paradise Lost*, with clear though fragmentary counterparts in *Moby-Dick* and *Heart of Darkness*, in *The Waste Land, A Portrait of the Artist as a Young Man*, and in Faulkner's "The Bear." Although there are many variations on the mythic themes and structures which shape these works, some appear to be indispensable: (1) being lost in a maze; (2) penetrating the heart of the maze and encountering successfully the "bi-form monster," a conflicted creature, half-brute, half-human, at its center; (3) deliverance from the maze, usually with a guide; and (4) communication of this heroic crisis of individuation to the culture of the hero—not primarily to celebrate the hero's achievement but to restore or preserve or revitalize his culture. Dante's *Inferno* gets much of its energy from Dante the exile's devotion to his city. Along the same lines, Odysseus and Penelope, Theseus and Ariadne, Daedalus and Icarus, Aeneas and Anchises, Stephen and Bloom, Ike McCaslin and Sam Fathers find their revelations at the heart of a labyrinth, at Eliot's "still point of the turning world," have their visions, and bring back as much of the revelation as they can to the world from which they come.

The greatest nineteenth-century fictions deviate from this archetype of the hero's alienating and reorienting journey. Having lost or discarded the religious or mythic foundations that had provided narrative purpose and fulfillment, they reveal fractured, problematical, and ephemeral points of view. For many of us Dante's elaborately structured Hell is disturbing because most of the damned understand why they are consigned to the particular categories in which they find themselves. Utter disorientation has for us become a more compelling vision of Hell.

4 *Paradise Regain'd:* Self-Discovery in the Wasteland

So mighty is the spell that these [poetic] adornments naturally exercise, though when they are stripped bare of their musical coloring and taken by themselves, I think you know what sort of a showing these sayings of the poets make. For you, I believe, have observed them.

I have, he said.

Do they not, said I, resemble the faces of adolescents, young but not really beautiful, when the bloom of youth abandons them?

Plato, *The Republic*

Despite the austere manner in which it seems to eschew the traditional mythic allusions of epic, *Paradise Regain'd* may be seen as a deeply symbolic version of a "monomyth" (a word borrowed from *Finnegan's Wake*), an archetypal pattern in which the hero, according to Joseph Campbell, "ventures forth from the world of common day into a region of supernatural wonder"; then encounters and wins, with divine help, a victory over "fabulous forms"; and "comes back from this mysterious adventure with the power to bestow boons on his fellow man."[1]

With its primary emphasis on Jesus as the ultimate hero of myth, *Paradise Regain'd* may also be seen as combining elements of the fairy-tale hero:

Typically, the hero of the fairy tale achieves a domestic, microcosmic triumph, and the hero of myth a world-historical macrocosmic triumph: whereas the former—the youngest or despised child who becomes the master of extraordinary powers—prevails over his personal oppressors, the latter brings back from his adventures the means for the regeneration of his society as a whole.[2]

The "domestic microcosmic" aspect of *Paradise Regain'd* is evident in, among other things, the innocence and ignorance and youth of the hero. Although Jesus asserts, in his first meditations, his early aversion to "childish play" and dedication to "public good," he sets out without any idea of how he is to fulfill the ultimate role of which he is, nevertheless, assured:

> "To rescue *Israel* from the *Roman* yoke,
> Then to subdue and quell o'er all the earth
> Brute violence and proud Tyrannic pow'r,
> Till truth were freed and equity restor'd. . . ."[3]

His ignorance, lack of power, and submissiveness imply something like the initial weakness of the young would-be redeemer of folk tale, as does his dependence on his mother, a virtual matriarch in the absence of his Father, for what little information he has about his mission:

> "These growing thoughts my mother soon perceiving
> By words at times cast forth, inly rejoic'd,
> And said to me apart: high are thy thoughts
> O Son, but nourish them and let them soar
> To what height sacred virtue and true worth
> Can raise them, though above example high;
> By matchless deeds express thy matchless Sire."
>
> [1.227–33]

In his unannounced departure from home to undertake the inward adventure of self-discovery in the wilderness and in going back to his mother in the end—

> he unobserv'd
> Home to his mother's house private returned

—Jesus is, in a sense, tracing the monomyth in its essentially private and domestic mode of the fairy tale. To be sure, both the "growing thoughts" she fosters and the single, approving theophany of the Father, who announces, impersonally and laconically (according to Satan's report), "This is my son Belov'd, in him am pleas'd,"[4] sustain Jesus as he tries to fathom the perplexed question of his identity as "Son of God" (an identity which Satan will also claim for himself), and he never questions the public end to which his career is dedicated, only the means.

The uncertainty about Jesus' specific mission and the means to its accomplishment is compounded by Milton's resolute confinement of the action of *Paradise Regain'd* to his inward psychomachia. From the public point of view, represented mainly by his mother and his discomfited disciples, he achieves nothing. They are kept ignorant of the whole adventure. The negative way of his quest, through denial and privation, qualifies Jesus as more quintessentially "private" than any of his predecessors in privations, such as Odysseus and Dante. Odysseus had a guide and a clearly defined goal through most of his wanderings and, though often hungry, never fasted for forty days. Dante had a more than competent guide in the *Inferno* who provided him with a minutely detailed plan of Hell.

Thus the "adventures" of Milton's hero are "microcosmic" as far as the public is concerned, and we readers alone are privileged to share with Milton a knowledge of the Son's secret quest. His actions, in the context of the epic tradition, are inactions, his return home at the end of the poem something less than an anticlimax, a return, apparently, to the *status quo ante* that appears to deflate the great expectations he had shared with his mother and to abrogate the implications of his Father's annunciation at the Jordan. It is interesting to try to imagine the homecoming scene: Mother: "Where did you go?" Son: "Out." Mother: "What did you do?" Son: "Nothing."

Paradise Regain'd is a fairy-tale version of the monomyth in other respects. Jesus, in this story, is, like many folklore heroes, the youngest son. He is, moreover, the youngest of three and thus occupies that special position of apparent inferiority and real inner strength that third sons in fairy tales often occupy. As Son incarnate he is a figure distinctly different from and, for the time being, separate from the Son of *Paradise Lost*, the "Second Omnipotence" (6.684). Of this omnipotent, omniscient figure the Son incarnate of *Paradise Regain'd* knows little, since, like other mortals, he is in most respects confined to seeing the divine through a glass, darkly. Satan is not alone in regarding him as distinct and separate from that Son who with "his fierce thunder drove us to the deep" (1.90) and shares his perplexity with his fellow devils:

"Who this is we must learn, for man he seems
In all his lineaments, though in his face
The glimpses of his Father's glory shine."

[1.91–93]

The Son of *Paradise Regain'd* is likewise confined to knowledge of the
Old Testament and, like Satan, to uncertain predictions about the
future. In knowledge, then, the contestants are evenly matched, and
Satan's uncertainty about the Son's identity is a demonic mirror of
the Son's own uncertainty. The critical difference between them lies
in Satan's compulsive and vain pursuit of knowledge about his
opponent, as distinct from the Son's imperturbable faith in the
adequacy of whatever knowledge God vouchsafes him. On the eve of
his ordeal he declares:

> "And now by some strong motion I am led
> Into this Wilderness, to what intent
> I learn not yet; perhaps I need not know;
> For what concerns my knowledge God reveals."
>
> [1.291–94]

This serene resignation, unhesitatingly supported by faith, is reflected in Jesus' quiet, unemphatic, laconic responses to Satan:

> "Who brought me hither
> Will bring me hence, no other Guide I seek."
>
> [1.335–36]

> "Why dost thou then suggest to me distrust,
> Knowing who I am, as I know who thou art?"
>
> [1.355–56]

Thus Jesus counters Satan's relentless attempts to goad him into
action or to declare his messianic intentions, with an intelligent
brevity of speech that instantly exposes the fraudulent motive behind
the temptation. The encounters have their comic aspect, as the
obsessed Satan, in Bergsonian fashion, repeats and repeats his vain
gambits and suffers one pratfall after another. The encounters dramatize the foredoomed failure of a lying and imprisoned intelligence to
enthrall a free one. The effect is to keep Satan in a state of frantic
uncertainty that reaches its highest pitch when Christ rejects the
benefits of Greek philosophy with this devastating response:

> "Think not but that I know these things; or think
> I know them not; not therefore am I short
> Of knowing what I ought: he who receives
> Light from above, from the fountain of light,
> No other doctrine needs, though granted true. . . ."
>
> [4.286–90]

The Son's gnomic utterances express essential truth unadorned, and his longer speeches, almost devoid of imagery and rhetorical complexity, also imply an innocence that can express itself artlessly. Against this artlessness Satan's figurative and involuted style is powerless.

Satan's desire for knowledge of the Son is in the service of his compulsion to convert him from trust in God to a premature exercise of his destined messianic role. The "wiser" older brother, we might say, tries to subvert the secret strength of the younger, a strength essentially beyond his comprehension. Such jealousy is a persistent element in folklore, as one sees in Cinderella and her older half-sisters, in Cordelia and her two evil older sisters, in Joseph and his brothers, and in many other cases. Satan's machinations are bound to fail, if only because he cannot dissociate knowledge from the corrupting, self-serving exercise of power, and he is therefore incapable of recognizing the Word incarnate. As in *Comus* and *Samson Agonistes* this hero is never seriously tempted, and the interest of his career lies elsewhere than in the drama of temptation. The suspenseless, virtually actionless nature of his encounters is characteristically Miltonic, implying that the human spirit is the arena where any real action occurs. If there is a dramatic element in *Paradise Regain'd*, it may be found in the Son's gradual self-definition, culminating in a sudden, blinding self-revelation.

It may also be found in the dramatized encounter between the Son, considered as self, and Satan, considered as ego. A similar relationship can be seen in Cordelia in conflict with Regan and Goneril. Although Satan and Regan and Goneril are older, they have never developed beyond the infantile ego, which can relate to others only in terms of its own drives and therefore cannot comprehend that infinitely larger entity, the achieved self. Thus too, as in countless fairy tales, *As You Like It* among them, the despised and often dispossessed youngest child defeats his evil older brother, even though the older brother seems to have the power to arrange things pretty much as he likes. For Milton and Shakespeare worldly power is anatomized as weakness, and other-worldly weakness as the only real strength.

An even more important fairy-tale aspect of the relation of Jesus and Satan is seen in the main model for *Paradise Regain'd*, The Book of Job. In both texts the Father withdraws during the trial of his favorite son, and Satan becomes his surrogate. Whereas Satan proposes the testing of Job and has divine permission to afflict him in any way he wishes, the Father in *Paradise Regain'd* takes the initiative in offering Jesus to Satan as a subject for temptation. In folklore terms this harsh paternal behavior would correspond to that stage in the young hero's development when the father is seen as an ogre. Job's wife and friends seem bent on persuading him to take such a view, but they fail. The idea, of course, never occurs to Jesus, because his faith is founded on an unshakable trust in the divine goodness. Job's God finally speaks to him, though incomprehensibly, out of the whirlwind, but the only direct communication Jesus has with the Father is the brief theophany at the River Jordan. In view of Jesus' divine nature, that is sufficient. Unlike Job, the Son is given no rewards at the end of the poem. The point, I suppose is that there is nothing the Father could give him that he lacks. The Son's final utterance on the pinnacle of the Temple, "It is written, thou shalt not tempt the Lord thy God," is an impersonal declaration, in his Father's words, of the underlying truth which Satan has labored to destroy. As Jesus utters them, the words apply equally to himself and to Satan, but the accompanying miracle, which he does not anticipate, gives them a further and astounding application to himself. In refusing to tempt God, Jesus manifests the truth that he *is* God. Poised dizzily on the spire of the Temple, with, one would imagine, his arms outstretched to maintain his balance, the Son symbolizes the New Testament figure of the crucified Jesus triumphantly raised upon the apex of the Old Testament.

∽

We may now look back to other elements of the monomyth in its microcosmic, fairy-tale form in *Paradise Regain'd* to shed light on the vexed question of its genre.

The opening lines imitate, through Spenser, the discarded proem of the *Aeneid* and imply, in the "Virgilian progression," Milton's attachment to the idea of a threefold poetic career, from pastoral, through Georgic, to epic:

> I who erewhile the happy Garden sung
> By one man's disobedience lost, now sing
> Recover'd Paradise to all mankind,
> By one man's firm obedience fully tried
> Through all temptation, and the Tempter foil'd
> In all his wiles, defeated and repuls't,
> And *Eden* rais'd in the waste Wilderness.

"The happy Garden" emphasizes the pastoral aspects of *Paradise Lost*, but the prelapsarian labors of Adam and Eve in "lopping and propping" their garden and their arduous labors after the Fall, whether in Adam's sweaty toil to win his bread or in Eve's childbirth labors, imply the Georgic tradition, going back to Hesiod's *Works and Days*, and summed up in the Virgilian phrase, *labor improbus*. "The happy Garden," lost "by one man's disobedience," gives place, in *Paradise Regain'd*, to "the waste Wilderness," an inversion of Eden's "wilderness of sweets." Now, Milton seems to say, we come to the true epic, the recovery of Paradise "to all mankind" through the unmatched heroic achievement of "one man's firm obedience fully tried/Through all temptation" and the "raising" of Eden in compensation for its earlier razing.

Paradise Regain'd thus completes the central myth of loss and redemption projected from the very beginning of *Paradise Lost* and affirmed emphatically at its close in Michael's final promise to Adam of "a paradise within thee happier far" (12.587). Once the enclosed garden of Eden is seen as an irrecoverable and *local* paradise, the way is open for Adam and Eve to take the first steps in the human saga that will lead to the mission of Jesus in the wilderness. Like them he *wanders*, the verb suggesting resignation.

If *Paradise Regain'd* is to be construed in some ways as the culminating epic in Milton's career, at least from his point of view, we must try to understand why its austere style succeeds despite its exclusion of many of the features of epic: heroic *action*, divine interventions, allusiveness, sublimity, and figurative richness. The repression of these grand aspects of the traditional epic is clearly appropriate to the themes of privacy and deprivation which provide the thematic keynote to Jesus' ordeal. The negative way is reflected in the privations of this chastened style. The style also suggests the essential humility of Jesus and corresponds to the fairy-tale aspect of the solitary adventures of a little-known youth. Finally, by directing our attention toward the inward journey, a meditation in process, the austerity annuls the outer copiousness and richness of setting that are appropriate to traditional epic. The polychromatic garden gives way to a monochromatic desert. The fecundity of Eden yields to the sterility of the trans-Jordanian wilderness. The total effect is to contract the infinite variety of *Paradise Lost* into a desolate and largely featureless milieu in which topographical details are almost entirely irrelevant.

The Son's forty-day journey differs from the voyages of Odysseus, Gilgamesh, Aeneas, Dante, Beowulf, or Satan (in *Paradise Lost*) in having no conscious geographical goal. His point of departure is the Jordan, where he was baptized, but the time is not specified:

> So they in Heav'n their Odes and Vigils tun'd.
> Meanwhile the Son of God, who yet some days
> Lodg'd in *Bethabara*, where *John* baptiz'd,
> Musing and much revolving in his breast,
> How best the mighty work he might begin
> Of Savior to mankind, and which way first
> Publish his Godlike office now mature,
> One day forth walk'd alone, the Spirit leading,
> And his deep thoughts, the better to converse
> With solitude, till far from track of men,
> Thought following thought, and step by step led on,
> He enter'd now the bordering Desert wild,
> And with dark shades and rocks environ'd round,
> His holy meditations thus pursu'd.

> [1.183–95]

The present participles contribute to the rapt, musing mood of this passage, suggesting the passivity of the traveler. "One day" he walked forth alone: the temporal vagueness is augmented by the line, "He enter'd now the bordering Desert wild." When is "now"? When he entered the desert. Temporal vagueness here suggests the "once upon a time" with which fairy tales begin, and it discounts the importance of chronology. In the forty days that follow, chronology is all but forgotten, and place, to the extent that it is described at all, does not mark progression in a journey; its notations are purely symbolic or for atmosphere, the Son's "holy meditations" being interrupted only by nightfall or by Satan's visitations. Such places, in most instances, are unconnected by time or movement or geographic relation to any other "place." Only inner time and place matter, as Jesus meditates on the time and place and manner in which he may "first / Publish his Godlike office now mature," a public event that does not occur in the poem. His inward journey, then, has nothing to do with the times or places where events occur, except for the culminating pinnacle of the Temple. The passage, in its simplicity, may seem to anticipate the style of Wordsworth on one of his reflective excursions into the natural scene, except that it is quite devoid of Wordsworth's unceasing interest in the natural scene. Jesus' detachment from his milieu is another major manifestation of the intense inward focus of his experience.

Outwardly the emptiness and topographical bleakness of the wilderness reflect both the privacy and the privation of the hero's quest. Inwardly, it may serve as it often does in both fairy tale and myth, as a field free for the free exercise of unconscious impulses. In emptying himself of will and submitting to a blank and undifferentiated environment, in exposing himself to Satanic suggestion, Jesus also submits to the repertoire of visions and ideas projected on that blankness by the Satanic imagination. In his sharing of these visions, despite his resolute rejection of the implications Satan finds in them, must there not be, in Jesus' own imagination, a degree of participation? For him as well as for the Tempter, they have meaning and interest. Were he utterly indifferent to them, the whole experience would be meaningless, and he would not be moved, as he sometimes is, to make extended analytical rejections of the motives for action that Satan fallaciously claims for them. In response to Satan's argument that it is the Son's urgent duty to seize "Occasion's forelock" and assert himself as Messiah, Jesus defines his role with compelling cogency and force:

> "All things are best fulfill'd in their due time,
> And time there is for all things, Truth hath said.
> If of my reign Prophetic Writ hath told
> That it shall never end, so when begin
> The Father in his purpose hath decreed,
> He in whose hand all times and seasons roll.
> What if he hath decreed that I shall first
> Be tried in humble state, and things adverse,
> By tribulations, injuries, insults,
> Contempts, and scorns, and snares, and violence,
> Suffering, abstaining, quietly expecting
> Without distrust or doubt, that he may know
> What I can suffer, how obey? who best
> Can suffer, best can do, best reign, who first
> Well hath obey'd; just trial e'er I merit
> My exaltation without change or end."

[3.183–97]

Repeatedly, Satan projects a polychromatic and animated image of one culture or another, crammed with exotic names and compelling details. He is a geographer and historian, the custodian, as it were, of time and place. Invariably, however, Jesus nonsuits his gambits by rejecting the temptation to seize the time and place for the beginning of his career, and his language is as insistently abstract as Satan's is specific. Despite its austerity, however, the Son's style has a sinuous, interconnected clarity and an intellectual tightness whose sublime simplicity cancels Satan's virtuosity. Since Satan has intimations of his doom, and since the Son's reign will be eternal, Satan's point of view is limited to specific historical opportunities which the Son can serenely refuse. Offers of power, of fancied strange delights, and threats of violence cannot shake his twofold piety as Son of God and Son of Man.

At key moments in the poem the wilderness through which the Son wanders is presented as a maze or labyrinth. And so it must seem to one fixated on time, space, and goal, like Satan:

> The way he came not having mark'd, return
> Was difficult, by human steps untrod;
> And he still on was led, but with such thoughts
> Accompani'd of things past and to come
> Lodg'd in his Breast, as well might recommend
> Such solitude before choicest Society.
>
> [1.297–302]

Dwelling amongst untrodden ways, this second Adam tests his progenitor's admission to the independent-minded Eve that "solitude is sometimes best society" (*PL* 9.249); unlike Eve, who is "amazed" by the physical and rhetorical involutions of the Serpent, the Son, with Providence his guide, never questions the validity of the route he follows. Though isolated and physically disoriented in the waste-land, Jesus nonetheless achieves Satan's vain boast in *Paradise Lost* that "the mind is its own place" in the calm confidence he evinces: "Who brought me hither / Will bring me home, no other guide I seek" (1.335) and reminds Satan of his ghastly discovery that he is "never more in Hell than when in Heaven" (*PL* 1.420). "Oracles are ceast," he declares, and continues:

> "And thou no more with Pomp and Sacrifice
> Shalt be inquir'd at *Delphos* or elsewhere,

At least in vain, for they shall find thee mute.
God hath now sent his living Oracle
Into the World to teach his final will,
And sends his Spirit of Truth henceforth to dwell
In pious Hearts, an inward Oracle
To all truth requisite for men to know."

[1.457–64]

In dismissing oracles like "Delphos," Jesus is differentiating himself
from a long line of epic heroes whose rites of passage require a guided
visit in pursuit of visionary or oracular knowledge in the underworld,
as Odysseus visits Tiresias, Aeneas the Sybil and the spirit of
Anchises, as Dante traverses Hell with Virgil, or as Guyon descends
to the cave of Mammon. In the wilderness Jesus thus enacts the
double role of heroic seeker of Truth and the source of "all truth
requisite for men to know." "Place" is again displaced, and the
ancient identification of Delphi as the navel of the world is replaced
with the Christian revelation of the oracle within. Thus Jesus' rite of
passage is distinguished from all others in being a descent into the
truth within himself, the individuation there achieved being independent, virtually, of the time or place where it occurs. His enunciation
of this truth exposes Satan's essential unreality:

To whom our Saviour with unalter'd brow:
"Thy coming hither, though I know thy scope,
I bid not or forbid; do as thou find'st
Permission from above; thou canst not more."
   He added not; and Satan bowing low
His grey dissimulation, disappear'd
Into thin air diffus'd; for now began
Night with her sullen wing to double-shade
The Desert; Fowls in thir clay nests were couch't;
And now wild Beasts came forth the wood to roam.

[1.493–502]

These lines, which end book 1, typify a pervasive characteristic of
Milton's wilderness setting. It is low and earthbound and largely
two-dimensional. There are one scene in Heaven, two devilish consis-
tories held somewhere in the air, and a brief apotheosis when Jesus is
borne up by flights of angels from the pinnacle of the Temple, but the
earthbound milieu, eschewing the upward and downward sublimities

of action in *Paradise Lost,* reflects the persistently humble vision of Jesus' *via negativa,* as well as the peripatetic meditative mode of his quest. Notable also is the negative quality of the scene. Into this monochromatic landscape doubly shaded at nightfall the Prince of Hell, now, in Milton's brilliant phrase, "a grey dissimulation . . . disappears into thin air diffus'd," assuming, or being absorbed into, the insubstantiality of his new status as Prince of the Air. Even birds nest on the ground. What little energy is left in the waning light is transferred rather perfunctorily to unspecified wild beasts who now "come forth the woods to roam." We are witnessing them through the serenely indifferent eye of the Son. All the conventional elements of romantic horror are here, as in countless scenes in Spenser's fairy land, or in Macbeth's spine-chilling "Light thickens, and the crow makes wing / To the rooky wood," but Milton somehow contrives to divest them of horror. The tone, like the scene, does not reflect but, rather, absorbs the horror, leaving the Savior "unalter'd."

That Jesus does not "alter" in response to any of the temptations again suggests that, unlike other heroes undergoing rites of passage, his individuation has already been substantially achieved before the story begins. The self into which he descends at the outset of his meditations is perfect and fully formed. His ordeal, then, is a matter rather of self-discovery than of self-fullfillment.

The Tempter, in the first encounter, may be seen as a "threshold guardian" on the borders of a zone of magnified power. Beyond him "is darkness, the unknown, and danger; just as beyond the parental watch is danger to the infant and beyond the protection of his society danger to the member of the tribe."[5] Jesus is capable of converting this zone of danger to beneficial uses, whereas a more conventional hero would jeopardize not only himself but his "tribe," as does Eve in her fatal solitary excursion. As threshold guardian and Prince of the Air, Satan has power over space and time, moving the Son of God up and down and around at will and simultaneously exchanging his "grey dissimulation" (reminiscent of Archimago) for a repertoire of ephemeral identities that counterpoint the Son's unchanging self. Satan, as the quintessential ego, is fundamentally unchanged through all his metamorphoses, a threshold guardian through whom Jesus passes as easily as Alice going through the looking glass.

If Jesus has already achieved the fundamental goal of true selfhood before the events of *Paradise Regain'd* begin, the poem may seem to lack action, to amount to little more than a series of demonstrations of his spiritual perfection, with all the activity left to that energetic virtuoso, Satan. On the other hand, the main action of the poem may, paradoxically, be a kind of inaction, Jesus' persistent determination to refrain from untimely or inappropriate deeds. If, as we have seen, the fairy-tale hero "achieves a domestic, microcosmic triumph," this occurs in Jesus' private interior victory. If the hero of myth achieves "a world-wide macrocosmic triumph," this is the inevitable and undoubted consequence of Jesus' secret victory. The fact that Milton utterly ignores Jesus' active career indicates his conviction that it is the destined sequel to his ordeal in the desert.

The series of temptations must then be regarded as moments in a process of self-discovery. "Wand'ring the woody maze" for forty days of total deprivation, he undergoes the temptation to turn stones into food (and thus enact the social gospel of charity), the manifold temptations of the banquet (2.302–405), the offers of wealth and political power to redeem Israel (2.406–86), of glory (3.1–144), of "zeal and duty" in assuming the throne of David (3.145–250), of world empire (3.251–443), of Roman "wealth and power, /Civility of Manners, Arts, and Arms,/ And long Renown" (4.44–194), and of the rich delights of Greek culture (4.195–366). Milton is thus recapitulating major episodes in the epic tradition that he is radically revising, and Satan's attitude toward such achievements is quite orthodox, according to tradition. After the offer of Greece fails, "quite at a loss, for all his darts were spent" (4.366), Satan turns to other strategies to shake his steadfast victim. Returning him to the wilderness ("What dost thou in this world?"), he employs all the special effects in his repertoire to harass and disturb the Son: darkness, cold, ugly dreams, thunder, "fierce rain with lightning mixt, water with fire / In ruin reconcil'd," hurricane winds, "infernal ghosts and hellish furies" who howl, yell and shriek, and brandish fiery darts. But these Dantean apparitions are, like the dismal night of their occurrence and the impresario conducting them, "unsubstantial" (399). On the fair morning that ensues, the Son answers Satan's solicitous inquiries with a stroke of deflating *sprezzatura*, "Mee worse than wet thou find'st not" (4.486). Clearly, there is dramatic interest in the interplay between Satan's versatile arts and the artlessness of the Son's rejoinders. Perhaps, on the other hand, the Son's artlessness is really the art that conceals art in the spontaneous simplicity of truth.

This last encounter with specious terrors and double darkness is a hyperbolic reprise of the first, and the two episodes bracket the seven temptations enumerated above, analogues, perhaps, for the seven deadly sins, isolating the visionary mode of Christ's ordeal in the wasteland from events in the "real" world which precede and follow them: the Son's baptism and his triumphant stand on the pinnacle of the Temple.

Incarnation has cut the Son off from all direct access to the Father (except for the epiphany at Jordan), and the action of the poem consists, in the last analysis, in the gradual discovery, through essentially *human* resources, of the nature of his career as Son of God and savior of mankind. The climax on the Temple spire is a culminating revelation of his divine identity, one in which the *Logos* moves beyond the realm of discursive language and debate to an almost wordless epiphanic mode. His rescue and succor by the angels are outside the framework of the action proper, and a nine-word coda brings him back to the point of his departure: "Hee unobserv'd / Home to his Mother's house private return'd." From a public standpoint, he has achieved nothing. From Milton's point of view of the *via negativa* as the essential way, he has fulfilled his quest so perfectly that not a trace of it can be discerned at the poem's end except by those who have the privilege of sharing Milton's vision.

My conclusion is that *Paradise Regain'd* is an epic poem that radically modifies traditional aspects of epic—grandeur, hero, actions, and style. The career of the meditative hero, outwardly inactive, must be rendered in a style shorn to a large extent of those qualities that contribute to the grandeur of traditional epic; rich and elaborate imagery (there are almost no similes in the poem); classical allusions; rhetorical, metrical, and syntactical inversions, suspensions, and variations; and sensuous sound patterns that have so much to do with the incantatory and sonorous effects of the *Aeneid* or *Paradise Lost*. Vocabulary is abbreviated. The diction is chastened.

All such tendencies toward a lower and more austere style appear most conspicuously in the narrative passages and in the speeches of the Son. Since Satan's speeches are repeated invitations to regress into an inappropriate and outmoded course of heroic deeds, his language tends to be more conventionally epic. The temptations he offers re-create experiences and deeds that are central to earlier epic—prowess in battle, self-glorification, elaborate banquets, the advancement of an ethnic or national destiny, even the great philosophic and literary achievements of ancient Greece—and which undergird so much of *Paradise Lost*. An outstanding example is Satan's animated account of Rome:

> "Many a fair Edifice besides, more like
> Houses of Gods (so well I have dispos'd
> My Airy Microscope) thou mayst behold
> Outside and inside both, pillars and roofs
> Carv'd work, the hand of fam'd Artificers
> In Cedar, Marble, Ivory or Gold.
> Thence to the gates cast round thine eye, and see
> What conflux issuing forth or ent'ring in,
> Praetors, Proconsuls to thir Provinces
> Hasting or on return, in robes of State:
> Lictors and rods, the ensigns of thir power,
> Legions and Cohorts, turms of horse and wings:
> Or Embassies from Regions far remote
> In various habits on the *Appian* road,
> Or on th'*Aemilian*, some from farthest South,
> *Syene*, and where the shadow both way falls,
> *Meroë*, *Nilotic* Isle, and more to West,
> The Realm of *Bocchus* to the Blackmoor Sea. . . ."
> [4.55–72]

These seventeen lines are part of a sentence that extends to twenty-four lines and which forms but a small portion of Satan's sinuous, variegated representation of Rome, geographical, political, architectural. The epic emphasis on power, wealth, and culture, to which we can supply analogues in *Paradise Lost*, lacks, nevertheless, a point of view or a vision that can discern any real meaning behind all this detail. The accounts of Hell and Eden in *Paradise Lost* are unified by coherent values, but this vivid heterogeneity is devoid of insight. Satan can supply an engaging tableau of imperial Rome with a lot of busy going and coming, and he can indicate its greatness by a catalogue of exotic places it governs, but there is no inkling of any authentic purpose or principle underlying this inventory. "Fam'd Artificers" reminds us of Daedalus, but neither the most famous of ancient mythopoeic artists nor any artist or work of art is here. Rome is an ornamental and inchoate anthill rendered in a relentlessly materialistic mode. This fact is obviously related to the fact that everything Satan has to offer is specious, but it also suggests that, in the course of his degeneration, the heroic rebel has lost whatever appreciation of the heroic he once had. Jesus unerringly exposes the hollowness of the proffered vision:

> "Embassies thou show'st
> From Nations far and nigh; what honor that,
> But tedious waste of time to sit and hear
> So many hollow compliments and lies,
> Outlandish flatteries?"
>
> [4.121–25]

Satan's speech has some of the momentum and cumulative power that is so evident in *Paradise Lost*, with "the sense variously drawn out from one verse into another," but the offer ends in anticlimax as he feebly concludes, "to me the power / Is given, and by that right I give it thee" (4.103–04). Since he cannot identify any recognizable value in the gift, he is easily put down by the laconic simplicity of Jesus' rejoinder.

Jesus' apparent inaction, "deeds above heroic / Though in secret done," is heroic conduct of a unique order, since on it depends not only the restoration or preservation of a nation but the opportunity for the salvation of all mankind. Only an achievement of this illimitable magnitude can cancel the consequences of the Fall. Unlike Adam and Eve, the hero of such an ordeal must achieve his triumph by resolutely denying himself any form of self-assertion, any impulse of the will that might lead him to exercise his power prematurely and to some limited end, like Achilles or Aeneas. The acts of Jesus, then, are a disciplined and total obedience to the promptings of the Spirit. With the rejection of traditional modes of heroic behavior, Milton must find a form and a style that adequately express the *via humilis* Jesus pursues. By blending the usual epic preoccupation with the sublime with the humbler mode of the fairy tale, the dualistic style of *Paradise Regain'd* is responsive both to the secret character of Jesus' ordeal and to its enormous implications for the human race. Jesus' experiences in the wilderness are folklore and romance, much influenced by Spenser, while their public consequences are celebrated in the sublime epic quality of the climactic epiphany and apotheosis.

The interaction of Satan's and Jesus' styles may be understood as a conflict between two modes of epic value, patterned, it may be, on the aggressive and self-assertive Achilles as contrasted with the much-enduring Odysseus. Whatever power Satan still has, no one has ever thought of him as the hero of this poem. Irrevocably lost, his vain hope is to subvert the power of the new hero through second-hand versions of old epic temptations. Ultimately the difference in their utterances goes beyond modes of action, values, and styles. Satan's speeches are self-defeating because they are governed solely by the egoistic compulsion toward personal power, and they mask a hollowness. Jesus' speeches are always in the service of belief in the transpersonal divine, and he speaks with the sublime simplicity of Truth.

Since the hero of *Paradise Regain'd* is both man and God incarnate, his self-defining ordeal, though limited to an inscrutable sense of divine destiny and to a purely human wisdom supported by that sense of destiny, puts him in a different class of heroes from the others under consideration. Nonetheless the privation of knowledge about his divine career places Jesus firmly among the other heroic figures whose rites of passage yield revelations that lead to the founding of a new society or the restoration of an old one. Thus *Paradise Regain'd*, in following the self-denying and self-fulfilling career of Odysseus and in rejecting systematically the collective, secular vision of the Roman empire, shows strong affinities with the mythical *via negativa* of the *Odyssey* and the *Inferno*, while rejecting implicitly both the philosophic individualism of later Greek culture and the collectivistic, power-centered social principles of the *Aeneid*. In his final epic Milton has succeeded brilliantly in producing a hero apparently stripped of traditional heroic power, in the mode of the unestablished Nobody of Homer's *Odyssey*, one who exemplifies, through his total rejection of appeals to the ego and his profound, godlike, aversion to the exercise of godlike power toward inadequate ends, the essential reality of the achieved self.

Paradise Regain'd, then, appears to be a palinode of the *Aeneid* and a liberal, enfranchised version of the *Inferno*. Milton does not need the elaborate Augustinian and Thomistic categories of sin which are deployed so elaborately in the *Inferno*. While Milton's hero encounters more tempting versions of damnation than Dante can depict in his hideously stratified Hell, the Son of God, in his divine intuitions, his wise passiveness, his established self, is indifferent to the manifold modes of sin, except to the degree that Satan offers opportunities for him to violate his mission. Milton's Jesus, as God incarnate, exemplifies the *coincidentia oppositorum*, the union of opposites, that establishes him as the ultimately heroic antihero.

5 *The Prelude*: Wordsworth's Irresolute Novel of the Self

But the summit of what Keats unkindly called the "egotistical sublime" was achieved by Wordsworth. He conceived his incompleted masterpiece, The Recluse, *on an analogy with the traditional epic form, and particularly with Milton's* Paradise Lost. *But before beginning this work, it seemed to Wordsworth "a reasonable thing that he should take a review of his own mind," and record his findings in the fourteen autobiographical books of* The Prelude. *And, once chosen, the epic subject of* The Recluse *turns out to be a very modern one; namely, "the sensations and opinions," as Wordsworth tells us, "of a poet living in retirement," incorporated in a poem of which "the first two parts . . . will consist chiefly of meditations in the Author's own person."*

M. H. Abrams

Wordsworth's *Prelude* is the outstanding Romantic example of what John Freccero, in discussing the *Divine Comedy*, calls "the novel of the self."[1] Freccero makes the point that the author of a successful "novel of the self," in writing about the crisis of his growth, must suffer a kind of death of the ego, a separation of the recorder from the actor, since only the fully achieved self can authentically record its former experiences in the ordeal of individuation, as in the *Confessions* of Augustine. In Wordsworth's poem, the consciousness of the poet has few signs of such a transformation. The ego observed and the observing ego are continually intermixed, and we find countless passages in which Wordsworth wishes to persuade us of the objective or archetypal value of experiences that are contingent and personal. Point of view, tone, style, structure are all subject to shifting winds, as in the poet's opening description of his newly found freedom:

> Oh there is blessing in this gentle breeze
> That blows from the green fields and from the clouds

And from the sky: it beats against my cheek,
And seems half-conscious of the joy it gives.
O welcome Messenger! O welcome Friend!
A captive greets thee, coming from a house
Of bondage, from yon City's walls set free,
A prison where he hath been long immured.
Now I am free, enfranchis'd and at large,
May fix my habitation where I will.
What dwelling shall receive me? In what vale
Shall be my harbour? Underneath what grove
Shall I take up my home, and what sweet stream
Shall with its murmurs lull me to my rest?
The earth is all before me: with a heart
Joyous, nor scar'd at its own liberty,
I look about, and should the guide I chuse
Be nothing better than a wandering cloud,
I cannot miss my way. I breathe again;
Trances of thought and mountings of the mind
Come fast upon me: it is shaken off,
As by miraculous gift 'tis shaken off,
The burthen of my own unnatural self,
The heavy weight of many a weary day
Not mine, and such as were not made for me.[2]

[1.1–25]

There are many striking things about this passage as the beginning of
a poem that implicitly claims epic status. Not the least is the large
self-consciousness that informs what has been, traditionally, the most
anonymous part of an epic. Random natural phenomena are rendered, through a hesitant pathetic fallacy, as sympathetic attendants
on the enfranchised poet. The breeze "seems half-conscious of the joy
it gives." The entire natural setting is transformed into a scenario
ministering to the poet's mood and exists only in the context of his
own wishes.

Perhaps even more striking is the zest with which Wordsworth
celebrates his disorientation and homelessness. Although he claims
that he is free to make his home wherever he chooses, there are only
rare moments in the poem when he is settled enough in one place as
to be at home. If epic is often preoccupied with the relation of the
concept of home to self-discovery, Wordsworth here seems to be

claiming in homelessness a virtue which would have sent shudders through an Odysseus or an Aeneas. The thrust of the passage is overwhelmingly and insistently centrifugal, and, in place of the quest for a defined goal, we find an apostrophe to the delights of random-ness, a randomness that is reflected in the shifting grammatical modes of self-reference; alternations between first-and third-person verbs that imply a kind of enthusiastic indeterminism about the speaker's identity, which hovers, as it were, between *him* and *me*.

Goalless, homeless, without a concrete self-description, Wordsworth sets out from the despised city with no guide but a wandering cloud and no motive but "freedom." To consecrate, build, and defend the city is one of the highest social and cultural concerns of traditional epic. One need only think of Odysseus' devotion to Ithaca, or the importance of Rome to Aeneas, or Dante's fascination with the Florence that has betrayed him, or the obsession of Joyce's characters with the minutest details of dull, dirty Dublin, to see this. It is another indication of the placelessness dominating the opening of *The Prelude* that Wordsworth should so casually dismiss what, for better or worse, was the cultural center of his civilization. This is not a criticism but an observation, and indeed there were plenty of good reasons for hating nineteenth-century London. Yet the Miltonic allusion is relevant to the point: "The earth is all before me." This is quite a different statement from that at the end of *Paradise Lost*:

> The World was all before them, where to choose
> Thir place of rest, and Providence thir guide. . . .
>
> [12.646–47]

Wordsworth has dropped the place of rest and taken a wandering cloud instead of Providence.

Thus we have an epic journey with a point of departure but no destination. To an extent the design is like that of *Paradise Regain'd*, where Christ has no topographical goal as he wanders in the wilder-ness; but his meditations, unlike Wordsworth's, are highly struc-tured, and his submission to the promptings of the Spirit is utterly different from Wordsworth's submission to the promptings of his mood.

The entire narrative of *The Prelude* is a series of starts, of new beginnings, under the guise of sequential development, episodes intermixed with random and often vague philosophical disquisitions. Wordsworth has, along with other epic features, jettisoned the philosophic and religious armatures that shape most epics, and the growth of the poet's mind is not often reflected in the coherent growth of his ideas. The poem tends at times to reflect upon its own making in a curious way, as in this passage that follows the opening paragraph:

> Thus far, O Friend! did I, not used to make
> A present joy the matter of my Song,
> Pour out, that day, my soul in measur'd strains,
> Even in the very words which I have here
> Recorded: to the open fields I told
> A prophecy: poetic numbers came
> Spontaneously, and cloth'd in priestly robe
> My spirit, thus singled out, as it might seem,
> For holy services: great hopes were mine;
> My own voice chear'd me, and, far more, the mind's
> Internal echo of the imperfect sound;
> To both I listen'd, drawing from them both
> A chearful confidence in things to come.
>
> [1.55–67]

The Friend (Coleridge) is not individualized and he comes across as just another vague persona both for Wordsworth himself and for his reader. This is as far from the strenuous sense of purpose and shared experience that pervades other epics as one could get. Dante offers perhaps the most extreme contrast, with his sequence of tightly articulated experiences.

Soon, predictably, the mood of optimism collapses:

> if my mind,
> Remembering the sweet promise of the past,
> Would gladly grapple with some noble theme,
> Vain is her wish; where'er she turns she finds
> Impediments from day to day renew'd.
>
> [1.137–41]

Part of the drama of *The Prelude* inheres in such alternating periods of creativity and frustration. The poem is repeatedly threatened with its own destruction, a threat inseparable from the way in which it is conceived. As a forthright and spontaneous account of significant moments in Wordsworth's life, it must inevitably concern itself with experiences of doubt. Dante the poet has in all respects a firmly established perspective from which he can look back on the experi-

ences of Dante the pilgrim, but Wordsworth's recording self is not
nearly so distinct from his experiencing self. In fact, in the opening
phase of the poem, they are the same. This is reflected in the
atemporality of the opening. We are told nothing about the stage in
life in which the poet finds himself. An indifference to time seems to
be part of the new "freedom" he is celebrating, but such indifference
deprives the opening of a retrospective dimension.

After such vicissitudes in trying to get his poem started,
Wordsworth suddenly shifts his focus from rather general observations on the difficulties of composition to vivid recollections of his
childhood in the valley of the Derwent:

> Oh! many a time have I, a five years' Child,
> A naked Boy, in one delightful Rill,
> A little Mill-race sever'd from his stream,
> Made one long bathing of a summer's day,
> Bask'd in the sun, and plunged, and bask'd again
> Alternate all a summer's day, or cours'd
> Over the sandy fields, leaping through groves
> Of yellow grunsel, or when crag and hill,
> The woods and distant Skiddaw's lofty height,
> Were bronz'd with a deep radiance, stood alone
> Beneath the sky, as if I had been born
> On Indian Plains, and from my Mother's hut
> Had run a abroad in wantonness, to sport,
> A naked Savage, in the thunder shower.
>
> [1.291–304]

This passage bursts with energy, and the flexible rhythms and accents
of the verse transmit the experience empathically. The weary mood
has given way to an imaginative recreation of the sensibility of a child
who is innocent of any need or impulse for reflection. The passage
that follows about nesting and trapping is equally vivid, as is the all
too famous incident of stealing the boat and the brilliant account of
ice skating, "Proud and exulting, like an untired horse, / That cares
not for its home" (1.459–60). The spontaneity, however, cannot
survive:

> Uncouth assemblage was it, where no few
> Had chang'd their functions, some, plebeian cards,
> Which Fate beyond the promise of their birth

Had glorifi'd, and call'd to represent
The persons of departed Potentates.

[1.548–52]

Rather than a fusing of memory and event in the successful recreation of childhood delight, we find here the patronizing whimsy of an adult perspective.

Book 1 ends with two points: (1) "the hope . . that I might fetch / Invigorating thoughts from former years, / Might fix the wavering balance of my mind" (648–50); and (2), as Wordsworth looks ahead to the rest of his poem, the prospect that "I will forthwith bring down, / Through later years, the story of my life. / The road lies plain before me; 'tis a theme / Single and of determin'd bounds . . ." (666–69). "The wavering balance of the mind" has been manifest in the alternations of mood and attitude already noted. That the story of Wordsworth's life is "single and of determin'd bounds" raises central questions about the unity of *The Prelude*. At this stage of our inquiry we can say that the postulated unity of the poem lies only in the alleged continuity of Wordsworth's ideas and experiences; in other words, the unity arises mainly from the fact that all these things happened in the life of the man who is writing about them.

This unity is promptly questioned early in book 2:

A tranquillizing spirit presses now,
On my corporeal frame: so wide appears
The vacancy between me and those days,
Which yet have such self-presence in my mind
That, sometimes, when I think of it, I seem
Two consciousnesses, conscious of myself
And of some other Being.

[2.27–33]

The alleged singleness of theme is challenged by this sense of the gap between the childhood sensibility of experience and the mature sensibility of narrative relation, and the random accounts of village pleasures that follow suggest only that these activities were hallowed by intrinsic joy and sentimental recollection. An enlarging sympathy with natural phenomena is then recounted—love of the sun, the moon, the darling vale—but the question arises as to what these responses have to do with the specific development of Wordsworth's own mind. Instead of animating specifics, Wordsworth next proceeds to celebrate "the spirit of religious love / In which I walked with Nature" (2.376–77), "An auxiliar light . . . from my mind which on the setting sun / bestow'd new splendor" (2.387–89), the "bliss ineffable" with which "I felt the sentiment of Being spread / O'er all that moves" (2.419–21). These assertions claim little more than anyone would expect: that the growing imagination, in response to the evidence of harmony in nature at its most benign, will become deeply aware of a principle of natural coherence. A later phrase about "communing with God and Nature" (2.446) leaves undeveloped the repeated claim that such moments of natural sympathy were indeed authentic moments of religious insight. The argument is circular: they are religious moments because the imaginative response seems to testify to their religious character, but, beyond this assertion, there is no testimony as to the specifically religious content of these moments.

Book 3, "Residence at Cambridge," is an unblushing account of a period of truancy. Wordsworth seems to have valued the place chiefly because of its illustrious associations with men like Spenser, Milton, and Newton, and he enjoyed the variety of human types among his peers while standing aside from them: "I was the Dreamer, they the dream; I roam'd / Delighted through the motley spectacle" (3.28–29). The insights he had accumulated before Cambridge did not serve him as a scholar. There is not a hint in his account of university life that he read or learned anything, and so his general satire on the stodgy, formalistic quality of the place is undermined by the fact that he daff'd this world aside and bid it pass as a grotesque spectacle. Again the specifics necessary to justify his aversion are either absent or superficial, and while his attitude toward the abuses of higher education is like Pope's, unlike Pope, he does not make the gravamen stick by supplying evidence. The university experience is thus reduced to an anti-intellectual reflex in favor of an unshaped leisure that seems to have contributed nothing to the growth of his mind. The child of love and duty has been transformed into an idle scoffer. It is hard to see any continuity between the two.

Wordworth's Cambridge experience leads to another observation of *The Prelude's* status as epic. Chief among the functions of the great epics of the past is their celebration and preservation of their cultural heritage. As noted earlier, they contain the genetic code of the culture from which they spring, the social, political, moral, religious, artistic, poetic, and intellectual traditions that shape and animate that culture.

Residence at Cambridge is an extended dismissal of this all-important epic tradition, as the poet, faced with the opportunity to absorb his intellectual heritage, repeatedly regresses into the consoling communings with Nature that had governed his earlier life. We shall explore further this bold departure from the example of past epics. Suffice it to note here that, except for some commonplace allusions to *Paradise Lost, The Prelude* shows no signs of attempting, like its predecessors, to include and rework parts of them or to enhance, through rich mimesis, the suggestive implications of his own poem. This is one reason for the dominating subjectivity of Wordsworth's poem and for the curious way in which it keeps referring to its own process of generation.

Regression is the theme of book 4, "Summer Vacation," essentially a repetition of Wordsworth's earlier sojourns in the happy valley: the snow-white church, the aged Dame, the accustomed bed. With little to support the claim, he now finds

> How Life pervades the undecaying mind,
> How the immortal Soul with God-like power
> Informs, creates, and thaws the deepest sleep
> That time can lay upon her; how on earth,
> Man, if he do but live within the light
> Of high endeavours, daily spreads abroad
> His being with a strength that cannot fail.
>
> [4.155–61]

The alternation of objective and subjective vision is brilliantly conveyed through a simile at the midpoint of the book:

> As one who hangs down-bending from the side
> Of a slow-moving Boat, upon the breast
> Of a still water, solacing himself
> With such discoveries as his eye can make,
> Beneath him, in the bottom of the deeps,
> Sees many beauteous sights, weeds, fishes, flowers,
> Grots, pebbles, roots of trees, and fancies more;
> Yet often is perplex'd, and cannot part
> The shadow from the substance, rocks and sky,
> Mountains and clouds, from that which is indeed
> The region, and the things which there abide
> In their true dwelling; now is cross'd by gleam

Of his own image, by a sunbeam now,
And motions that are sent he knows not whence,
Impediments that make his task more sweet;
—Such pleasant office have we long pursued
Incumbent o'er the surface of past time
With like success; nor have we often look'd
On more alluring shows (to me, at least)
More soft, or less ambiguously descried,
Than that which now we have been passing by,
And where we are still lingering.

[4.247–68]

The leisurely movement of this passage evokes a hushed, meditative, pleasantly perplexed mood in which objective reality and its reflected images are intermixed. A similar passage in *Walden*, where Thoreau is fishing at night, watching the stars' reflections in the pond and feeling tugs and twitches on his line from fishes in the depths, serves to suggest mysterious contacts with remote forces. Not so here, where observation is crossed by a fleeting but interesting note of narcissism. Where objects and reflections of objects are mingled, where does one find reality? When the observer is observed by himself, what assurance is there that his observations are true? Self-consciousness may conceal consciousness of the self: "The very garments that I wore appear'd / To prey upon my strength, and stopp'd the course / And quiet stream of self-forgetfulness" (4.292–94). A glorious sunrise restores his confidence in his powers: "I made no vows, but vows / Were made for me; bond unknown to me / Was given, that I should be, else sinning greatly, / A dedicated spirit" (4.341–44). This is yet another instance of Wordsworth's alternating doubt and conviction of his poetic destiny and also another instance of the way in which the poem repeatedly begins itself anew. Bouts of blank self-consciousness obliterate, again and again, the visionary power. This time solipsism is overcome by Wordsworth's encounter with a remarkable old soldier, who, in his stoic desolation reminiscent of the leech-gatherer, is one of the few characters in the poem to call forth the poet's gift for imaginative sympathy with another. Other characters tend to serve only as elements in his milieu; he achieves very little sympathetic communication with them. Here, however, he overcomes his aversion to the bedraggled, ghastly, meager figure and succors him, paying tribute to his calm acceptance of his fate: "My trust is in the God of Heaven / And in the eye of him that passes me" (4.494–95). "With quiet heart" Wordsworth goes on to seek his own "distant home" (4.504).

The episode works an important transformation in the mind of the poet. Happily, he leaves its meaning for us to grasp without supplying any moralizing interpretation. It is a major turning point in the poem and forms a context for the memorable dream of the Bedouin Arab ascribed to the Friend. Hartman's comments on the dream are illuminating:

> The Guide, who has a stronger presence here than in any other episode, is the initiation-master, who guides the poet, but only to a more radical loss of Way. His symbols, the emblems of the human spirit, of revelations achieved by man by himself, suggest two *akedot* or fundamental ways in which man binds the world to himself. They exalt not only the human mind but also nature, and are therefore nature-things (stone, shell) and mind-things (books). Poetry paradoxically foresees a destruction of these bonds. The chase in which the Dreamer is both pursuer and pursued, mingles emotions of fear and desire. Just as a desire to cleave to the Guide is engendered by the Poet's fear, so, on following the Guide, a visionary fear arises. One question that must be answered before the dream can be understood is exactly what the dreamer desires or fears, the two being linked as in "blast of harmony." A clue furnished as to the character of that link by other episodes is that they also center on the "anxiety of hope": hope is heightened to the point where its imaginative and even apocalyptic character appears.[3]

As initiation-master the Arab guide has the power to help the poet through the rite of passage of his individuation crisis. As an exotic oriental figure he represents mysteries hitherto remote from the poet's experience. As an object of fear and desire he represents the conflicting attraction and repulsion generated by the approach to the *mysterium tremendum.*[4] As an object of flight and pursuit he reflects the poet's terrified ambivalence toward the crisis he may undergo. The alternatives he faces are the death of nature or the death of imagination, and, if Wordsworth is to succeed in his ordeal, he must ally himself with the powers of the imagination which, in the long run, are threatened by submission to nature. The "Desert Sands," which yield to "the fleet waters of the drowning world" (5.135–36) are shadowy adumbrations of the flight of the Israelites from Egypt through the Red Sea and across the desert toward Jordan, a traditional type (implicit in the opening of the *Inferno*) of conversion. Although Wordsworth characteristically fails to make the allusion specific, there is more than enough in the whole dream to establish it as a central, full, and rich expression of the conversion crisis and the crisis of individuation and the major encounter, for the poet of *The Prelude*, with truly supernatural, numinous powers.

Significantly, the Dream is followed by an unprecedented tribute to the sublime power of epic:

> And yet it seems
> That here, in memory of all books which lay
> Their sure foundations in the heart of Man;
> Whether by native prose or numerous verse,
> That in the name of all inspired Souls,
> From Homer, the great Thunderer; from the voice
> Which roars along the bed of Jewish Song;
> And that, more varied and elaborate,
> Those trumpet-tones of harmony that shake
> Our Shores in England; from those loftiest notes
> Down to the wren-like warblings, made
> For Cottagers and Spinners at the wheel,
> And weary Travellers when they rest themselves
> By the highways and hedges; ballad tunes,
> Food for the hungry ears of little Ones,
> And of old Men who surviv'd their joy;
> It seemeth, in behalf of these, the works
> And of the Men who fram'd them, whether known,
> Or sleeping nameless in their scatter'd graves,
> That I should here assert their rights, attest
> Their honours; and should, once for all, pronounce
> Their benediction; speak of them as Powers
> For ever to be hallowed; only less
> For what we may become, and what we need,
> Than Nature's self, which is the breath of God.
>
> > [5.198–222]

Nowhere else in *The Prelude* does Wordsworth pay such a sounding tribute to his predecessors, classical, biblical, and English. If the conclusion celebrates Nature's self, it is that Nature which, traditionally, is the Book of God. What Wordsworth may have gained through his ordeal is the freedom to abandon a simplistic response to Nature, often indistinguishable from his own projections, to a Nature that has a more authentic existence established by God. In any event, the poet, in this great passage, allies himself passionately with the great epic (and balladic) traditions he has hitherto ignored.

The sequence in *The Prelude* that centers on the poet's attempted, or partly or fully completed crisis of individuation depends on a key episode that can be read in several different ways. The archetypal motif of "crossing the Alps" turns out to be an anticlimax. The crucial pass, as often happens in real life, has been traversed without Wordsworth's or his Friend's having been aware of it. Without guides, they set out in pursuit of "a lofty mountain" (6.506), which they climb with eagerness only to learn from a passing peasant that their way lies downward: "to the place which had perplex'd us first / We must descend" (6.514–15), and as they make their way down, "hard of belief," they find that they have crossed the Alps. Aspirations frustrated, they have penetrated the critical point of the journey, which they feel should be a manifestly high point, only by a reluctant and ignorant descent. Reality contradicts and disappoints their expectations. It is inviting to see this moment in the journey as corresponding to a whole tradition of epic crises in which the hero must reach his goal by the *via humilis* rather than the *via sublimis*. Dante begins his journey with his eyes fixed on the Mount of Purgatory, but the three beasts stand in his way, and Virgil appears to tell him that he must descend through the agony of the Inferno before he can reach the base of the mountain on which his desires are fixed. The way down, or the way counter to one's intentions, is the way to the true goal. Aeneas must descend to the underworld before he can achieve his end. Odysseus laments when he learns from Circe that, before he can pursue his homeward way, he must visit the dead at the periphery of the world. The Son of God discovers that he can achieve his divine mission only by refraining from actions that would, by worldly standards, normally lead to it. Somewhat the same, though more obscure, is Wordsworth's discovery that what looks to desire and common sense like the way up must be the way down. To adopt Eliot's philosophic Greek motto, the way up and the way down are the same, with the necessary proviso that the way down is an indispensable stage in the hero's fulfillment of his goal. If these conjectures are right, then the mode of contradiction everywhere manifest in Wordsworth's moving account of an infernal passage through the Alps comes through to us as a well-established and traditional feature of the epic quest:

> The dull and heavy slackening that ensued
> Upon those tidings by the Peasant given
> Was soon dislodg'd; downwards we hurried fast,
> And enter'd with the road which we had miss'd
> Into a narrow chasm; the brook and road
> Were fellow-travellers in this gloomy Pass,
> And with them did we journey several hours
> At a slow step. The immeasurable height
> Of woods decaying, never to be decay'd,
> The stationary blasts of water-falls,
> And every where along the hollow rent
> Winds thwarting winds, bewilder'd and forlorn,
> The torrents shooting from the clear blue sky,
> The rocks that mutter'd close upon our ears,
> Black drizzling crags that spake by the way-side
> As if a voice were in them, the sick sight
> And giddy prospect of the raving stream,
> The unfetter'd clouds, and region of the heavens,
> Tumult and peace, the darkness and the light
> Were all like workings of one mind, the features
> Of the same face, blossoms upon one tree,
> Characters of the great Apocalypse,
> The types and symbols of Eternity,
> Of first and last, and midst, and without end.
>
> [6.549–72]

What distinguishes this amazing passage from most of Wordsworth's other representations of the natural scene is otherness. The optimistic celebration of communion with nature in the preceding books here gives place to a profound and pervasive sense of its mysterious autonomy, its union of opposites, an epiphany remote from human wishes. The somber stream, which might be one of the rivers of Dante's Hell, is no companionable Derwent. The simultaneous decay and immortality of the woods escapes the happy cyclic and seasonal character of trees in Wordsworth's happy vale. The breath of winds, so often seen as an emblem of inspiration by the poet, is here frozen into "winds thwarting winds." Sublime expectations are thwarted by "the sick sight and giddy prospect of the raving stream." The impression is one of total alienation. Unconsoling, indifferent, re-mote, and terrible, this vision of nature has an authentic objective status that sets it apart from the many earlier projections upon nature of a sympathetic benignity.

The sublime and inaccessible mystery of this experience leads Wordsworth to a new vision of the inner unity of natural beauty and natural terror. Intimations of apparently conflicting order and chaos, "Tumult and peace, the darkness and the light," lead to the apocalyptic vision of what looks like phenomenological incoherence as "The types and symbols of Eternity." The experience here affirmed is that of an ultimate reality that is the *coincidentia oppositorum*, a profound sense of the essentially paradoxical nature of reality. The vision does not prevail for long, however, and book 5 peters out as travelogue. Nevertheless this extraordinary vision will remain as one of the touchstones of *The Prelude*.

"Residence in London," book 7, is a countervision. In a socially alien and culturally corrupt milieu, Wordsworth becomes again the detached observer rather than the visionary participant. The Jonsonian chaos he depicts in London is contrasted in every way with the vision of conflicting natural forces as "all like workings of one mind, . . . The types and symbols of Eternity." The striking conjunction of opposites in book 6 now finds its countertheme of a superficial and distracting heterogeneity, always, apparently, different and diverting, always, in reality, vapid manifestations of the same banality. London, in Wordsworth's account, mainly resolves itself into false art, into a false mimesis of experience constantly offering the new without providing renewal. The heterogeneity of popular urban culture, as Wordsworth sees it, is reflected in the pervasive motif of metamorphosis in this book, and the key idea is of an art that "apes" reality.

To survive, Wordsworth must look to the mountain, to the natural forms from which his memory draws strength. But he encounters, in the tumult of the city, a man who functions for him as something like the saving exemplar he found in the Old Soldier, a blind and speechless man who wears a placard as blank as his countenance. The blind mute incarnates the opposite of everything that London seems to be. He is a taciturn critic of its character. London is full of spectacles he cannot see. London is full of speech, song, and music to which he is indifferent. The keynote of London is agitated movement, and he does not move. Amidst the phenomenological frenzy that is London, the blind man is established as a silent

and unresponsive center of something utterly detached from the
activities of the city. Within a "parliament of monsters" the poet is
fascinated by this apparition:

> And once, far-travelled in such mood, beyond
> The reach of common indications, lost
> Amid the moving pageant, 'twas my chance
> Abruptly to be smitten with the view
> Of a blind Beggar, who with upright face,
> Stood propp'd against a Wall, upon his Chest
> Wearing a written paper, to explain
> The story of the Man, and who he was.
> My mind did at this spectacle turn round
> As with the might of waters, and it seemed
> To me that in this Label was a type,
> Or emblem, of the utmost that we know,
> Both of ourselves and of the universe;
> And, on the shape of the unmoving man,
> His fixèd face and sightless eyes, I look'd
> As if admonish'd from another world.
>
> [7.608–23]

Immobilized, blind, silent, his identity divulged only by the "written
paper" he wears, the Blind Man suggests a Tiresias-like figure,
suggestive, symbolic, but, to Wordsworth, obscure. His immobility
and silence imply, with his blindness, the traditional visionary functions of the seer. But this seer says nothing, and we are not told the
message on his breast. The blindness strikes Wordsworth as an
admonition "from another world." In contrast to the poet's intense
visual engagement with the inchoate phenomenology of London, the
detachment of the Blind Man is significant. Surprisingly, the encounter suggests to the poet new views of what he has seen in old guise,
"The calmness, beauty of the spectacle" (603). The moment suggests
a wisdom that is both more submissive to experience and more open.
The fact that his "mind did at this spectacle turn round" suggests the
at least momentary achievement of something like the experience of
conversion.

    This unexpected revelation anticipates, as John Hodgson shows,
the culminating experience of conversion on Snowdon in book 13.
Having escaped bondage to the senses in London's distracting
Bartholomew Fair, Wordsworth "defamiliarizes" and "substantiates"
an "apparition 'from another world.' "[5] Beneath the label and behind

the blind, blank expression, Wordsworth senses a hidden truth, "As if admonish'd from another world."

The moment of vision is, however, gradually eroded in books 8 and 9, "a period in Wordsworth's life that parallels the time between the Fall and final loss of Paradise."[6] The anticipated forward movement of the poem promised by the symbolic descent to the underworld in crossing the Alps and by the visionary moment in London is not fulfilled. "Retrospect" (book 8) is a long and rambling assemblage of memories on the declared theme of love of Nature leading to love of mankind. The participants at the pleasant fair beneath Helvellyn (a manifest contrast to the chaos of Bartholomew Fair), the shepherd and his sagacious dog, the dignified laborer free and working for himself, and innumerable other humble tillers of the soil receive high praise, but in no case is there any impression of the bilateral relationships normally present in one human's love for another. Wordsworth describes these figures as ideal types and praises them, but he does not communicate with them. This fact suggests that they lack the autonomy of characters imaginatively and sympathetically conceived and that they are projections of the poet which he uses to illustrate and explore the human condition as he conceives it. The arbitrary, unilateral process is suggested by a sudden observation that "Thus sometimes were the shapes / Of wilful fancy grafted upon feelings / Of the imagination . . ." (8.383–85). This experience may help to account for the spineless structure of book 8 and a large part of book 9.

Only when Wordsworth has established his one real friendship in the poem (besides the friend, Coleridge), with Beaupuy, do his tentative and random observations about the French Revolution begin to crystallize. The opening of the book, with its image of the meandering river returning back upon itself, is a clear acknowledgment of the retrograde, perhaps regressive, tendencies at the heart of *The Prelude*, tendencies that here are explicitly connected to the mood of solitary freedom with which the poem began:

> Free as a colt at pasture on the hill,
> I ranged at large, through the Metropolis
> Month after month. Obscurely did I live,
> Not courting the society of Men. . . .

> [9.18–21]

There follow some of the poem's most vivid social descriptions and most acute reflections on political movements and institutions, given focus by the admired Beaupuy, who "perish'd fighting in supreme command / Upon the Borders of the unhappy Loire" (9.431–32). Perhaps Beaupuy's commitment unto death to the cause he fights for—so different from Wordsworth's position as a detached but sympathetic observer—makes him a central figure in the poem. Beaupuy also has a depth of sympathy and firmness of belief that set him apart from most of the other characters, and the friendship between the two men involves real exchanges of ideas and feelings.

But the brave idealism Wordsworth found in Beaupuy could not survive the manifold terrors committed by both sides in the Revolution or Britain's opportunistic intervention in the war. After an exhaustive examination of respective rights and wrongs, Wordsworth, for the first time in the poem, loses his confidence in the essential goodness of human nature and "Sick, wearied out with contrarieties, / Yielded up moral questions in despair" (10.899–900). This protracted psychomachia seems to me to be worthy of being called truly heroic, and its heroic nature is marked by the poet's unstinting honesty, courage, and concern. At last, "Nature's self [defined as the Breath of God], by human love / Assisted, through the weary labyrinth / Conducted me again to open day . . ." (10.921–23). Dorothy (unnamed) provides the clue by which the poet emerged from the labyrinth of human brutality to resume his career. The distribution throughout the poem of themes of the rite of passage shows how protracted is the ordeal that here culminates in a qualified victory: "One great Society alone on earth, / The noble Living and the noble Dead" (10.968–69). The moment is capped by a suggestive allusion to Eleusis: "O flowery Vale / Of Enna! is there not some nook of thine, / From the first playtime of the infant earth / Kept sacred to restorative delight?" (10.1003–05). Enhancing allusion here suggests the fusion in nature and man of the principles of death and rebirth.

With this preparatory ordeal the poem moves on in book 11 to explore the impairment and restoration of the imagination. The book begins as a retrospect of the poem's development up to this moment and thus constitutes another new beginning. In the second paragraph the poet claims an orderly development in the preceding books that in fact they cannot support:

> This History, my Friend, hath chiefly told
> Of intellectual power, from stage to stage

Advancing, hand in hand with love and joy,
And of imagination teaching truth
Until that natural graciousness of mind
Gave way to over-pressure of the times
And their disastrous issues.

[11.42–48]

This is true enough of the crisis induced by the French Revolution and its consequences, but it appears to ignore by design the alternations of mood and inner conflict noted earlier. For some reason Wordsworth wishes at this point to claim for *The Prelude* a steady development in experience and belief that is not there. One obvious reason would be that he was troubled by his sense of the poem's regressive tendencies and its frequent contradictions and second views of experience. A deeper reason may be that the poet needs to repress the essentially alternating character of his ordeal, in which, quite typically, the shortest way home is the longest way round, in which descent must be a necessary precursor to ascent. At any rate the passage seems to deny the agonistic complexity of the journey as we know it. The point is accentuated by the fact that Wordsworth immediately undermines his optimistic assertion by describing a new phase in his psychomachia in which he employs Reason against, one presumes, Imagination: "Thus strangely did I war against myself; / A Bigot to a new Idolatry / Did like a Monk, who hath forsworn the world / Zealously labour to cut off my heart / From all the sources of her former strength . . ." (11.74–78). Prospero-like, he sees himself as trying "to unsoul . . . / Those mysteries of passion which have made, / And shall continue evermore to make . . . / One brotherhood of all the human race" (11.84–88). The fraternal assertion is made in the face of the terrible accounts of fraternal murder in book 10. Wordsworth simply tries to recover himself from the evidence of human unregeneracy he has so tellingly reported. So book 11 opens with some striking instances of denial and wish-fulfillment, and it returns to a much earlier general affirmation in "The life of nature, by the God of love / Inspired, celestial presence ever pure . . ." (11.99–100). This beneficent power seems to exist apart from the many manifestations of evil in book 10. The poet takes refuge in "craving combinations of new forms" (11.192), in Nature, "rejoicing to lay the inner faculties asleep" (11.195). The renewal of his imagination is related to two visionary episodes: the encounter with the girl and her pitcher, the gibbet, and the naked pool nearby and, oddly enough, the death of his father. The first clearly synthesizes intimations of life and death. The second might have unconsciously liberated him to focus again on a Nature that is consistently maternal. The book ends thus:

> Behold me then
> Once more in Nature's presence, thus restored
> Or otherwise, and strengthened once again
> (With memory left of what hath been escaped)
> To habits of devoutest sympathy.
>
> [11.393–97]

The brief account of his father's death, a father unmentioned elsewhere in the poem, and this concluding assertion of the restoration of Nature (and, one presumes from the title of the book, Imagination) seem unavoidably related. The restoration is an escape back to an earlier condition. The fixating power of early experiences, working counter to growth, repeatedly returns the poem to beginnings, however strong the poet's conscious drive to move forward.

The acknowledged crisis of books 10–12 ends with one more assertion of renewed power to the Friend:

> Nor is it, Friend, unknown to thee, at least
> Thyself delighted, who for my delight
> Hast said, perusing some imperfect verse
> Which in that lonesome journey was composed,
> That also then I must have exercised
> Upon the vulgar forms of present things
> And actual world of our familiar days,
> A higher power, have caught from them a tone,
> An image, and a character, by books
> Not hitherto reflected. Call we this
> But a persuasion taken up by thee
> In friendship; yet the mind is to herself
> Witness and judge, and I remember well
> That in life's every-day appearances
> I seem'd about this period to have sight
> Of a new world, a world, too, that was fit
> To be transmitted and made visible
> To other eyes, as having for its base
> That whence our dignity originates,

That which both gives it being and maintains
A balance, an ennobling interchange
Of action from within and from without,
The excellence, pure spirit, and best power
Both of the object seen, and eye that sees.

[12.356–79]

As Hodgson says, "The healing of Wordsworth's imagination by nature described in books 10–12 in truth simply repeats the process of its original shaping by nature in books 1–4, and for that matter repeats the process of its shaping by London in books 7–8."[7] Books 10–12 seem, then, to retreat, under the disillusioning experience of revolution and politics, to an earlier mode of belief, despite the poet's claim to have now had "sight / Of a new world," stimulated by his reflections, during a walking trip in the Salisbury Plain, on the human sacrifices and astrological rituals practiced by the Druids at Stonehenge. The *frisson* of the sacrificial altar and "The desart visible by dismal flames" yields to his being "gently charm'd, charm'd, / Albeit with an antiquarian's dream" as he meditates vaguely on "a mystery of shapes." The episode seems desultory and unsubstantiated, and we must ask ourselves if it has the imaginative power to support the optimistic asseverations of the apostrophe to Coleridge (quoted above) with which book 12 ends. What might have been material for a vital encounter with primitive mysteries of ancient Britons and an authentic experience of the numinous is rendered as an uninformed and undisciplined tourist's reverie. The dismal horror and serene beauty Wordsworth feels are left unassimilated and unresolved.

Fortunately the same criticism cannot be leveled at the culminating episode of *The Prelude*, the extraordinary ascent of Snowdon by moonlight, one of the earliest sections of the poem composed. Even in this culminating vision of universal harmony, however, Wordsworth, though accompanied by a "Band" of climbers and led by an experienced guide, characteristically conveys no sense of a common bond, his inclination to solitude bordering on solipsism, marked, with unwitting humorlessness, by "I, as chanced, the foremost of the Band":

              With forehead bent
Earthward, as if in opposition set
Against an enemy, I panted up

With eager pace, and no less eager thoughts.
Thus might we wear perhaps an hour away,
Ascending at loose distance each from each,
And I, as chanced, the foremost of the Band;
When at my feet the ground appear'd to brighten,
And with a step or two seem'd brighter still;
Nor had I time to ask the cause of this,
For instantly a Light upon the turf
Fell like a flash: I look'd about, and lo!
The Moon stood naked in the Heavens, at height
Immense above my head, and on the shore
I found myself of a huge sea of mist,
Which, meek and silent, rested at my feet:
A hundred hills their dusky backs upheaved
All over this still Ocean, and beyond,
Far, far beyond, the vapours shot themselves,
In headlands, tongues, and promontory shapes,
Into the Sea, the real Sea, that seem'd
To dwindle, and give up its majesty,
Usurp'd upon as far as sight could reach.
Meanwhile, the Moon look'd down upon this shew
In single glory, and we stood, the mist
Touching our very feet; and from the shore
At distance not the third part of a mile
Was a blue chasm; a fracture in the vapour,
A deep and gloomy breathing-place thro' which
Mounted the roar of waters, torrents, streams
Innumerable, roaring with one voice.
The universal spectacle throughout
Was shaped for admiration and delight,
Grand in itself alone, but in that breach
Through which the homeless voice of waters rose,
That dark deep thoroughfare had Nature lodg'd
The Soul, the Imagination of the whole.

[13.29–65]

"What makes the scene particularly remarkable and unusual,"
Hodgson says, "is its structural reflexivity or *redoublement*, its
repetition of itself."[8] This "layering and doubling of its features"
conveys a genuine implication of "presence beneath presence, power

beyond power," the agent of this doubling being the thick mist that Wordsworth sees from his standpoint on the flanks of Snowdon as "a huge sea of mist," an enchanting landscape of "headlands, tongues, and promontory shapes" that "shot themselves . . . Into the Sea, the real Sea." In a brilliant passage Hodgson unfolds Wordsworth's *redoublement* of the already doubled imagery, pursuing it by turns from two distinct though complementary perspectives. "From one viewpoint he seeks to understand the essences of his twin subjects, to know what mind and nature are; from the other, he seeks to understand their powers, to know what they can do. Thus Wordsworth's meditation upon this complex analogy epitomizes the entire philosophical inquiry of *The Prelude*."[9] The "hidden underpresence" of the real topography of sea and mountains is "a figure of the ever-invisible spiritual or ideal world, the infinite realm of spirit and power underlying, informing, and exalting nature. . . . Substantiation is thus Wordsworth's defense against the existential anxiety: underpresence valorizes presence, depth constitutes the significance of surface."[10] This sudden, sublime, and specifically divine dual vision of a double natural phenomenon Hodgson sees mirrored and formally reversed in the London epiphany in book 7, when the poet's attention is arrested by the blind beggar. There he moves from motley heterogeneity to unity; here, from apparent unity to a mystical apprehension of the doubleness of Nature and of Mind. The mist simultaneously conceals and reveals; the mind of the poet both sees and envisions, through the "metaleptic" extension of his emblem.[11] Within the austere metaphysical limitations of *The Prelude* this climactic scene is the most complete and imaginatively powerful symbol one can hope for.

The compelling imaginative force of this climactic experience and its manifold links to other major episodes like the encounter with the blind man in the central book or the Simplon Pass experience, while indicating major stages in the thematic and structural development of *The Prelude*, only emphasize the recurrent weaknesses in much of the poem. Even if we grant the verve and vividness of such famous recollections of childhood as the long summer days playing by and in the Derwent and the kinesthetic delight of river skating by starlight or the "ministry of fear" manifested in the promiscuous borrowing of the rowboat or the mixed terror and delight of stealing birds' nests from windswept cliffs, such "spots of time" remain local and isolated *aperçus* in the intended overall design. Even if, furthermore, we recognize the poet's lapses into ennui, alienation, and creative blankness as unavoidable dead ends in his wayfaring, false turns as he tries to make his way through an unusually indeterminate labyrinthine course, the total impression of the poem is of a work too full of random events and dilatory philosophizing on these events. The poet of the *Inferno* has an integrated retrospective view of the ordeal of pilgrimage, a pilgrimage that has formed the poet's recording self. In the apparently random wanderings of Jesus in *Paradise Regain'd*, we participate in the process of his self-discovery as he submits to the promptings of the Holy Spirit, sharing in his profoundly meditative journey in an inward visionary mode that annihilates both the desert landscape and the anxieties and fraudulent tableaux urged on him by Satan. In contrast to the Son of God's unwavering dedication to restoring Paradise within the waste wilderness and to Dante's increasingly authentic responses to the highly structured desolations of Hell, the wayfaring Wordsworth, guided by his impulsive surrender to fluctuating impressions of Nature's fluctuating moods, is bent on reading intimations of immortality through the benign and admonitory phenomena of the landscapes through which he wanders. Onto the natural he projects a highly selective and subjective benign Providence. His paradise is without serpents. The poem's easy optimism finds evil only in personal failures and in corrupting social and political institutions.

From his visionary ordeals what can Wordsworth contribute to the enlightenment of his culture? Despite his programmatic title to book 8, "Love of Nature Leading to Love of Mankind," his deepest response to society, beyond the spontaneous sociability of childhood in books 1–2, is to withdraw, an impulse from which much of the best English poetry of the seventeenth century was written. But the Horatian tradition of retirement and contemplation, as exemplified by the great English poets of that period, was inseparably related to a corresponding commitment to public responsibility, as a comparison of Marvell's "The Garden" and "Horatian Ode" suggests. In the context of the epic quest, *The Prelude* ends with its hero pursuing his sublime personal romance far from the cities of God and man, aloof from contemporary culture and essentially detached from the traditional values that have sustained or revitalized it. Curiously enough, *The Prelude*, like the *Iliad*, projects a conception of egocentric heroism that implicitly denies the associations of men bound by love, law, and ritual without which there can be no society.

6 The Epic of Indeterminacy: Don Juan

Now there is nothing gives a man such spirits,
Leavening his blood as cayenne doth a curry,
As going at full speed—no matter where its
Direction be, so 't is but in a hurry,
And merely for the sake of its own merits;
For the less cause there is for all this flurry,
The greater is the pleasure in arriving
At the great end of travel—which is driving.

Don Juan

In his dedication to *Don Juan*, Byron chides Southey and Wordsworth for assuming that "Poesy has wreaths for you alone," and adds: "There is a narrowness in such a notion, / Which makes me wish you'd change your lakes for ocean." The isolated, introspective, parochial qualities Byron finds in these Lake poets is juxtaposed with the expansive, universal implications of the ocean, implications richly fulfilled in *Don Juan*. Byron goes on to charge Southey and Wordsworth with the base vice of self-love, depicts himself as one "wandering with pedestrian muses," and invokes Milton as the model of the true poet:

> If fallen in evil days on evil tongues,
> Milton appealed to the Avenger, Time,
> If Time, the Avenger, execrates his wrongs,
> And makes the word "Miltonic" mean "*Sublime*,"
> *He* deign'd not to belie his soul in songs,
> Nor turn his very talent to a crime;
> *He* did not loathe the Sire to laud the Son,
> But clos'd the tyrant-hater he begun.[1]

The last half of the stanza refers to Southey's time-serving poems, but the whole stanza and the ones following it strike a note satirical

133

and sublime that stands out in the amazing medley of styles employed in the course of the poem.

In canto 3 Byron extends his charge against Wordsworth to include banality:

> He wishes for "a boat" to sail the deeps—
>   Of ocean?—No, of air; and then he makes
> Another outcry for "a little boat,"
> And drivels seas to set it well afloat.

[98]

To this he adds a criticism of Wordsworth's indifference to the classical tradition and to the poetry of his predecessors:

> If he must fain sweep o'er the ethereal plain,
>   And Pegasus runs restive in his "Waggon,"
> Could he not beg the loan of Charles's Wain?
>   Or pray Medea for a single dragon?
> Or, if too classic for his vulgar brain,
>   He fear'd his neck to venture such a nag on,
> And he must needs mount nearer to the moon,
> Could not the blockhead ask for a balloon?

[99]

These attacks on Wordsworth's bathos and narrow vision, to whatever extent they are justified, are important guideposts to Byron's concept of true poetry. It must have range and variety; it must be capable of the sublime or heroic; most of all, it must encompass experiences that are not mere matters of self-concern.

As I have tried to show, Wordsworth's greatest problem in *The Prelude* is the unstable character of his narrative persona. Often it is absorbed in recreating the past experience that the mature persona, who should put that experience in a new perspective, has lost. Often, too, the lack of narrative structure and of well-articulated beliefs leads to effusive, incantatory celebrations of higher truths that are simply projections. Without epistemological awareness and some attachment to the manifold traditions of epic, *The Prelude* seems to hang in a metaphysical void, a condition aggravated by the paucity of specific reference in much of the descriptive writing.

If Wordsworth the narrator tends to lose his later identity in his younger self, Byron, in contrast, tends to overwhelm or usurp the identity of Don Juan. Reflections on his hero's experiences often lead to extended disquisitions on the poet's own kaleidoscopic impressions of life, impressions full of shock, surprise, cynicism, indignation, and pathos. This usurpation is a function of the vacuous nature of the hero. Throughout his astonishingly various wanderings, Juan seldom manifests a capacity for either reflection or growth. Taciturn, more given to quick-witted reactions than to well-thought-out actions, without goal or defined purpose, Juan seems, at least in the first half of the poem, to represent an infantile ego governed by instinct. He is adaptable enough to acquire manners, but not character.

In contrast to Wordsworth's continual effort to give shape and coherence to *The Prelude*, Byron repeatedly celebrates the aleatory randomness of *Don Juan*, a randomness reflected in the dazzling medley of subjects and styles he employs. He uses Juan's experiences to explore a multiplicity of views on the human condition. They contradict, jostle, and qualify each other, leaving the reader to find some unity or coherence.

If the hero cannot grow, his story can have only a beginning. No conceivable finish could truly end the poem. Without an ending, it can have no middle. Without a middle, in which the critical trans-formative experience for the hero normally occurs, there can be no climax. Hence, like *The Prelude, Don Juan* is a series of beginnings, in which Byron jocularly plays havoc with the traditional structures and motifs of epic and resolutely deconstructs his chosen myth. "I want a hero, an uncommon want," and so he picks, casually, Don Juan. Soon after Byron makes a mock obeisance to narrative structure in epic:

> Most epic poets plunge "in medias res"
> (Horace makes this the heroic turnpike road),
> And then your hero tells, whene'er you please,
> What went before—by way of episode. . . .
>
> [I.6]

> That is the usual method, but not mine—
> My way is to begin with the beginning;
> The regularity of my design
> Forbids all wandering as the worst of sinning. . . .
>
> [7]

The beginning is, inevitably, *ab ovo*, the birth of Juan in Seville, leading to an account of his early growth and education and of the early pangs of puberty, which render him a lonely, moody adolescent. The youth's mother, a moralistic bluestocking, has devised a system for his moral education that is totally and comically remote from reality, while being apparently blind to the growing passion of her son and a beautiful young matron whom she pretends to regard as her best friend. There are hints that she plays the procuress in this affair to revenge herself on her husband. In any event romantic passion has its denouement in bedroom farce, and Juan is sent on his travels, while Donna Julia languishes in a convent. For all its frivolousness, the opening episode sets a major theme of the poem by its exposure of hypocrisy and ignorance of human nature in conventional manners and institutions. In an episode entirely governed by instinct, chance, and the self-ignorance of the lovers, Byron boldly reasserts his epic intentions:

> My poem's epic, and is meant to be
>   Divided in twelve books; each book containing,
> With love and war, a heavy gale at sea,
>   A list of ships, and captains, and kings reigning,
> New characters; the episodes are three:
>   A panoramic view of Hell's in training,
> After the style of Virgil and of Homer,
> So that my name of Epic's no misnomer.
>
>   [200]

After this declaration, Byron characteristically drops the subject in the twenty-two remaining stanzas of canto 1 in order to digress facetiously on the literal truth of his poem; on the excellence of Milton, Dryden, and Pope and the dullness of Wordsworth, Coleridge, and Southey; on the sadness of having reached the advanced age of thirty; on fame; on death. In canto 2 he willfully breaks the unity of the Haidée episode on the grounds that the canto has grown long enough:

> In the mean time, without proceeding more
>   In this anatomy, I've finish'd now
> Two hundred and odd stanzas as before,
>   That being about the number I'll allow
> Each canto of the twelve, or twenty-four;
>   And, laying down my pen, I make my bow,
> Leaving Don Juan and Haidée to plead
> For them and theirs with all who deign to read.
>
>   [216]

This assertion, equivocal as it may be, is abruptly shattered by the delayed, abbreviated, and irreverent invocation with which canto 3 opens, "Hail, Muse! et caetera," and the stanza with which it abruptly ends:

> I feel this tediousness will never do—
>   'Tis being *too* epic, and I must cut down
> (In copying) this long canto into two;
>   They'll never find it out, unless I own
> The fact, excepting some experienced few;
>   And then as an improvement 'twill be shown:
> I'll prove that such the opinion of the critic is
> From Aristotle *passim*—see *Poietikes*.

Such arbitrary manipulation of epic unity moves into the first stanza of canto 4: "Nothing so difficult as a beginning / In poesy, unless perhaps the end. . . ." Canto 6 ends with the throwaway couplet, "Meanwhile, as Homer sometimes sleeps, perhaps / You'll pardon to my Muse a few short naps."

One more example should clarify what Byron is up to in his ostentatious disregard of epic conventions. This one occurs in the middle of canto 12, which, by Virgilian or Miltonic models, would be the final book of the poem:

> But now I will begin my poem. 'Tis
>   Perhaps a little strange, if not quite new,
> That from the first of Cantos up to this
>   I've not begun what we have to go through.
> These first twelve books are merely flourishes,
>   Preludious, trying just a string or two
> Upon my lyre, or making the pegs sure;
> And when so, you shall have the overture.

[54]

Byron is celebrating the invertebrate, improvised character of his own poem and suggesting at the same time that epic continuity and coherence are not available to the modern poet. The implication of all this jocular challenging of epic conventions is that contemporary experience cannot be shaped to epic form, and the ultimate reason for this is that modern culture does not provide the religious, moral, social, and mythic foundations which can sustain a shared and unified view of life. In the face of this futility Byron chooses to emphasize process, movement, and change as essential aspects of reality that challenge all institutions and established forms. His tale is "A nondescript and ever-varying rhyme, / A versified Aurora Borealis, / Which flashes o'er a waste and icy clime . . ." (7.2). The "ever-varying rhyme" lights up in evanescent flashes both the appearances of life and the wasteland that lies behind it. In place of the creative benignity of Wordsworth's sun we have in *Don Juan* ever-changing and intermittent gleams of light.

If the poem has an organizing principle it may be one of startling contrasts. The comic, social view of marriage in canto 1, cast in the spirit of Congreve, is opposed in canto 2 by the agony and pathos of the shipwreck. The ordeal of thirst, hunger, exposure, cannibalism, and death in turn gives way to the idyllic fulfillment of love in the encounter of Haidée and Juan. Society, annihilated in the shipwreck, shows signs of being restored in canto 3, but the heedless lovers are destroyed by Haidée's father in canto 4. Haidée dies with her unborn child, and Juan is sent into slavery in Turkey. Enslavement, however, turns out to be something of a lark, and Juan easily escapes to take part in the appalling siege of Ismail. Thence, having won his spurs, he is wafted to St. Petersburg to participate in a luxurious life as lover of the lubricious Catherine the Great. Exhausted by his duties there, he is given leave to go to England, where, in an endless English country visit, he has a platonic affair with the beautiful Aurora Raby, whose name, perhaps, suggests her rather unstable character. The final episode of the uncompleted poem is Juan's midnight encounter with the ghost impersonated by the Countess of Fitz-Fulke (note the deflationary Regency overtones of her name), the only intimation of the supernatural in the whole poem.

Despite the extraordinary episodic variety of Juan's adventures, he is no picaresque hero, for he lacks the cunning and opportunism of the *picaro*. Rather, with a few exceptions, Juan is a passive figure who caroms from one encounter to another and catalyzes the deeds of other characters. Foresight or hindsight would disqualify him for the part.

There are, nevertheless, frequent intimations of epic themes scattered through the poem. Don Juan has the courage and physical strength of a hero. In both the shipwreck and the siege he acts resolutely. When he is washed ashore on Haidée's island we think of Odysseus' corresponding experience on Nausicaa's island, but the resemblance only heightens the difference in mood and value between the two incidents. The domestic and social values exemplified in the *Odyssey* are totally absent from *Don Juan*, and the king of this island turns out to be only a murderous brigand. As a kind of Circe, Gulbeyaz tries vainly to work her magic on the hero, and nothing follows from the encounter. The significance of Ismail is indeterminate, however full of horrors. The affair with Catherine is a travesty. The sojourn in England, which really constitutes a *nostos* (although Juan is nominally Spanish), divulges no real signs of restoration or return, only a sense of prevailing ennui. The hero's long and strenuous journey has got him nowhere, and the final "revelation" is an appropriately anticlimactic breaking off of a potentially endless tale.

The events precipitated by Juan are interesting, but Juan is rarely so. Byron seems deliberately to have devised a hero utterly devoid of complexity, curiosity, or motive, with the idea that the real interest of his poem must be sought elsewhere. What really absorbs our attention is the poet's manifold response to the nominal subject of his tale as reflected in his intellectual brilliance, moral insight, and stylistic virtuosity. In contrast to his naive hero, Byron is inexhaustibly alert and responsive to the matter of his tale.

An instance of this is the balanced sympathy and detachment with which he presents Julia's conflicting feelings:

> How beautiful she look'd! her conscious heart
> Glow'd in her cheek, and yet she felt no wrong:
> Oh Love! how perfect is thy mystic art,
> Strengthening the weak, and trampling on the strong!
> How self-deceitful is the sagest part
> Of mortals whom thy lure hath led along!—
> The precipice she stood on was immense,
> So was her creed in her own innocence.
>
> [1.106]

Julia's situation is somewhat like that of Eve in *Paradise Lost* when she insists to Adam on being free to expose herself to temptation to prove her innocence. Young, passionate, childless, married (presumably by arrangement) to an unsympathetic man twice her age who has been having an affair with Juan's mother, fortified against temptation only by feeble conventions, her surrender seems inevitable. Yet, for all his sympathy, Byron does not let her off easily. Her capacity for self-deception, her brazen response when challenged by her husband, even the self-dramatizing tone of her farewell note to Juan, "written upon gilt-edged paper / With a neat little crow-quill, slight and new," embossed with a sunflower and the motto "*Elle vous suit partout*," imply that she has to some extent been corrupted, like Francesca, by the decadence of her milieu. Essentially alone, like most of the women in *Don Juan*, her capacity for survival is nil. There is probably no reason to believe that Julia is worse off as an unbelieving votaress in a convent than she was in the hypocritical desolation of her social and domestic life, and Byron allows her to recede into the past as he delivers his own bitter-sweet elegy to the enchanting illusions of first love:

> No more—no more—Oh! never more, my heart,
>   Canst thou be my sole world, my universe!
> Once all in all, but now a thing apart,
>   Thou canst not be my blessing or my curse:
> The illusion's gone for ever, and thou art
>   Insensible, I trust, but none the worse,
> And in thy stead I've got a deal of judgment,
> Though heaven knows how it ever found a lodgment.
>
>   [1.215]

Byron's farewell to first and passionate love, which continues in a tone more wry in the succeeding stanza, is one testimony to his mature perspective. The various instances of social irony and of self-irony with which the first canto ends help to convert the Romantic egotism of Julia and Juan into an instance of the process of disillusionment which seems the necessary companion of growing up. It is a wholly different tone that Byron brings to bear on Juan's pathetic and absurd departure into exile from Cadiz:

> "And oh! if e'er I should forget, I swear—
>   But that's impossible, and cannot be—
> Sooner shall this blue ocean melt to air,
>   Sooner shall Earth resolve itself to sea,
> Than I resign thine image, oh, my fair!
>   Or think of anything, excepting thee;
> A mind diseased no remedy can physic—"
> (Here the ship gave a lurch, and he grew sea-sick.)
>
>   [2.19]

Juan's clichés are like those Byron attributes to Wordsworth, but at least Juan is young and nauseated and here attempting, desperately, to mediate between totally incompatible physical and emotional states. As Byron observes of love, "Against all noble maladies he's bold, / But vulgar maladies don't like to meet" (22). What has happened here does not occur in epic or romance: the claims of the heart alternate with spasms of vomiting. However inclusive traditional epic may be, its characters are never visited by "vulgar illnesses." Whatever illness Apollo visited on the Achaians in book 1 of the *Iliad*, the victims simply died in impersonal swarms, the prey of dogs. Heroes are otherwise wounded, and most of them die, but none are ever sick: sickness is outside the decorum of epic. It gets back into literature through mock epic: in Marvell's "Flecknoe" and "Last Instructions to a Painter" in *The Dunciad*; in Swift.

George Ridenour has emphasized the theme of falling as central to *Don Juan*.[2] In a passage reminiscent of the invocation to book 7 of *Paradise Lost*, Byron expresses a Miltonic anxiety that poetic aspiration may lead to a Satanic fall:

> For oftentimes when Pegasus seems winning
>   The race, he sprains a wing, and down we tend,
> Like Lucifer when hurl'd from heaven for sinning;
>   Our sin the same, and hard as his to mend,
> Being Pride, which leads the mind to soar too far,
> Till our weakness shows us what we are.
>
> [4.1]

Byron, wandering with the Horatian pedestrian muses, eschewing (most of the time) the epic sublime, avoids hubris of this sort, although he finds it in some of his contemporaries. He avoids it by a comprehensiveness of attitudes that is aware simultaneously of high and low aspects of human experience. Thus the thoughtless self-absorption of the lovers, touching in its intensity, is nevertheless doomed by their lack of foresight, and their romantic Eden is inevitably vulnerable when Lambro returns. For Lambro the affair is a gross affront to his rights, and he deals with it according to his unambiguous code: "But I must do my duty—how thou hast / Done thine, the present vouches for the past" (4.46). When two incompatible attitudes collide, the more realistic one, if backed by superior power, must prevail. We indulge in the dreamy love idyll, but we accept its inevitable collapse:

> Valour was his, and Beauty dwelt with her:
> If she loved rashly, her life paid for wrong—
>   A heavy price must all pay who thus err,
> In some shape; let none think to fly the danger,
> For soon or late Love is his own avenger.
>
>   [4.73]

If *The Prelude* attempts epic status in the absence of myth, coherent quest, social values, and cultural institutions—in the absence, also, of the cosmic values in which the *Odyssey, Paradise Regain'd*, and the *Paradiso* are firmly anchored—*Don Juan*, as a totally other kind of Romantic epic, is filled with the various kinds of heroic activities, values, and images that are the matter of epic. For the wanderer, Juan, life is filled with alternations between love affairs, in which he plays the passive role of Odysseus with Calypso and Circe, appalling and agonizing experiences in shipwrecks and war that outdo Homer in horror, and relatively low-keyed sojourns in milieus that are either extraordinarily exotic or as familiar as the great house parties that are a fixture of the nineteenth-century English novel. If this truncated narrative has a pattern, it is a movement from familiar social institutions in Juan's youth and adolescence in Spain, through a variety of exotic experiences, back to the familiar and slightly boring milieu of the Amundevilles' country place. Uneducated, untouched by parental influences, devoid of any cultural commitments but with natural good temper and good manners, Juan wanders in and out of engagements in which chance involves him. Only under the pressure of some unavoidable challenge does he act. As detached as Wordsworth's mind, both growing and mature, from the cultural inheritance of Western man and from the myths and concepts on which his civilization is based, Juan has no capacity—nor even any curiosity—about interpreting life as it passes. He simply is impelled from one adventure to another. As we have seen, he has little capacity for psychological or spiritual growth. How could he, when he lacks any real interest in the past or the future?

If Wordsworth as poet and hero was irrepressibly reflective and articulate in *The Prelude*, Byron in *Don Juan* has supplied a hero who almost never speaks and a commentator who is rarely silent. To whatever extent Byron sympathizes with his hero, he feels impelled to comment endlessly on Don Juan's experiences from viewpoints that extend from the sublime to the ridiculous.

Byron's "ever-varying rhyme," his alternation in style from the true sublime, in the tribute to Milton, to the biting Juvenalian sublime, as in his annihilating attack on Castlereagh, to the good-humored "honest simple verse" of the pedestrian muses that conceals beneath its mask of candid simplicity a devastating exposure of Southey's apostasy, to the declamatory indignation of Julia at her husband's suspicions, to the lyric and elegiac notes that pervade the account of the love of Juan and Haidée, to the Romantic sublime of

> They looked up to the sky, whose floating glow
>   Spread like a rosy Ocean, vast and bright;
> They gazed upon the glittering sea below,
>   Whence the broad Moon rose circling into sight;
> They heard the waves' splash, and the wind so low,
>   And saw each other's dark eyes darting light
> Into each other. . . .
>
> [2.185]

—all these dazzling and masterful shifts of style and tone demonstrate Byron's rich capacity to respond and to accommodate his poem to a vast medley of experiences that requires an extraordinary flexibility in point of view. Like Dryden and Pope, Byron can mediate brilliantly between high, middle, and low without building his poem on the established cultural and aesthetic consensus that is fundamental to the social vision of Augustan poetry. While he can adopt easily the stylistic virtuosity and finish of Augustan poetry, and while he is utterly at home in a wide variety of societies, Byron is fundamentally an outsider, an exile writing of the vicissitudes of human experience from a point of view that is spontaneous, free, unconventional, and inexhaustibly inventive. Characteristically, one judgment will elicit a counterjudgment. In commenting on the lines just quoted, Ridenour observes of the lovers:

> . . . it is precisely because of the completeness of their harmony with nature that they are not exempt from sharing in its less idyllic manifestations. Such involvement in the natural, while it makes possible something so beautiful as the love of the two young "birds," implies also a participation in the vicissitudes inevitable to a fallen nature, particularly in its subjection to mutability.[3]

This shrewd insight, that something like the first law of motion is at work in the vision of *Don Juan*, that idyllic nature must necessarily have its evil corollary, is a mark of honesty and comprehensiveness of view. It may be that Wordsworth's alternating moods in the face of a nature to which he attributes an almost unvarying benevolence and a particular maternal affection toward himself grow out of his reluctance to admit nature's dangerous ambivalence. One might add, following Ridenour, that human nature at its extremes, as in the lust of Catherine the Great and the sterility of Castlereagh (in the dedication), shows that "the Byron of *Don Juan* . . . is less concerned with 'reconciling' opposites than with implying their moral equivalence."[4]

Within the pervasive themes of love and war, traditionally associated with epic, Byron tends to satirize the pretensions of both love and glory. He intuits the moral design of the *Iliad*, which raises fundamental doubts about the validity of either when carried to an extreme. "It does not, then, seem reckless to suggest that, in his lesser way and from his essentially secular and predominantly rationalist point of view, Byron is attempting as radical a redefinition of the nature of epic and the epic hero as was Milton in *Paradise Lost*."[5] Or, as Michael Cooke observes,

> *Don Juan* stands as more than a thing of flashy juxtapositions; it is created as a universe of the unpredictable, containing, as Byron had once said of his mind, "500 contradictory contemplations, though with but one object in view." It abounds in untoward developments, like *The Prelude*, but unlike that work results in no final, all-encompassing serenity. Conceding nothing to "that vice-nature custom," Byron advances before us with a "dedication" that is at best a rebuke, and hardens into a denunciation; he promises an epic which on inspection does not so much revise as revoke the epic tradition.[6]

Writing in a later study on the problems of *Don Juan*, Cooke observes that Byron's "contemplation of 100 cantos of *Don Juan*, a number so magnificent as to leave scant time for Byron's daily business of love and war . . . , but in Byron's own concept of it . . . unfinishable, inasmuch as he meant to discourse in it *de rebus cunctis et quibusdam aliis*": on everything and more besides, should remind

us of the "warrant Byron obtained from his time" to write "the
unfinishable poem . . . a signal romantic contribution to the form
and vital entelechy of poetry itself."[7]

For Cooke the problem of the long poem for the Romantics was
that "the long poem could not, in reality or in mortality, be made
long enough. Which is to say, it could not be infinite."[8] The problem
of the long Romantic poem, Cooke says, "lay not in the collapse of
sustaining philosophical structures."

One must point out, that if the Romantic poet—and Byron
especially—felt his project thwarted by the fact that he could not
write "infinitely," then his disappointment was, at the least, naive. If
his great predecessors, within their allotted spans, could produce such
self-contained and complete long poems as the *Iliad, Oydssey,
Aeneid, Paradise Lost,* and *Paradise Regain'd,* such despairing reactions to the fact of human mortality do no credit to a poet of Byron's
awareness of the limitations of mortality, temporally speaking, on
man's creative yearnings. The failure of the long Romantic poem was
due not to the early deaths of many of its practitioners—Keats,
Shelley, and Byron—but to the collapse of "sustaining philosophical
structures" and the loss of the mythic and numinous contexts which
for centuries had made it possible for a living poet to complete a living
and self-sustaining poem. If one extends the implication that the
Romantics were haunted by the fact that they could not live long
enough to write an "infinite" poem, the *Weltschmerz* of those who
age but are immortal comes to mind. Wordsworth lived long and had
the chance to revise *The Prelude* over more than half a century. Yet
one could imagine Wordsworth afflicted with immortality and seeking vainly, like Tennyson's Tithonus, for a terminal illness to rescue
him from infinite senescence:

> The woods decay, the woods decay and fall,
> The vapours weep their burthen to the ground,
> Man comes and tills the field and lies beneath,
> Me only cruel immortality
> Consumes: I wither slowly in thine arms,
> Here at the quiet limit of the world,
> A white-haired shadow roaming like a dream
> The ever-silent spaces of the East,
> Far-folded mists, and gleaming halls of morn.

> [1–9]

Imagine Wordsworth of *The Prelude* compelled forever to stay in the Alpine pass that leads to Locarno:

> The immeasurable height
> Of woods decaying, never to be decay'd,
> The stationary blasts of water-falls,
> And every where along the hollow rent
> Winds thwarting winds, bewilder'd and forlorn,
> The torrents shooting from the clear blue sky,
> The rocks that mutter'd close upon our ears,
> Black drizzling crags that spake by the way-side
> As if a voice were in them, the sick sight
> And giddy prospect of the raving stream. . . .
>
> [6.555–64]

For the decrepit but undying Tithonus the horror is the mortal, seasonal cycle which he can, with diminishing interest, witness, but never again share. For Wordsworth there is an opposing horror—of an immemorial natural scene that seems impervious to the natural cycles of decay, death, and rebirth.

These collateral witnesses do much to express Byron's lack of interest in the completion of a poem from its very beginning clearly recognized as uncompletable. Whatever ending Byron could entertain occurred at Missalonghi. For Byron, as we have seen, the Lake poets are egotistical, metaphysically mad, and opportunistic. To exorcise them he invokes Milton, Dryden, and Pope. As Ridenour reminds us, with his discussion of the pervasive theme of the Fall in *Don Juan*, Byron's epic is, in many ways, earthbound and pedestrian. Among its other virtues, *Don Juan* maintains a close touch with empirical reality, balanced with every human intuition Byron could bring to bear upon it. The result is usually a strikingly honest awareness of man's fate in all its aspects. Byron's concern with aging—at thirty—is only one indication of his commitment to the aspirations and disappointments of mortality. *Don Juan* is indeterminate with respect both to the hero's destiny and to his inadequate powers of reflection; yet, among the other realities of life it not only accepts but passionately affirms is the potential of personality, or, in Jung's terms, the acceptance of the challenging ordeal of selfhood.

As we have seen, *Don Juan*, by its apparently random narrative, repeatedly denies any capacity for epic completion. Moreover, it consistently undermines through frequent attacks the idea of epic as heroic, thematically harmonic, and founded upon an archetypal myth. One stanza will do for many:

> An honest gentleman at his return
>   May not have the good fortune of Ulysses;
> Not all lone matrons for their husbands mourn,
>   Or show the same dislike to suitors' kisses;
> The odds are that he finds a handsome urn
>   To his memory—and two or three young misses
> Born to some friend, who holds his wife and riches—
> And that *his* Argus—bites him by the breeches.
>
> [3.23]

Such a jocose, irreverent rendering of a moment of pathos in the *Odyssey* is an instance of Byron's revocation rather than revision of epic tradition. If it implies that Homer's view of experience is too idealized and selective, it is not only a cheap joke but a deliberate ignoring of the comprehensiveness of the *Odyssey's* vision, in which Penelope, Telemachus, a few old retainers, and a decrepit hound are alone against a horde of rapacious suitors in their fidelity to their lord and master. If, on the other hand, we see it as one of Byron's many insistent reminders that ordinary human beings usually fall short of human, not to mention heroic, standards, it comports with Byron's commitment to the reality of ordinary experience as a major truth.

The episodic, changing, and unpredictable character of Don Juan's journey challenges the epic stature Byron seriously (and sometimes humorously) claims for his poem. The Horatian epigraph *difficile est proprie communia dicere* is rendered in one manuscript as "Whate'er the critic says or poet sings / 'Tis no slight task to write on common things." To write appropriately of *communia* is difficult for a number of reasons. If *communia* are common topics or common-places, the difficulty arises from the characteristic banality of such subjects. But a quite different interpretation is possible—that it is difficult to write appropriately of what is common to mankind when the story is episodic and individualistic. This seems to accord with Byron's declaration late in the poem that

> The difficulty [Horace's word again] lies in colouring
>   (Keeping the due proportions still in sight)

With Nature manners which are artificial,
And rend'ring general [*communia*] that which is especial.
                                                                    [15.25]

Although these lines are directed specifically at the artificial society
exemplified by Norman Abbey, they can apply also to the random,
aleatory, melodramatic character of Juan's career, a career which the
hero does virtually nothing to shape. An uncentered, homeless
cosmopolite, he observes, like Odysseus, the manners of many
different people, but, unlike that hero, rarely draws conclusions from
his observations.

Reflection is reserved for—one might say usurped by—the poet,
who ostentatiously violates the ancient tradition of authorial anonymity by frequent and long digressions that undermine whatever
autonomy or personality Juan possesses. While it is true that, in the
later stages of the poem, Byron and Juan grow closer together—even
the difference in their ages seems to diminish—Juan only occasionally
achieves a coherent point of view. At the same time Byron goes to
great lengths to bring multiple and contradictory viewpoints to bear
on the story. As Ridenour says, "It is to Byron's interests (as well as
his taste) to undermine any systematic formulation of reality, to set
system against system, and to exalt the primacy of that immediate
experience . . . of which the poet is a peculiarly authoritative spokesman."[9] But then, the poet's authority as spokesman is based on views
of society that are the views of an exile, and though Byron may claim
that "the voyage is to be into the heart of social man,"[10] social man,
both in Juan's experiences and in his creator's comments, rarely has a
heart. This requires Byron in effect to invent various roles for his
characters and even for himself, and the question arises as to whether,
in all his metamorphoses, Byron achieves any more coherence of
personality than his Juan does.

As one example we can take Juan's bizarre adventures in a
Turkish harem in canto 5. The first two stanzas set the tone for the
episode:

When amatory poets sing their loves
     In liquid lines mellifluously bland,
And pair their rhymes as Venus yokes her doves,
     They little think what mischief is in hand;
The greater their success the worse it proves,
     As Ovid's verse may give to understand;

Even Petrarch's self, if judged with due severity,
Is the Platonic pimp of all posterity.

I therefore do denounce all amorous writing,
    Except in such a way as not to attract;
Plain—simple—short, and by no means inviting,
    But with a moral to each error tack'd,
Formed rather for instructing than delighting,
    And with all passions in their turn attacked;
Now, if my Pegasus should not be shod ill,
This poem will become a moral model.

In thus prefacing the only erotic canto of the poem, Byron is
facetiously adopting a prudish attitude while advancing with not
much subtlety his wish to give the poem a pornographic turn. The
adventure in the harem does nothing to advance "the voyage into the
heart of social man," unless the encounter with the imperious and
unsympathetic Gulbeyaz contributes any insights. Indeed it is a
purely melodramatic erotic tale designed to titillate and amuse. It
does, however, reveal in Juan a hitherto unsuspected firmness of
character. He risks death by refusing to become a Muslim. He dons
women's clothes only under the threat of castration. He thwarts
Gulbeyaz's command to make love to her, affirming that love is for
the free, and is sentenced to death for his obstinacy. The utter
improbability of the harem atmosphere may be part of a deliberate
plan to put Juan in the foreground, and indeed from here on he
occupies a more prominent place in the poem. Gulbeyaz, with her
unbridled concupiscence and exotic attractions, recedes into the background, as Catherine the Great does later.

There are traces in this canto of the affair of Aeneas and Dido in
Aeneid 4, with the hero turning his back on the furious queen. The
massive door of Gulbeyaz's chamber is gilded bronze, carved in
curious guise:

Warriors thereon were battling furiously;
    Here stalks the victor, there the vanquished lies;
There captives led in triumph droop the eye,
    And in perspective many a squadron flies:
It seems the work of times before the line
Of Rome transplanted fell with Constantine.

                                                    [5.86]

These images, unlike Dido's, are not identified, nor can Juan, ignorant of history, identify them. That they may represent the fall of Rome is an ironic touch in the Virgilian context. At any rate there is nothing of the tears of mortal sorrow. The episode ends with the frustrated queen histrionically debating, like Dido, whether to kill herself or Juan. She decides upon the latter, although the plan miscarries.

The whole harem episode is a scherzo of unlikely encounters, mistaken identities, and, especially, of conflict between utterly incompatible values. Its lack of social coherence is part of its point. Social coherence is impossible where fathers imprison or murder their sons, where everyone is either a tyrant of limitless privilege, or a slave, where there are no laws, and where there are no rudiments of social life. The lonely, predatory malevolence of Lambro has been, as it were, institutionalized in Constantinople, and yet we must remember that, as a Greek, Lambro is one of the victims of Turkish tyranny. Thus the melodramatic, slightly lubricious, and violent character of the episode turns out to be a faithful expression of Byron's conviction that lust and violence are equivalents. Aesthetically, one might add, the culturally sterile milieu of the harem is incapable of producing true art. The grandiose vulgarity of the edifice evokes some telling comments from the poet in stanzas 59 and 63:

> Alas! Man makes that great which makes him little—
>   I grant you in a church 'tis very well:
> What speaks of Heaven should by no means be brittle,
>   But strong and lasting, till no tongue can tell
> Their names who rear'd it; but huge houses fit ill,
>   And huge tombs worse Mankind—since Adam fell:
> Methinks the story of the tower of Babel
> Might teach them this much better than I'm able.

> Yet let them think that Horace has expressed
>   Shortly and sweetly the masonic folly
> Of those, forgetting the great place of rest,
>   Who give themselves to Architecture wholly;
> We know where things and men must end at best:
>   A moral (like all morals) melancholy,
> And "Et sepulchri immemor struis domos"
> Shows that we build when we should but entomb us.

This last stanza exemplifies both the Horatian temper and the Horatian tone, and it also marks the facility with which Byron assimilates

Greek and Latin into his stanzas. Despite his delight in mocking aspects of epic, there is a strong mimetic tendency in *Don Juan* to adapt to it the perspective and insights of great ancient writers.

In canto 8 the siege of Ismail elaborates violence as a counter-theme to the theme of lust in canto 7. The violence in the earlier canto was between individuals; here it becomes a ghastly collective enterprise in which cruelty and courage are manifested on a grand scale. In the midst of the carnage and danger, Juan insists to his English comrade Johnson on rescuing and protecting a little Turkish orphan girl:

> Said Juan—"Whatsoever is to be
>   Done, I'll not quit her till she seems secure
> Of present life a good deal more than we."—
>   Quoth Johnson—"*Neither* will I quite insure;
> But as the least *you* may die gloriously."—
>   Juan replied—"At least I will endure
> Whate'er is to be borne—but not resign
> This child, who is parentless, and therefore mine."
>
> [100]

This is clearly another significant revelation of Juan's character. In canto 7 he boldly maintained his own integrity and freedom in the face of death. Here, in the midst of death, he affirms his obligation to Leila, as she will be known, and thus demonstrates strong feelings of sympathy and affection that have not appeared before. The act is wholly devoid of the egotism that, in Byron, seems almost insepara-ble from erotic love. A corresponding development occurs in the poet's celebration of the beleaguered old Turkish warrior:

> But flanked by *five* brave sons, (such is polygamy,
>   That she spawns warriors by the score, where none
> Are prosecuted for that false crime bigamy),
>   He never would believe the city won
> While Courage clung but to a single twig.—Am I
>   Describing Priam's, Peleus', or Jove's son?
> Neither—but a good, plain, old temperate man
> Who fought with his five children in the van.
>
> [105]

Byron concludes with a moving tribute:

> In the meantime, cross-legged, with great sang-froid,
>   Among the scorching ruins he sat smoking
> Tobacco on a little carpet;—Troy
>   Saw nothing like the scene around;—yet looking
> With martial Stoicism, nought seem'd to annoy
>   His stern philosophy; but gently stroking
> His beard, he puff'd his pipe's ambrosial gales,
> As if he had three lives, as well as tails.
>
>   [121]

The facetious last line is disappointing, even if it is an effort to imitate the insouciance of the pasha, whom M. C. Richards has described as the "centered self."[11]

Juan has proved his integrity and personal dignity in the ordeals of the harem, the abode of lust; in the hell of war, he has demonstrated a selfless concern for a helpless waif; finally, Byron, for once allowing his hero's actions to speak for themselves, has movingly presented, in the old pasha, an example of the achieved heroic self. These instances seem to add up to a critical change in the author and his hero and point to the possibility of significant developments in the characters of both.

When Juan becomes the royal favorite at the Russian court, this possibility of development seems to be thwarted, for the hero seems to regress to his earlier, more egocentric role. Now he is a figure of glamor because of his military exploits and his good looks, and there is a touch of narcissism in his dazzling new appearance:

> Suppose him sword by side, and hat in hand,
>   Made up by Youth, Fame, and an army tailor—
> That great enchanter, at whose rod's command
>   Beauty springs forth, and Nature's self turns paler,
> Seeing how Art can make her work more grand
>   (When she don't pin men's limbs in like a gaoler),—
> Behold him placed as if upon a pillar! He
> Seems Love turn'd a Lieutenant of Artillery!
>
>   [IX.44]

Or, as the next stanza indicates, a lieutenant of artillery turned into Cupid. For the first time in the poem we find Juan concerned about his appearance and his dress. He has become a work of art, something "made up" and "placed . . . upon a pillar." The glory he has won in battle now serves merely to increase his sex appeal. He has become a sex object, a sort of male pinup, immobilized by self-satisfaction. Yet implicit in this decorative amalgam of warrior and god of love are the terrible potential relations between lust and violence, as stanza 55 indicates:

> Oh thou *"teterrima causa"* of all *"belli"*—
>   Thou gate of Life and Death—thou nondescript!
> Whence is our exit and our entrance, well I
>   May pause in pondering how all souls are dipped
> In thy perennial fountain: how man *fell* I
>   Know not, since Knowledge saw her branches stripped
> Of her first fruit; but how he *falls* and rises,
> Since, *thou* hast settled beyond all surmises.

As part of the pervading theme of falling, this stanza associates the Fall, the failure of human knowledge, the interconnection of love, as the most terrible cause of war, with both death and birth, all cast in the pedestrian style of Horace rather than in the heroic sublime.

Meanwhile Juan, self-pleasing pleaser of the voracious Catherine, also suffers a fall:

> He, on the other hand, if not in love,
>   Fell into that no less imperious passion,
> Self-love—which when some sort of thing above
>   Ourselves, a singer, dancer, much in fashion,
> Or Duchess, Princess, Empress, "deigns to prove"
>   ('Tis Pope's phrase) a great longing, though a rash one,
> For one especial person out of many,
> Makes us believe ourselves as good as any.
>
> [68]

The more Juan becomes "an especial person" for Catherine, the less of a special person he becomes in himself, nor is there the slightest sign of any but carnal communication between them. Juan could resist the imperious demands of Gulbeyaz in the name of freedom, but the flattering attentions of the empress subvert his independence.

Juan's regression into egocentric passivity allows Byron to fill the void with strong observations on what is now called the life crisis. Canto 10, beginning with further reflections on the Fall, leads through a yearning to "leave land far out of sight," "to skim / The ocean of eternity," since "the roar / Of breakers has not daunted" him (4). Clearly bored with the empty routine of the Russian court, Byron is prepared to leave Juan as the submissive consort of a kind of Circe for a larger world of oceanic possibilities, much as Odysseus does after he leaves Circe. There is thus a split between speaker and hero wider than any seen heretofore, and Byron feels that he himself is at a crucial point in his life:

> And this same state [of Juan's life] we won't describe: we
>   would
>   Perhaps from hearsay, or from recollection;
> But getting nigh grim Dante's "obscure wood,"
>   That horrid equinox, that hateful section
> Of human years—that half-way house—that rude
>   Hut, where wise travellers drive with circumspection
> Life's sad post-horses o'er the dreary frontier
> Of Age, and looking back to Youth, give *one* tear;—
>
> I won't describe,—that is, if I can help
>   Description; and I won't reflect,—that is,
> If I can stave off thought, which—as a whelp
>   Clings to its teat—sticks to me through the abyss
> Of this odd labyrinth; or as the kelp
>   Holds by the rock; or as a lover's kiss
> Drains its first draught of lips:—but, as I said,
> I *won't* philosophise, and *will* be read.
>
> [27–28]

At Dante's age of thirty-five, at the frontier that marks the passage from the years of growth to the years of decline the refusal to reflect while in fact reflecting and the reference to "the abyss / Of this odd labyrinth," which assimilates the pervasive epic theme of the critical journey to the other world, mark this as a critical phase in the ordeal of the poet.

Typically, Byron moves on from this grave contemplation to treat death as manifested in the cure the court doctors prescribe for Juan's undiagnosed illness. The comic virtuosity and brilliance of this passage do not annul the profoundness of the ones quoted; its humor suggests an essential resource in facing what is seen as irreparable loss:

But here is one prescription out of many:
    "Sodae sulphat. 3vj. 3fs. Mannae optim.
Aq. fervent. f. 3 its. 3ij. tinct. Sennae
    Haustus" (and here the surgeon came and cupped him),
"R. Pulv. Com. gr. iij. Ipecacuanhae"
    *"(*With more beside if Juan had not stopp'd 'em).
"Bolus Potassae Sulpheret. sumendus,
Et haustus ter in die capiendus."

[41]

Senna is a powerful purgative, ipecac both an emetic and a purgative.
These and the other medicines are to be taken three times a day. Not
since the rough passage on the *Trinidada* has the hero been so sick, or
sick in such unheroic ways. The point of the joke is that, after months
of aimless self-indulgence at the Russian court, the hero is in need of
a drastic cleaning out. Byron mercifully leaves the conclusions for us
to draw. Nevertheless, that Juan's repletion, indigestion, and consti-
pation, together with his narcissistic fit of self-love, should occur
simultaneously with Byron's Dantean reflections on the central crisis
in human life establishes a rich and subtle parallel between their two
careers.

    In the concluding cantos Byron often seems committed to
devaluing whatever potentials for personal development he and his
hero may have. Canto 12 begins with another, excessively pessimistic
view of middle age. It touches superficially on Juan's routine in
England, interspersed with frivolous declarations such as "now I will
begin my poem" (54) and "Here the twelfth Canto of our introduction / Ends" (87), followed in the first stanza of canto 13 with the
announcement "I now mean to be serious." An elegiac eulogy on
Cervantes is followed by a desultory introduction to the Amundevilles with a superb description of the natural surroundings of
Norman Abbey (12.56–58), which are never mentioned again. A
similar incoherence is to be found in the purposeless house party with
its ill-matched and forgettable guests, and in the expectations Byron
arouses that Juan will have some culminating love affair with Adeline
or Aurora Raby. Adeline, however, "Knew not her own heart"
(14.91), while Aurora shows only a mild interest in Juan. Byron has
deliberately frustrated our expectations, as does Juan when (in 16.96)
he watches Adeline playing her social role and wonders whether she
is real; and his final experience in the poem is his grasp of "the hard

but glowing breast" of the ghost impersonated by Lady Fitz-Fulke.

From his sojourn with Queen Catherine to this ending six cantos later, Juan has made no significant decision and performed no action of note, except for his quick-witted treatment of the highwayman. He comes to England with great expectations about its legendary freedom and law, but makes no effort to learn about them. He reverts to the characteristic passivity of his much younger self, and his final erotic encounter, like his first, is contrived by an experienced and sensual woman. Byron's commentary increases in these final cantos, but in both action and commentary there appears to be a deliberate attempt to dismantle whatever coherence *Don Juan* has earlier developed.

In the context of this study the chief importance of *Don Juan* lies in its versatile and searching representations of the impossibility of attaining a true self in a world that is everywhere dominated by the claims of the ego, a world in which vital relationships with others and with the numinous are too superficial and temporary to permit the achievement of an authentic personal identity. The poem effectively annuls the archetypal thrust of true epic, in the process suggesting repeatedly the monomyth that has been lost.

7 The Ivory *Pequod* and the Epic of Illusion

Over Descartian vortices you hover. And perhaps, at mid-day, in the fairest weather, with one half-throttled shriek you drop through that transparent air into the summer sea, no more to rise for ever. Heed it well, ye Pantheists!

                                                            Moby-Dick

Where but in Moby-Dick shall we find such a terrifying picture of a man rejecting all connection with his family, his culture, his own sexuality even, expunging the colors from the rainbow, rejecting the stained imperfections of life for a vision of spotless purity and rectitude attainable only in death, drifting into the terrible future, jamming himself on, like a father turning into a raging child, toward a catastrophe which annihilates a whole world?

                                                        Richard Chase

Unlike many other epic ordeals, Ahab's furious quest for Moby Dick is marked by repeated rejections of opportunities for self-discovery. Against numerous, though sometimes faint or dubious, intimations of an intelligent or benign cosmos he opposes his insistence on a chaotic or malign universe and focuses his frustration and rage on the white whale that once took off his leg. From his own catastrophe he infers, somewhat like Achilles in his anger, a cosmic hostility on which he will wreak vengeance, whatever the cost to himself and others. In contrast to the universal malevolence Ahab construes from his dismemberment, Melville provides the example of the captain of the *Enderby*, who has lost an arm to Moby Dick, attributes his misfortune to the risks inherent in whaling, and, with good sense and good humor, refrains from further assaults on the creature. The two maimed captains are distinguished by Ahab's solipsistic, brooding rage and Captain Boomer's sociability. Boomer, of course, is superfi-

cial, for the denouement of the novel demonstrates beyond a doubt
that the white whale is capable of effective and total revenge against
his pursuers.

That a sperm whale can by force and guile destroy a whaling ship
as easily as he can snap off a man's leg leaves hanging a major
question Ahab does not ask: can the violence of the whale, unlike the
indiscriminate mass voraciousness of sharks, be an intelligible response to the cumulative acts of violence he has suffered from his
attackers? Though not explicitly stated, the motive of self-defense is
evident in passages which describe bull whales protectively surrounding mothers and their young. The implication is that the whaleman,
in his unconsidered assumption of a divine right to his great and
normally peaceful prey, provokes the counterviolence in what Ahab
perceives to be an instrument of a malign universe. Numerous
instances of bereaved whalemen's wives and children do not lead him
or most of the other partners in the hunt to recognize the agony
inflicted on these other warm-blooded creatures bound together by
ties of interdependence and love. Even Ishmael, who has an immediate experience of the whale's familial and tribal character in the Grand
Armada, is usually unaware of this striking cetological fact as he
exhaustively pursues the reality of the sperm whale. Perhaps the
enormous disparity in size between man and whale tends to alienate
the human observer.

A clue to the symbolism of *Moby-Dick* is ivory. On his first
night in New Bedford, Ishmael, short of funds, puts up at the dingy
Spouter Inn of Peter Coffin. To enter the inn's inner room he must
walk through "the vast arched bone of the whale's jaw, so wide, a
coach might almost drive beneath it."[1] Ishmael descends to his
inferno through the gate of false dreams of Homer and Virgil. What
he experiences past this threshold has the ambivalent character of the
visitations and visitings of the underworld found in the dreams of
Agamemnon and in Aeneas's encounters with the past and future of
Rome. For Ishmael, the ensuing experiences will have a problematical
reality.

The *Pequod*, onto which he carelessly signs himself and his black
cannibal mate, Queequeg, is bedecked with ivory embellishments,
"apparrelled like any barbaric Ethiopian emperor, his neck heavy with
pendants of polished ivory. She was a thing of trophies," an elaborate

ivory artifact that may remind us of the strange simulacrum of the dead Mezentius, with its ivory weapons, that Aeneas erects as a trophy after his victory in the *Aeneid*. The *Pequod* suggests a more barbaric magic: "A cannibal of a craft, tricking herself forth in the chased bones of her enemies. All round, her unpanelled, open bulwarks were garnished like one continuous jaw, with the long sharp teeth of the sperm whale" (p. 105). Ahab's craft of revenge is an intricate assemblage cannibalized with whales' teeth as a superstitious augmentation of her formidable technical powers of destruction. So casually does Melville mention these details that one might easily overlook the curious regression of the white American New England hunter into modes of symbolic magic that appear immediately savage and aberrant in exotics like Queequeg, Tashtego, or the sinister Fedallah.

Even the *Pequod's* tiller is of ivory. She is an artifact of cumulative destruction built from the bones of her chosen prey and "tricked out" as a whale, driven by the malign motives Ahab ascribes to Moby Dick. Unlike the authentic sperm whales she hunts, however, the *Pequod* has neither the organic unity nor the essential vitality of the great creatures she mimics, but she does have the avenging passion her obsessed captain can infuse into his crew, however futilely. For the time, we can hold to the idea that the *Pequod*, in a variety of ways, is Ahab's imitation of a sperm whale.

That the owners of the ivory *Pequod* are Quakers and thus committed by their faith to peace suggests that something of the whited sepulchre attaches to this ship and her bloody enterprise. The name Pequod, meaning "Destroyer," is another strange note, given that the largest settlement of Pequod Indians had been massacred in Mystic, Connecticut, by a large force of white settlers under a Captain Mason in 1637. The massacre was notable for the large number of women and children slain, and Mason's name lives on in the island near the mouth of the Mystic River awarded to him by the people of the colony. In the mid-1800s there were few Pequods in Nantucket, and one wonders why Melville should have gone so far afield to find such an inauspicious name. Possibly the name of a tribe almost annihilated by the whites hints at the colonist's propensity for destroying any creatures, whales or native Indians, that he can turn to profit or that stand in the way of his total mastery of the New World. In any event, the killer *Pequod* is intimately identified by its ornamentation with the prey that will destroy it and, by its name,

with the indigenous victims of colonial rapacity. Ultimately, the loss
of the *Pequod* is the fated reflex of the purposes to which she was
devoted and, in a larger view, a comment on the American version of
the *imperium sine fine*. As in *Heart of Darkness*, in *Moby-Dick* the
exploitation of "savages" and the acquisition of ivory go hand in
hand, and both stories of modern imperialism may share with the
Aeneid the sad intimation that such obsessively pursued gains may,
in the long run, belong among the illusions of the Gate of Ivory. In
the two novels some of the "savages" ironically have more real
humanity than most of the whites. Among the thirty-odd heteroge-
neous crewmen, Melville's most resourceful and generous character
is the cannibal Queequeg, while, of all those embarked on his tinpot
steamer, only the cannibals are of any use to Marlow.

The *Pequod* sails on Christmas night with the final pious adjura-
tions of the sepulchral and miserly Bildad and the somewhat cheerier
farewells of his irreverent partner, Peleg. They preside like mystic
threshold guardians over the *Pequod's* departure for voyages through
strange seas. It is they who have administered various initiatory and
inquisitory tests to candidates for the voyage, although they are
comically unable to establish a priority between piety and profit. That
the day of departure is the Nativity goes virtually unnoticed by all
the characters, a tacit indication, perhaps, of the pervasively Old
Testament emphasis that permeates the themes and motifs drawn
from Jonah and Job and questions of justice, judgment, punishment,
and vengeance. Bildad salutes the parting vessel with a hymn of Isaac
Watts based on Psalm 119 (*In exitu Israel de Egypto*), a hymn that
here invokes ironically the possibility of the experience of conversion
with which the *Inferno* begins:

> "Sweet fields beyond the swelling flood,
>   Stand dressed in living green.
> So to the Jews old Canaan stood,
>   While Jordan rolled between."
>
> [p. 145]

The providential theme of deliverance is, of course, utterly antithetical to the disastrous quest on which Ahab is bent, but the hollow
pietism of the true believers who hope to profit by the voyage
indicates, like Father Mapple's simple fundamentalism, a spiritually
bankrupt culture. Of all the Christians in *Moby-Dick*, only Star-

buck's ill-defined but deep conviction of Providence can command any respect, but that conviction cannot support Starbuck against the titanic obsession of cosmic evil to which Ahab, with occasional and important remissions, is ultimately dedicated.

If Ahab denies with the obsessive energy of his ego the possibility of conversion and, like Kurtz, almost succeeds in his megalomaniacal subjugation of his fellows to an awed and worshipful submission, the cultivation or preservation of more positive possibilities lies chiefly in the narrator of *Moby-Dick*, Ishmael, as, in *Heart of Darkness*, it does in Marlow. With Ahab and Kurtz frozen in attitudes of titanic egotism, these narrators, like "Milton" in *Paradise Lost*, undergo ordeals of individuation as they reflect on the experiences they are recounting. Because Marlow is virtually without companions in whom he can confide, his account is far more coherent and introspective than Ishmael's. Compared with Marlow, Ishmael is naive and disestablished, and in his precarious sense of self and purpose he resembles the naive, young, impressionable fairy-tale hero out of whose very weaknesses intuitions of truth may grow. As the only survivor of the ordeal of the *Pequod*, Ishmael, like Odysseus, will capture the promise of a survival that transcends his unique endurance of a disaster that destroys all his shipmates.

Ishmael, the major recording intelligence of *Moby-Dick*, is sufficiently involved in the manifold activities of the *Pequod* to supply a vivid and authentic account of the voyage. Driven by self-ignorance and curiosity, without financial resources, he, like Marlow, decides not to decide and takes his chances on a dubious voyage. Orphaned and homeless, Ishmael enters the scene with no orienting heritage beyond his education as a schoolmaster. His trial, so randomly assumed, will be to discover the realities underlying the extraordinary voyage of the *Pequod* and, in that process, himself.

The first stage of Ishmael's initiation after entering the Spouter Inn is his "marriage" to the black cannibal, Queequeg. White and nominally Presbyterian, Ishmael is appalled at the prospect of sharing a bed with his harpoon-carrying, idol-worshiping savage. Torn between a rootless alienation and an adventurous receptivity, Ishmael discovers, through Queequeg, a bond of affection that is new to him.

Queequeg, despite his apparent oddities, is a man assured of himself, with vivid recollections of his home, his princely status, his religion, and his family obligations. Queequeg has everything Ishmael initially lacks and needs. The satisfaction of these needs is marked by that first night together in a bed in the Spouter Inn where the bedmates share puffs of Queequeg's tomahawk-pipe and Ishmael awakes with Queequeg's arm around him.

Ishmael's bond with Queequeg is essential to his authority as recording persona of *Moby-Dick*. Their love and trust, elaborated in "The Monkey-Rope," "A Squeeze of the Hand," and other episodes, endorses Ishmael's veracity as raconteur of the voyage. Love and trust, the undertone of Melville's story has it, are the only authenticating tokens in an experience that would otherwise be simply a bizarre adventure. Starting with his Yankee assurance about values, despite his dismal incapacity to lay claim to any, Ishmael—self-named refugee—finds the rudiments of an identity through an unexpected friendship with a displaced cannibal prince who worships an idol named Tojo.

Identity, then, here inseparable from relationship, endows Ishmael with a point of view and the ability to recognize the deeply-riven character of Ahab, as he appears for the first time on the quarterdeck long after the *Pequod* has left Nantucket on its southerly course:

> Threading its way out from among his grey hairs, and continuing right down one side of his tawny scorched face and neck, till it disappeared in his clothing, you saw a slender rod-like mark, lividly whitish. It resembled that perpendicular seam sometimes made in the straight, lofty trunk of a great tree, when the upper lightning tearingly darts down it, and without wrenching a single twig, peels and grooves out the bark from top to bottom, ere running off into the soil, leaving the tree still greenly alive, but branded. (pp. 168–69)

Overloaded with symbolistic bifurcation, loaded as well with the familiar marks of the damned Romantic hero, the passage makes its point too insistently. Yet, there is Ahab, split but green, potentially fertile but branded like Cain with a passion that dare not tell its name. This passage, in which Melville apparently did not trust his reader to get the point, establishes firmly Ahab's dualistic nature. It requires no extraordinary insight to discern from these visible signs a split in Ahab's personality.

More interesting than the account itself is the observation by an old Gay Head Indian that the "seam" came upon Ahab "not in the fury of any mortal fray, but in an elemental strife at sea" (p. 169). The passage contributes, somewhat programmatically, to the development of a deep inner division in Ahab's spirit wherein his "barbaric" ivory leg stands both for the violent illusion of his quest and for his deep affinity for what is savage. Savagery, however, as we shall see, is a two-edged concept, and it may prove to be a critical test for anyone who brings, like Ahab, preconceptions rashly made about what is savage and what is civilized.

Like the ivory *Pequod,* Ahab is partly fabricated from his enemies. His responses to his dilemma are sometimes grotesquely comic. When Stubb politely reminds the captain that the pounding of his ivory leg keeps the mates below from sleeping, Ahab delivers a tirade. When Stubb retreats in humiliation and anger, Ahab retires on the poop to a chair made of ivory. He smokes his pipe, but finds it brings no solace and tosses it overboard in the first of a series of actions that reflect his growing alienation and, later, deliberate disorientation.

When he next appears on deck, Ishmael is puzzled by Ahab's brow: "Did you fixedly gaze, too, upon that ribbed and dented brow; there also, you would see still stranger footprints—the foot-prints of his one unsleeping, ever-pacing thought" (p. 216).

In an unaccustomed procedure Ahab musters the entire crew aft to take part in a ritual dedication to the death of Moby Dick. To the mainmast he nails an Equadorean doubloon as prize for the first man to raise "me a white-headed whale with a wrinkled brow and a crooked jaw" (p. 218). In an outburst of passion, self-pity, and what Jung has called "inflation," Ahab declares:

"Aye, Starbuck; aye, my hearties all round; it was Moby Dick that dismasted me; Moby Dick that brought me to this dead stump I stand on now. Aye, aye," he shouted with a terrific, loud, animal sob, like that of a heart-stricken moose; "Aye, aye! it was that accursed white whale that razeed me; made a poor pegging lubber of me for ever and a day!" Then tossing both arms with measureless imprecations he shouted out: "Aye, aye! and I'll chase him round Good Hope, and round the Horn, and round the Norway Maelstrom, and round perdition's flames before I give him up. And this is what ye have shipped for, men! to chase that white whale on both sides of the land, and over all sides of earth, till he spouts black blood and rolls fin out. What say ye, men, will ye splice hands on it, now? I think ye do look brave." (p. 219)

Despite his megalomania, Ahab has a shrewd talent for effective theatrical speech and gesture exceeding, Ishmael elsewhere concedes, that of czars and emperors, for, he says, "in this episode touching Emperors and Kings, I must not conceal that I have to do with a poor old whale-hunter . . . and, therefore, all outward majestical trappings and housings are denied me. Oh, Ahab! what shall be grand in thee, it must needs be plucked at from the skies, and dived for in the deep, and featured in the unbodied air!" (p. 199). Yet Ahab's appeals, designed to rouse a sense of fellowship in the crew that will render them his malleable instruments—"my hearties," "that is what ye shipped for," "splice hands"—are the devices of a manipulator. Ahab here enacts the role of a minor devil, a shrunken Satan, bribing his crew with the promise of a minuscule reward if they submit to his will.

Starbuck, decent, judicious, and moderate, demurs. He reminds Ahab that the ship's business is catching whales; that if Moby Dick should turn up in the pursuit of other sperm whales, he will go after him, but that "vengeance on a dumb brute . . . that simply smote thee from blindest instinct is Madness. To be enraged with a dumb thing, Captain Ahab, seems blasphemous!" (p. 220). Despite his moderation and decency, however, Starbuck cannot imagine the whale as a creature possessing will and intelligence, whether directed, as Ahab supposes, to malignant ends, or, as the novel sometimes implies, toward the fulfillment of needs remarkably like those of its human hunters.

Starbuck's vague benevolence simply clears the field for Ahab's obsession: "I see in him outrageous strength, with an inscrutable malice sinewing it. That inscrutable thing is chiefly what I hate; and be the white whale agent, or be the white whale principal, I will wreak that hate upon him" (p. 221). The ritual confirmation is completed when the harpooneers cross their lances over Ahab's hands and drink toasts from the sockets of their weapons to the death of Moby Dick, the rest of the crew following their example. Thus the thirty-odd partners in the *Pequod's* venture have been induced to surrender their wills, through a rite of communion, to a leader whose vision is an obsession of hatred. If the oath holds, Ahab will have succeeded in endowing his cannibal craft with the coordinated organic unity of its living prey. With this expectation, Ahab, back in his cabin after the ceremony, can "prophesy": "I will dismember my dismemberer. Now, then, be the prophet and the fulfiller one. That's more than ye, ye great gods, ever were" (pp. 226–27).

Whatever great gods Ahab has in mind, Christ, evidently, is not among them. That fact is yet another indication of the Old Testament orientation of *Moby-Dick* and Melville's conception of Ahab as an atavistic figure.

Even Ishmael is overwhelmed by the ceremony of communion. Chapter 41, "Moby Dick," opens with this important confession:

> I, Ishmael, was one of that crew; my shouts had gone up with the rest; my oath had been welded with theirs; and stronger I shouted, and more did I hammer and clinch my oath, because of the dread in my soul. A wild, mystical, sympathetical feeling was in me; Ahab's quenchless feud seemed mine. With greedy ears I learned the history of that murderous monster against whom I and all the others had taken our oaths of violence and revenge. (p. 239)

As part of his fascination with the problem of defining Moby Dick, Ishmael extends his view to include a congeries of facts, rumors, and superstitions about the white whale, all the time noting the credulousness of seamen and of whalemen in particular. Some consider Moby Dick to be ubiquitous, perhaps because of the speed with which he travels through the depths of the oceans. Others hold him to be immortal. More compelling than these speculations is Ishmael's need to probe the growth of Ahab's compulsion and its hypnotic power over his mates:

> How it was that they so aboundingly responded to the old man's ire—by what evil magic their souls were possessed, that at times his hate seemed almost theirs; the White Whale as much their insufferable foe as his; how all this came to be—what the White Whale was to them, or how to their unconscious understandings, also, in some dim, unsuspected way, he might have seemed the great gliding demon of the seas of life—all this to explain, would be to dive deeper than Ishmael can go. (p. 251)

To what extent the book provides answers to these central questions we must wait till the end to see. In the meantime we can note that in the epic tradition Ahab's communion rite is an atavistic renewal and unleashing of the primitive and individualistic violence that is expressed, *inter alia*, in the feuds of the houses of Pelops and Atreus, in the anger of Achilles, and in the vengeful fury of Juno. Ahab's blasphemous communion rite inverts and subverts the normal functions of the kinds of religious and social rituals that initiate true *communitas*. For a time hatred proves to be a stronger bond than love, and Ishmael surrenders himself "to the abandonment of the time and the place" and allows himself to see "naught in the brute but the deadliest ill" (p. 252).

In the next chapter, "The Whiteness of the Whale," Ishmael continues his reflections and conjectures in an elaborate meditation on a creature that may be a clue to the nature of the universe. He notes the ambivalence of whiteness, suggestive of purity and innocence, of pallor, death, and spiritual blankness, of nothingness, even, and of various possibilities between these extremes, in a highly effective consideration of the complex and ultimately unanalyzable central symbol of the book. Inevitably he is drawn beyond discursive reason to the meditative mode, for that alone can embrace the ambiguities and paradoxes that lie at the heart of myth and symbol.

Ahab, meanwhile, bending his wrinkled brow over his charts in his cabin, threads "a maze of currents and eddies, with a view to the more certain accomplishment of that monomaniac thought of his soul" (p. 267). The passage is full of mythic implications: Ahab is a Theseus threading the labyrinth of clues with his pencil to find the center where the monster lurks. With the malign human intelligence Ahab ascribes to him, Moby Dick is as veritable a monster as the Minotaur.

In this context, Virgil's use of Daedalus's representation at Cumae of the Cretan labyrinth as a sort of chart for Aeneas's descent into the underworld illuminates an episode in *Moby-Dick* that most readers find extraneous or intrusive: the celebration and unexplained death of Bulkington, the helmsman whom Melville represents as the essence of reliability and integrity. The night before the Trojan fleet reached Cumae, its chief navigator, Palinurus, mysteriously disappeared from his post, and his ghostly explanation to Aeneas contradicts what we know of the facts, leaving the suggestion that he willfully abandoned a voyage in which he no longer believed. The unexplained death of Bulkington is analogous to a degree, although Aeneas is fully competent to take over the navigation of his fleet, while Ahab, increasingly guided by his own unreasoning will, jettisons, destroys, or misuses his aids to navigation as he moves further and further into remote Pacific seas. Clearly there is no place for a Bulkington on this *Narrenschiff*. His mysterious death, however, serves, like Palinurus's, as a necessary sacrificial prelude to the entrance into the labyrinth, the central episode of the *Aeneid* and the concluding event of *Moby-Dick*.

In "Surmises" (chapter 46) Ishmael summarizes his intuitions about Ahab, above all Ahab's realization that he must keep Starbuck "magnetized" by his will and that, to this end, he must make an effort to kill other whales besides Moby Dick to sustain the crew's interest in the voyage and to avoid the charge of "usurpation." Hence the normative encounter of "The First Lowering" (chapter 47), which nonetheless exposes for the first time Ahab's ghastly boat crew, led by the sinister Fedallah, who is rumored to be the devil's agent. The symbolic values of black and white become violent antinomies in this unique figure of evil, "tall and swart," with a single fang-tooth projecting from his lips, funereally dressed in black but wearing "a glistening white plaited turban" (p. 291). This "phantom" is later seen as an extension of Ahab's shadow and then, as they face each other silently on the quarterdeck through a long night, as his double. The climax of this eerie interpenetration of personalities comes when Ahab, gazing at night over the taffrail, sees in the smooth ocean the reflection of Fedallah's eyes (p. 686). In this context Ishmael's observation in chapter 1 is significant. Speaking of the fascination the sea exercises over people of all sorts, he observes that "still deeper is the story of Narcissus, who because he could not grasp the tormenting, mild image of the fountain, plunged in it and was drowned" (p. 26). What Ishmael marks as a self-destructive potentiality in himself and others, he develops later in a memorable passage in "The Mast-Head" (chapter 35):

There is no life in thee, now, except that rocking life imparted by a gently rolling ship; by her, borrowed from the sea; by the sea, from the inscrutable tides of God. But while this sleep, this dream is on ye, move your foot or hand an inch; slip your hold at all; and your identity comes back in horror. Over Descartian vortices you hover. And, perhaps, at midday, in the fairest weather, with one half-throttled shriek you drop through that transparent air into the summer sea, no more to rise for ever. Heed it well, ye Pantheists! (pp. 214–15)

This enchanting passage could have contributed to Auden's poem on Breughel's "Death of Icarus"[2] in its conjunction of serenity and terror and in its evocation of the dizzyingly hypnotic paradoxicality of such oceanic reflections, with their teasing hints that some deeper truth lies on the other side of the mirror. As Feidelson says of this passage:

> Like the water-gazer of Chapter I, the youth at the mast-head is in quest of the "phantom of life." When his own personal life and the infinite life of the sea blend together into a world soul, he seems to have attained the object of his quest. But this pantheistic mood is destroyed by his sudden awareness of the danger of death. He realizes that a pantheistic dreamer who "loses his identity" in the world soul is like one who is physically drowned in the sea.[3]

Ahab's phantasmagoric coalescence of vision with that of the devilish Fedallah may then imply a narcissistic projection of egotistical hatred as a perversion or elaboration of narcissistic self-love in a more sharply focused pursuit of the "phantom of life." The coalescence of vision implies, in any event, Ahab's commitment to his chosen conviction of the essentially malign character of cosmic reality, a conviction that he has just affirmed in rejecting Starbuck's final, moving appeal to give up the mad pursuit with the hubristic cry, "Is Ahab, Ahab?" (p. 685). From the promise of love and fellowship he has just seen in Starbuck's eyes, Ahab now sees eyes that confirm his dismissal of his potential self. The moment is tragic in its Lear-like defense of the inflated ego. As we have noted before, in Jungian psychological theory, the loss of the ego, especially when it feels itself threatened by the possibility of individuation, seems to the tragic hero, in his undeviating pursuit of his willed vision, death. This moment of illusion, interpreted by Ahab as a moment of self-affirmation, masquerading as anagnorisis, may or may not be, in Melville's conception, the moment of Ahab's damnation. Obviously, Melville is not writing his epic to Jung's prescriptions, and we must not dismiss the possibility that he has a view of man's fate and the possibilities of his life even more somber than what we find in Shakespearean tragedy.

ᕙᕗ

To these questions we shall return later. Let us consider further the intermediate alternations of narrative points of view that gradually build our knowledge of the *Pequod's* voyage into an epic that rivals its great precursors as the bible of a heroic culture. One "biblical" feature of epic is its preservation of the *techne*, the essential practical and aesthetic arts of a culture. Whatever else they provide, traditional epics record the arts and customs that are seen as vital to the preservation and survival of the cultures from which they spring. From Hesiod, Homer, Virgil, or Dante one could learn the arts that make life in the community possible and make it worthy of our commitment. To put it another way, the *mythos* that produces the culture and gives it purpose and grace is expressed from day to day in the work of its members, whether that work entails war, agriculture, art, or the manifold rituals sanctifying or consecrating its manifold institutions. Thus a handbook of whaling could be compiled from *Moby-Dick*. This *techne* has superadded to it extensive instances of the art of governing a community and, as in the *Odyssey* or the *Aeneid*, detailed directions, both pragmatic and sacramental, on how to achieve the shared and recognized goals of a society and of the people involved in its adventures. The pages devoted in Melville to the anatomy of whales, their habits and legends, the customs and procedures of whaling crews, and, above all, the techniques of capturing, killing, dismembering, and rendering whales, which at times seem to mimic the anatomical precision of the *Iliad* in its accounts of weapons, maneuvers, and wounds, clearly serve in much the same way to preserve the essential techniques on which a heroic culture depends.

Those details are not germane to our immediate interests. Suffice it to say that after all the vivid whaling material in the central chapters of *Moby-Dick*, provided by an omnivorous cataloguer of information, we reenter the predominantly impressionistic mode of "The Doubloon" (chapter 99), the portion of Melville's book that challenges comparison with *Iliad* 18 and *Aeneid* 10 in presenting an artifact that is a symbolic center of the epic. Like the shield of Aeneas, and even more like its prototype, the shield of Achilles, the Equadorian doubloon Ahab nails to the mainmast as a reward to the man who first sights Moby Dick is the uniquely central icon of the book. Sharing the portentousness of Virgil's shield and the rich complexity of Homer's, Melville's artifact also reflects the manifold impressions of various members of the *Pequod's* crew. At the same time it reflects the manifold epistemological modes of apprehension, ranging from the most simplistically objective to the most subtly subjective, that lie at the heart of the book's exhaustive exploration of reality.

First the data: the doubloon "on its round border . . . bore the letters, REPUBLICA DEL ECUADOR:QUITO."

> So this bright coin came from a country planted in the middle of the world, and beneath the great equator, and named after it, and it had been cast midway up the Andes, in the unwaning clime that knows no autumn. Zoned by those letters you saw the likeness of three Andes' summits; from one a flame; a tower on another; on the third a crowing cock; while arching over all was a segment of the partitioned zodiac, the signs all marked by their usual cabalistics, and the keystone sun entering the equinoctial point at Libra. (p. 550)

We must ask ourselves not only what this emblem means in itself and how the interpretations of its meanings reveal the ideas and feelings of those who comment on it, but also what symbolic function it serves in *Moby-Dick* as a whole. The details of the coin indicate a strong interest in balance, equality, and geographic centrality. "Equador," "the middle of the world," "beneath the great equator," "cast midway up the Andes," "the keynote sun," and "the equinoctial point at Libra," the zodiacal sign whose scales augment the fulcral significance of the doubloon as symbol—all these insistent specifications indicate a fixed and central point in space and time, while the coin's having been struck "in the unwaning clime that knows no autumn" implies that, like the shields of Achilles and Aeneas, the doubloon is a timeless work of art. Undoubtedly one symbolic function of the doubloon is to evoke an established, land-oriented stasis in a world that otherwise seems to manifest only flux, disorientation, and change. The coin clearly stands in symbolic opposition to the apparently random course of the *Pequod* and, especially, to its alienation and disorientation as marked by Ahab's labyrinthine charts, by his destruction of the quadrant that can find the ship's position from "the keynote sun," and by the reversed magnetism that affects the ship's compasses in the electrical storm. The symmetry of the three Andean peaks suggests not only the three masts of the *Pequod* but also the three crosses at Calvary and the Trinity (the last an obvious association in the coin of a Roman Catholic country). As a whole, the coin, in its perfect circularity, in its symmetry of design, and in the precious material of which it is made, expresses aspects of perfection related to its static, unchanging, immortal character; yet, even so, its name implies a potential ambiguity that unsettles these assurances. At any rate, it functions as a touchstone, as the various observations of the ship's crew show.

First Ahab:

> "There's something ever egotistical in mountain-tops and towers, and all other grand and lofty things; look here,—three peaks as proud as Lucifer. The firm tower, that is Ahab; the volcano, that is Ahab; and the undaunted, victorious fowl, that, too, is Ahab; all are Ahab; and this round gold is but the image of the rounder globe, which, like a magician's glass, to each and every man in turn but mirrors back his own mysterious self." (pp. 550–51)

Thus Ahab, master of place, time, and space, projects his fantasies, somewhat as Satan in *Paradise Regain'd* tries to project his vain imaginations. In the sign of Libra and its zodiacal opposite, Aries, he finds a desperate alternation of equinoctial storms: " 'So be it, then! Here's stout stuff for woe to work on. So be it, then' " (p. 551). Ahab finds in the doubloon the confirmation of his egotistical obsession.

Next Starbuck, who begins with the surmise that " 'The old man seems to read Belshazzar's awful writing,' " an utterly false intimation bred of his own desperation. He sees on the doubloon " 'A dark valley between three mighty, heaven-abiding peaks, that almost seem the Trinity, in some faint earthly symbol. So in this vale of Death, God girds us round; and over all our gloom, the sun of Righteousness still shines a beacon and a hope' " (p. 551). And that is Starbuck's own somewhat egotistical, but benign, reading.

Stubb's thoughts are refreshingly material and limited: " 'I'd not look at it very long ere spending it' " (p. 552). He interprets the zodiacal signs with the help of an almanac, but, distracted by the book, concludes with a whimsical view of man's life in twelve parts (p. 554).

Next Flask, even more obtuse, who calculates:

> "I see nothing here, but a round thing made of gold, and whoever raises a certain whale, this round thing belongs to him. So, what's all this staring been about? It is worth sixteen dollars, that's true; and at two cents the cigar, that's nine hundred and sixty cigars. I won't smoke dirty pipes like Stubb, but I like cigars, and here's nine hundred and

sixty of them; so here goes Flask aloft to spy 'em out."
(p. 554)

Flask's reductive calculus fails, even at this lowest level of response, to estimate the value of the doubloon, and Melville allows himself to take a crack at that familiar American type, the clever boob.

In his study of *Moby-Dick*, Edward Edinger, a Jungian analytical psychologist, stratifies the psychological functions of the *Pequod's* four officers:

> Ahab, as the representative of Melville's superior function, thinking, needs further scrutiny. Melville's descriptions of the other three officers, Starbuck, Stubb, and Flask, make it quite definite they refer to the functions of intuition, sensation, and feeling, respectively. Thus, by a process of elimination, if Ahab is to be given the superior function, this must be thinking. But the picture given of Ahab does not completely support this conclusion. He is not a clear thinker. He seems to be a magnified, enraged version of Flask, the feeling function, whose chief characteristic is his feeling of vengeance against whales. Late in the book, Ahab says,
>
> > "Ahab never thinks; he only feels, *that's* tingling enough for mortal man! To think's audacity. Thinking is, or ought to be, a coolness and a calmness; and our poor hearts throb, and our poor brains beat too much for that."[4]

Edinger's attempt here to distribute among the four officers of the *Pequod* the various functions of the psyche is a systematic error that blinds him to the unsystematic, but much more vital, psychological potentials of the *Pequod's* entire crew. He concludes that, "when the time comes, and the laws of life demand the old ruler sacrificed, the question arises, as with Ahab and his crew, whether or not the superior function will succeed in carrying the rest of the personality with it down to destruction."[5]

Edinger's comment is one instance—very rare in his work—of a dogmatic misapplication of psychological theory to a fiction that cannot be understood in such restricted, hierarchical terms; thus, he unwittingly illustrates the kind of blinding bias that prevents Ahab, Starbuck, Stubb, and Flask from seeing aright the image of the doubloon.

It is not surprising, then, that the only characters who can apprehend some truth in the doubloon come to it without preconceptions. Thus Queequeg silently compares the signs tattooed on his body with the signs on the doubloon, seeming to intuit correspondences between two works of symbolic art. Fedallah, as a Parsee fire-worshiper, bows to the image of the sun. Perhaps much more significantly, Pip, the little black boy unhinged by a terrible accident, can nevertheless conceive of the doubloon as the ship's navel, thus making the richest of intuitions in what Ishmael calls his "crazy-witty way" (p. 556). The primitive *omphalos*, as Feidelson notes, could be the center of the earth, as in Apollo's shrine at Delphi. Like Greenwich, that serves as the central point determining all other geographic (and spiritual) positions. In this respect the Equadorian doubloon could, if rightly used, orient the *Pequod* in many ways. Nailed to her mainmast, however, the doubloon, borne through courses determined only by the madness of her captain, becomes much more like that other navel, the *omphalos* of the sea where Circe brutalizes her alienated victims and bewitches them out of all thought of home. Such opposed potentialities in the coin express the profound symbolic duality of the doubloon. Ishmael's account, related, of course, long after the event, is the only one that can include the complex implications of Pip's wiser madness, and it suggests that, after his initial subjection to the compelling egotism of Ahab, unlike most of his shipmates he could achieve a view of the symbol in all its mystery and integrity that the others disintegrate. Hence it seems reasonable to see Ishmael, in this key chapter, as having begun to achieve a wholeness of view that he clearly lacked before. Looking back at his disorienting experience in "The Try Works" (chapter 95), we may see signs of his growing individuation. There, at the helm, Ishmael was bewitched by the infernal spectacle before him: "the rushing *Pequod*, freighted with savages and laden with fire, and burning a corpse, and plunging into the blackness of darkness, seemed the material counterpart of her monomaniac commander's soul" (p. 540). Appalled and entranced by these impressions, he suddenly discovers with horror that he seems to have allowed the ship to reverse her heading, as in fact she does later when the magnetism of her compasses is reversed. What has really happened is that Ishmael, exhausted and full of dread, has unconsciously reversed his own position:

> I could see no compass before me to steer by; though it
> seemed but a minute since I had been watching the card, by

the steady binnacle lamp illuminating it. Nothing seemed
before me but a jet gloom, now and then made ghastly by
flashes of redness. Uppermost was the impression, that
whatever swift, rushing thing I stood on was not so much
bound to any haven ahead as rushing from all havens
astern. . . . Lo! in my brief sleep I had turned myself
about, and was fronting the ship's stern, with my back to
her prow and the compass. In an instant I faced back, just in
time to prevent the vessel from flying up into the wind, and
very probably capsizing her. (p. 541)

Ishmael's unconscious has forced him to turn away from the infernal
course along which Ahab drives his ship to face the wished-for
direction of "all havens astern," and in the process very nearly
permits the *Pequod* to turn, in what would be a catastrophic jibe.
From this experience he reaches a Dantean conclusion:

Look not too long in the face of the fire, O man! Never
dream with thy hand on the helm! Turn not thy back to the
compass; accept the first hint of the hitching tiller; believe
not the artificial fire, when its redness makes all things look
ghastly. To-morrow, in the natural sun, the skies will be
bright; those who glared like devils in the forking flames,
the morn will show in far other, at least gentler, relief; the
glorious, golden, glad sun, the only true lamp—all others
but liars! (pp. 541–42)

From this reorienting reflection Ishmael advances to a firm
distinction between a wisdom "that is woe" and a woe, like Ahab's
that is "madness":

And there is a Catskill eagle in some souls that can alike
dive down into the blackest gorges, and soar out of them
again and become invisible in the sunny spaces. And even if
he for ever flies within the gorge, that gorge is in the
mountains; so that even in his lowest swoop the mountain
eagle is still higher than other birds upon the plain, even
though they soar. (p. 543)

This complex image suggests that, amid the depths and glooms and
intermittent elations of life, man can achieve a stabilizing reconciliation of opposed experiences, something akin to the reconciliation of

the *via sublimis* and *via humilis* at the center of the *Divine Comedy*. Whether he sinks or soars, the Catskill eagle preserves his integrity and imperturbable verve. As the only creature who, according to legend, can look directly at the sun, the eagle embodies also the clarity of vision and equilibrium toward which Ishmael seems to be moving.

If, as has been observed, Ishmael recedes into the background after "The Doubloon," his new equilibrium and breadth of vision, together with a fatalistic sense that there is no way by which he can hope to alter Ahab's design, help to explain why Melville now mainly entrusts the final events of the *Pequod's* career to an omniscient narrator. As Ahab draws closer to his goal, it is also essential that he occupy the foreground in the final working out of the tragedy.

The denouement begins with yet another encounter between Ahab and Starbuck that results in a merely temporary suspension of the captain's fell purpose. The first mate reports a bad leak and asks that orders be given for emptying the holds of the leaking casks and rigging the pumps. Ahab abruptly denies the request. Starbuck asks him to consider what the owners would say if so much valuable cargo were negligently lost, to which Ahab arrogantly responds: "What cares Ahab? Owners, owners? Thou art always prating to me, Starbuck, as if the owners were my conscience. But look ye, the only real owner of anything is its commander; and hark ye, my conscience is this ship's keel.—On deck!" (p. 605). Starbuck expresses his resentment; Ahab draws a musket from the rack and aims it at him. Starbuck unflinchingly stands his ground, declaring, "Thou has outraged, not insulted me, sir, but for that I ask thee not to beware of Starbuck; thou wouldst but laugh; but let Ahab beware of Ahab; beware of thyself, old man" (p. 605).

This terrific scene increases the prestige of Starbuck and, in a curious way, plants in Ahab a seed of admiration and affection for his first mate as well as a new, though temporary, capacity for reflection. He gives the orders, "and the Burtons were hoisted" (ibid.).

Ahab's now more ambivalent sense of a universal mystery in things emerges in his reverie as he surveys the tattooed patterns on the body of Queequeg, who was thought to be mortally ill but has made an inexplicable recovery.

> This tattooing has been the work of a departed prophet and
> seer of his island, who, by those hieroglyphic marks, had

written out on his body a complete theory of the heavens and the earth, and a mystical treatise on the art of attaining truth; so that Queequeg in his own proper person was a riddle to unfold; a wondrous work in one volume; but whose mysteries not even himself could read, though his own live heart beat against them; and these mysteries were therefore destined in the end to moulder away with the living parchment whereon they were inscribed, and so be unsolved to the last. (p. 612)

It is these hieroglyphs that evoke from Ahab "that wild exclamation of his—'Oh, devilish tantalization of the gods!' " (ibid.).

If the doubloon, as I have argued, serves to some extent as a central icon like Achilles' shield, is there not a corresponding symbolism in the mysterious images tattooed on his body which Queequeg, like Achilles, cannot interpret, images, it should be noted, that Queequeg has painstakingly carved upon his coffin? Queequeg's seemingly miraculous recovery from a severe illness and his transference of the images from his body, "destined to moulder," to the more enduring material of the "coffin buoy" that will save Ishmael alone of all the *Pequod's* crew, imply inescapably that the images Ahab finds tantalizing in their inscrutability symbolize the interlocked mysteries of life and death. Confronting these deeply interfused aspects of the ultimate, Ahab will strive to split them apart, his instrument being the destroyer *Pequod* with all her lovingly described weaponry, her piercing and probing lances and keen dividing blades.

What the discursive reason finds contradictory the mythic imagination finds possessed of a unity profound beyond the reach of analysis. In the first stages of their relationship, according to Edinger, Queequeg was, to Ishmael, "the primitive shadow figure,"[6] the unconscious side of the novice whaleman's personality that strikes Ishmael with fear and loathing. The alienation that the white, Presbyterian, "civilized" merchant sailor feels for the dusky, pagan, cannibal savage is related in a jocular, comically melodramatic style. Little by little the malleable white youth and the self-assured cannibal prince overcome the obvious differences that separate them. On waking after reluctantly sharing what had been the matrimonial bed of the keeper of the Spouter Inn, Ishmael finds himself embraced by Queequeg's arm, "tattoed all over with an interminable Cretan labyrinth of a figure" (p. 52). Henceforth Ishmael's development will be marked by a developing sympathy and respect for his companion. For a while their roles will be reversed, as Ishmael finds in his exotic savage friend qualities of mind and spirit that he himself lacks. Ishmael, the alienated orphan, whose casual commitment to the whaling voyage is an impulsive flight from his land-bred melancholia, gradually surrenders his habitual attitude toward "savages" and opens his mind and spirit to Queequeg's superior wisdom and achieved self-respect. The process can be noted in his recognition of Queequeg's spiritual self-discipline in the long, immobile fast of Ramadan; in Queequeg's generosity in insistently sharing with Ishmael half his fortune; and, above all, in Queequeg's extraordinary articulation of mind and body when he rescues, on the voyage from New Bedford to Nantucket, "with a long living arc of a leap" (p. 95), the "bumpkin" who had insulted him. With a self-sufficiency that is quite spontaneous, Queequeg, having saved both passenger and vessel, "put on dry clothes, lighted his pipe, and leaning against the bulwarks, and mildly eyeing those around him, seemed to be saying to himself—'It's a mutual, joint-stock world, in all meridians. We cannibals must help these Christians'" (pp. 95–96).

If Ishmael is, for a time, Queequeg's figurative wife, Queequeg, again in a reversal of roles, functions in some ways as his anima figure, first experienced as "the primitive shadow figure" and then, as he understands the "savage" better, as a guide to the release and conscious assimilation of his own primitive feelings. For Ishmael, to enter into an increasingly close and vital friendship with Queequeg is truly to embark upon the dark voyage of self-discovery. Unlike Ahab's attempts to establish the savage as a monolithic projection of his tortured will, Ishmael's growing awareness of and response to what is savage in the universe and in himself is rendered beneficial by being admitted to his conscious mind:

> I felt a melting in me. No more my splintered heart and maddened hand were turned against the wolfish world. This soothing savage had redeemed it. There he sat, his very indifference speaking a nature in which there lurked no civilized hypocrisies and bland deceits. Wild he was; a very sight of sights to see; yet I began to feel myself mysteriously drawn towards him. (pp. 83–84)

The complementarity between the civilized and savage friends and the accompanying integration of what had, to Ishmael, first seemed stark and irreconcilable opposites, has here, as Edinger notes,[7] a correspondence to the familiar pattern of Yang and Yin, which, happily, resembles a black whale and a white whale sharing a circle. Something like this symbol seems to be expressed in Ishmael's experience, before the climactic battles with Moby Dick, at the quiet center of an enormous pod of whales:

> And thus, though surrounded by circle upon circle of consternations and affrights, did these inscrutable creatures at the centre freely and fearlessly indulge in all peaceful concernments; yea, serenely revelled in dalliance and delight. But even so, amid the tornadoed Atlantic of my being, do I still for ever centrally disport in mute calm; and while ponderous planets of unwaning woe revolve round me, deep down and deep inland there I still bathe me in eternal mildness of joy. (pp. 498–99)

This enchanting experience restores the vital integrity of the symbolic mode as the expression of profoundest truth, inaccessible to the splintering mode of discourse. For a moment Ishmael has a vision of unrefracted reality that leads, not to the terrifyingly blank whiteness he envisioned earlier in "The Whiteness of the Whale," but to an indivisible interrelation of opposites. Ishmael apprehends something like Eliot's "still center of the turning world," but he apprehends it in a way that is characteristically Melvillean in its rich and loving attention to detail. One is struck by the dynamism of the moment, as in the labyrinthine dance on Achilles' shield or the labyrinthine maneuvers of the young horsemen performing the Troy Game in the *Aeneid*. Melville, without alluding to Homer or Virgil, nonetheless seems to have synthesized, in a living symbol, the aggressive aspects of the *lusus Troiae* (in the defensive actions of the bull whales at the circumference of the pod) and the harmonious power of the mazy dance at Knossos (in the serene revel at its center). For the moment, "the tornadoed Atlantic" of Ishmael's being coexists inseparably with his "ever centrally disporting himself in mute calm."

In contrast to Ishmael's movement toward a centered self, marked in this episode by a serene abandonment of egoistic anxiety, Ahab continues on what he had determined to be the inexorable and fated course of his will to "strike through the mask" of appearances to reach the ultimate secret of universal malignity. Having commanded the blacksmith to forge him a harpoon of the hardest and sharpest alloy, he insists on tempering the glowing steel in blood drawn from the *Pequod's* three harpooneers. The earlier compact into which he had, with formidable manipulative skill, compelled the crew he now reconfirms in a diabolic baptismal ritual. Before that great scene, Melville has indicated the opposite courses on which Ahab and Ishmael are embarked:

> Nor, perhaps, will it fail to be eventually perceived, that behind those forms and usages [of shipboard conduct at sea] . . . he sometimes masked himself; incidentally making use of them for other and more private ends than they were legitimately intended to subserve. That certain sultanism of his brain, which had otherwise in a good degree remained unmanifested; through those forms that same sultanism became incarnate in an irresistible dictatorship. For be a man's intellectual superiority what it will, it can never assume the practical, available supremacy over other men, without the aid of some sort of external arts and entrenchments, always, in themselves, more or less paltry and base. This it is, that for ever keeps God's true princes of the Empire from the world's hustings; and leaves the highest honors that this air can give, to those men who become famous more through their infinite inferiority to the choice hidden handful of the Divine Inert, than through their undoubted superiority over the dead level of the mass. (p. 198)

If Ishmael has, amid the pod of whales, intimations of "the Divine Inert" and yields his will to it, Ahab is devoted to satanic activism and ritualizes his devotion in baptizing the blood-tempered instrument of his vengeance: " 'Ego non baptizo te in nomine patris, sed in nomine diaboli,' deliriously howled Ahab, as the malignant iron scorchingly devoured the baptismal blood" (p. 621).

The cannibalistic steel forms the point to his fell purpose. This horrific scene is followed by idyllic and lyrical descriptions of the beauty of the sea at its most benign, when, as Ishmael remarks, "All this mixes with your most mystic moods; so that fact and fancy, halfway meeting, interpenetrate, and form one seamless whole" (p. 623). Even Ahab is not proof against such benevolent supernatural solicitings: "Nor did such soothing scenes, however temporary, fail of at least as temporary an effect on Ahab. But if these secret golden keys did seem to open in him his own secret golden treasuries, yet did his breath upon them prove but tarnishing" (p. 623).

Meanwhile, however, Fedallah's malign influence on Ahab continues to grow, as, in the only words he speaks in the whole book, he prophesies that "hemp alone can kill thee" (p. 632), a Delphically misleading oracle that Ahab interprets as guaranteeing his personal immunity in any future encounters with Moby Dick. In his vertiginal egocentricity Ahab destroys the ship's quadrant. From now on the *Pequod*, no longer capable or orienting herself by the sun, will navigate by dead reckoning. Soon afterward, Ahab delivers an ultimatum of self-sufficiency:

> "No fearless fool now fronts thee. I own thy speechless, placeless power; but to the last gasp of my earthquake life will dispute its unconditional, unintegral mastery in me. In the midst of the personified impersonal, a personality stands here." (p. 641)

This is his response to the St. Elmo's fire playing eerily through the rigging. Against the placelessness he ascribes to the spirit of fire, Ahab maintains that he is, himself, the center of all things: " 'Though but a point at best; whenceso'er I came; whereso'er I go; yet while I earthly live, the queenly personality lives in me, and feels her royal rights' " (p. 641).

This perplexing idea of Ahab's, that his will somehow incorporates both his hitherto solely masculine aggressive drive to vengeance on his attacker and an unexpected claim to the "queenly rights" of his personality, is illuminated by Edinger's gloss:

> The Queen is the anima, that figure we have looked for in vain in *Moby-Dick*. Ahab is identified with the anima. We have already noted that for Ahab the anima has not been separated from the mother monster. Hence her manifestations, in identification with the ego, are primitive and undifferentiated. His moodiness and outbursts of affect are symptoms of anima possession.[8]

Presumably, to be possessed by the anima is the opposite of possessing the anima, as in the syzygistic integration we have traced in

Ishmael's relation to Queequeg. If Ahab's shadow is the dark side of his personality, he here usurps its function and simply declares it to be that other part of his nature whose rights must be recognized. Perhaps, then, Ahab, in an egotistical assertion of his will, is here claiming for himself a wholeness of being that he has failed to achieve. His possession by the "queenly" anima, in contrast to Ishmael's reconciliation with what he had at first perceived as the hostile "shadow" of the cannibal Queequeg, is, then, but one more striking instance of his monomaniacal conception of "truth" as a monad he is destined to apprehend as a uniquely gifted personality. He would make, as Enobarbus says of Antony, his will lord of his reason: but, overreaching Antony, Ahab would make his will both master and mistress of a truth that Melville conceives as an amalgam of things that reason can apprehend only as contradictions.

If Moby Dick is the focus of his hostility to the underlying savagery of reality, Ahab is projecting onto the whale his own monomania. His surrender or loss of accoutrements and instruments that might arm him against his foe are illuminated by contrast with the process of loss and deprivation through which Odysseus discovers himself. To take another example, we may think of Ahab, without quadrant or tack-log in the wilderness of the sea, as possessing the potential for vision that Faulkner's Ike McCaslin has in "The Bear" when, having surrendered his compass, watch, and gun, he abandons his intention of killing the titanic, legendary Old Ben, maimed, like Moby Dick, and experiences through this surrender a vision of the great spirit that manifests the wilderness. That Old Ben has something of an anima function for Ike is implied, possibly, by his cousin's insistence, after the event, on reading Keats's lines, "She cannot fade, though thou hast not thy bliss, / Forever wilt thou love and she be fair." Negative capability and the Divine Inert are, then, both manifestations of a capacity to accept the indivisible symbolic unity of true vision.

But Ahab, like Achilles in his berserk rage, cannot maintain his single-minded assault on the absolute without remissions. The closer he gets to the anticipated fulfillment of his purpose, the more powerful are the counterforces arising from his unconscious. Like Homer, Melville dramatizes these conflicts. Starbuck, like Patroclus, lovingly solicits his attention to the promptings of his nature that he has struggled to keep buried. For Patroclus to live, Achilles must surrender his fixed revenge. Starbuck, unlike Patroclus, cannot—or will not—allow himself to submit without a final effort to make his captain save himself and his crew. When this fails, he thinks of killing Ahab, but that is no more within his power than a speechless submission would be.

A more powerful catalyst than Starbuck in the Faustian struggle for Ahab's soul is the weakest member of the *Pequod's* crew. When the sailor from the Isle of Man thinks to himself, after the loss of quadrant and tack-log, that to Ahab "Nothing's happened; but to me, the skewer seems loosening out of the middle of the world" (p. 658), he has abandoned hope. Yet, in the eleventh hour of the tragedy that Ahab will bring on himself and all but one of his shipmates, he is suddenly aware of little Pip, the black boy deranged by his abandonment in a desperate encounter with a whale, in which he imagined he was dragged down "to wondrous depths" in "the unwarped primal world" (p. 530). The black waif, obsessed by Stubb's callous charge of cowardice, and even more by the terrors of his abandonment, hails Ahab: "Captain Ahab! sir, sir! here's Pip trying to get on board again" (p. 659). The Manxman waves him off the quarterdeck: "Peace, thou crazy loon." Ahab, however, in a rare moment of compassion, rebukes the Manxman:

> "The greater idiot ever scolds the lesser," muttered Ahab, advancing. "Hands off from that holiness! Where sayest thou Pip was, boy?"
>
> "Astern there, sir, astern! Lo, lo!"
>
> "And who art thou, boy? I see not my reflection in the vacant pupils of thy eyes. Oh God! that man should be a thing for immortal souls to sieve through! Who art thou, boy?"
>
> "Bell-boy, sir; ship's-crier; ding, dong, ding! Pip! Pip! Pip! One hundred pounds of clay reward for Pip; five feet high—looks cowardly—quickest known by that! Ding, dong, ding! Who's seen Pip the coward?"
>
> "There can be no hearts above the snow-line. Oh, ye frozen heavens! look down here. Ye did beget this luckless child, and have abandoned him, ye creative libertines. Here boy; Ahab's cabin shall be Pip's home henceforth, while Ahab lives. Thou touchest my inmost centre, boy; thou art tied to me by cords woven of my heart-strings. Come, let's down."

"What's this? here's velvet shark-skin," intently gazing at Ahab's hand, and feeling it. "Ah, now, had poor Pip
but felt so kind a thing as this, perhaps he had ne'er been
lost! This seems to me, sir, as a man-rope; something that
weak souls may hold by. Oh, sir, let old Perth now come
and rivet these two hands together, for I will not let this
go."

"Oh, boy, nor will I thee, unless I should thereby drag
thee to worse horrors than are here. Come, then, to my
cabin. Lo! ye believers in gods of all goodness, and in man
all ill, lo you! see the omniscient gods oblivious of suffering
man; and man, though idiotic, and knowing not what he
does, yet full of the sweet things of love and gratitude.
Come! I feel prouder leading thee by thy black hand than
though I grasped an Emperor's." (pp. 659–60)

Ahab's sudden pivotal compassion for unaccommodated Pip clearly
owes a great deal to Lear's engagement, in the storm on the heath,
with Poor Tom and the Fool. For a moment, Ahab's fatal intent is
shunted off the iron rails of his resolution. But where Lear's anagnorisis is a vital stage toward his ultimate affirmation of love, Ahab's is a
momentary, essentially egocentric, and histrionic assertion of his
own powers of sympathy in the face of heaven's malignity. Given the
nature of his titanic self-concern, Ahab cannot sustain this mood for
long. In "The Cabin" (chapter 129) Ahab fears that his love for Pip
will, homeopathically, cure him of his monomania:

"If thou speakest thus to me much more, Ahab's purpose
keels up in him. I tell thee no: it cannot be."

"Oh, good master, master, master!"

"Weep so, and I will murder thee! have a care, for
Ahab too is mad. Listen, and thou wilt often hear my ivory
foot upon the deck, and still know that I am here. And now I
quit thee. Thy hand!—Met! True art thou, lad, as the
circumference to its center. So: God for ever bless thee; and
if it come to that,—God for ever save thee, let what will
befall." (pp. 672–73)

Once more, Ahab arrogates the "center" to himself and thus rejects
the loving and pitiful "double" that might have saved him. The
gesture of compassion, with its infidel blessing, is another renuncia-

tion of Ahab's residual human affinities. Pip, for a moment, has been surrogate for the young son and wife he abandoned on Nantucket in order to pursue his revenge.

Ahab's recognition of Pip's need to "come aboard" and Pip's sensitivity to the "man-rope" constituted by their handgrip provide an abortive version of the mutuality of Ishmael and Queequeg, linked together in the risky joint-stock enterprise of "The Monkey-Rope," in the relaxed and dreamy making of the sword mat, and, above all, in the benign mutualities of "A Squeeze of the Hand."

From this moment Ahab resumes what he regards as the fatal tracks of necessity. Night and day he appears on the quarterdeck in his "stone-carved coat and hat" (p. 675), indifferent to all vicissitudes of weather. Nonetheless, he chooses Starbuck to superintend the line by which he is hoisted into the rigging to look for the white whale. It is a daring choice, since Ahab is betting his life on Starbuck's reluctant submission. Far from expressing the mutual trust of Ishmael and Queequeg tied together by their "monkey-rope," however, Ahab is here domineering over the spirit of his guardian.

Aloft in the rigging, Ahab encounters a predatory bird. "Wheeling and screaming round his head in a maze of untrackable swift circlings," it towers to an enormous height, then "spiralizes downwards" and removes Ahab's hat (p. 678). Pipe, quadrant, tack-log, compass, hat: as these are abandoned or lost, the course of the *Pequod* is increasingly the plaything of her captain's maniacal spirit. The seabird's flight, to which Ahab is utterly indifferent, indicates that there are labyrinthine secrets of the air correlative to the labyrinthine secrets of the deep manifested by Moby Dick on which he is darkly fixated.

In a brief encounter with another whaling ship inappropriately named the *Delight*, the *Pequod* is "baptized" by the splash of a corpse consigned to the deep, a victim of the white whale. Ahab sails on, regardless, and the *Delight's* crew hail him, pointing to the coffin of Queequeg, now rigged astern as an improvised lifebuoy: " 'In vain, oh, ye strangers, ye flee our sad burial; ye but turn us your taffrail to show us your coffin' " (p. 680). The coffin-lifebuoy is to be the last of a series of richly ambiguous symbols that express the inversions and reversals of meaning that have characterized the voyage of the *Pequod*.

Our involvement in the approaching crisis of Ahab's obsession is greatly intensified by his astonishingly open disclosure to Starbuck of

"the desolation and solitude" of his life, which suggests that the
agony inflicted on him by Moby Dick has been only a particularly
painful episode in a lifetime of excruciating loneliness:

> "Forty years of continual whaling! forty years of privation,
> and peril, and storm-time! forty years on the pitiless sea!
> for forty years Ahab has forsaken the peaceful land, for
> forty years to make war on the horrors of the deep! Aye and
> yes, Starbuck, out of those forty years I have not spent
> three ashore. When I think of this life I have led; the
> desolation of solitude it has been: the masoned, walled-
> town of a Captain's exclusiveness, which admits but small
> sympathy from the green country without—oh, weariness!
> heaviness! Guinea-Coast slavery of solitary command!—
> when I think of all this; only half-suspected, not so keenly
> known to me before—and how for forty years I have fed
> upon dry salted fare—fit emblem of the dry nourishment of
> my soul!—when the poorest landsman has had fresh fruit
> to his daily hand, and broken the world's fresh bread to my
> mouldy crests—away, whole oceans away, from that young
> girl-wife I wedded past fifty, and sailed for Cape Horn the
> next day, leaving but one dent in my marriage pillow—
> wife? wife?—rather a widow with her husband alive! Aye, I
> widowed that poor girl when I married her, Starbuck; and
> then, the madness, the frenzy, the boiling blood and the
> smoking brow, with which, for a thousand lowerings old
> Ahab has furiously, foamingly chased his prey—more a
> demon than a man!". (p. 683)

This threnody surprisingly reveals Ahab's recognition in the evening
of his life, that his determination masked the horrible waste of his
life. Too insistently, perhaps, Melville has him recount the forty
years in which, like the Israelites, he has wandered in the wilderness,
forty years of sterile privation without any prospect of reaching the
promised land, forty years which implicitly evoke the forty days of
Jesus' contrastingly fruitful ordeal. The insistent repetitions evoke
Ahab's repeated experience of utter alienation and reveal him to be,
like Pip, simply another waif in the whale fishery. This horrible
knowledge, up to now, he says, " 'only half-suspected, not so keenly
known to me before,' " suggests that his obsessive pursuit of Moby
Dick has been a frantic effort to project on the whale his sense of

desolation. The psychological process by which he has transferred his growing awareness of a lifetime of desolation and projected it onto his "disaster" is much like that by which Achilles transforms his feelings of bereavement and guilt after the death of Patroclus into his obsessive attempts to dishonor the corpse of Hector. This is not to suggest, of course, that there are not existential motives that, in the case of both tragic heroes, go far beyond their personal experiences of loss, or that there are not times when Achilles and Ahab in their rage share intimations of the madness of vital truth. It is not simply his obsession that led Ahab to his striking earlier assertion to Starbuck:

> "All visible objects, man, are but pasteboard masks. But in each event—in the living act, the undoubted deed—there, some unknown but still reasoning thing puts forth the mouldings of its features from behind the unreasoning mask. If man will strike, strike through the mask! How can the prisoner reach outside except by thrusting through the wall? To me, the white whale is that wall shoved near to me. Sometimes I think there's naught beyond. But 'tis enough."
> (pp. 220–21)

Melville sustains alternative conceptions of Ahab's epistemological position—that the prison he would break out of is his own construction; and, on the other hand, that it has an existential reality independent of his special preoccupations. In the first instance, his attempt to "strike through the mask" by slaying the whale is plainly self-destructive, given the identities established between him and Moby Dick. The fatal blow he intends, like that Achilles delivers against Hector, who is wearing Achilles' old armor stripped from Patroclus, will inevitably rebound against himself. Against the objective possibility that a malign or indifferent divinity has hidden himself behind the inscrutable phenomena of the universe, Ahab's motive to strike through the mask is truly heroic. As Edinger observes, "Ahab's attack against the whiteness of Moby Dick represents the heroic effort of the ego, through creative imagination, to refract and dismember the infinite, boundless, transpersonal energy, by embodying it in specific images."[9] The ambiguous whiteness of the whale, as Ishmael read it, embraces the opposed possibilities of spiritual purity and deathlike pallor. Against the riddle of its sphinx-like blankness Ahab directs the disintegrating force of his blood-tempered lance.

Yet Ahab, despite his occasional commitment to a purpose greater than mere personal revenge and his intermittent intimations of natural and human benevolence that might momentarily block or derail his vengeful intent, is nevertheless dominated in the long run by pride, his psychomachia resembling that of Satan in *Paradise Lost*:

"O then at last relent: is there no place
Left for Repentance, none for Pardon left?
None left but by submission; and that word
Disdain forbids me, and my dread of shame
Among the Spirits beneath, whom I seduc'd
With other promises and other vaunts
Than to submit, boasting I could subdue
Th' Omnipotent."

[4.79–86]

Ahab's remark to Starbuck, already referred to—" 'Talk not to me of blasphemy, man; I'd strike the sun if he insulted me' " (p. 221)—parallels the opening of Satan's soliloquy, with its expression of hatred for the sun.

Another significant episode in Ahab's psychomachia occurs when he refuses to allow the *Pequod* to interrupt the pursuit of Moby Dick to help the stricken *Rachel* search for a lost boat crew which includes its captain's young son. That the next ship encountered is the misnamed *Delight*, which has just lost five men to Moby Dick, clinches the point that Ahab's attempt to appease his own sense of desolation by avenging himself on the white whale must tend toward the same deadly consequences.

In the final episodes of Ahab's career, his globe-circling wanderings contract to a point. Hurled overboard in the first day's chase by Moby Dick, he is drawn into a whirlpool caused by the whale's violent maneuverings:

So revolvingly appalling was the White Whale's aspect, and so planetarily swift the ever-contracting circles he made, that he seemed horizontally swooping upon them. And, though the other boats, unharmed, still hovered hard by; still they dared not pull into the eddy to strike, lest that should be the signal for the instant destruction of the jeopardized castaways, Ahab and all; nor in that case could they themselves hope to escape. With straining eyes, then,

they remained on the outer edge of the direful zone, whose
centre had now become the old man's head. (p. 694)

The pursued whale and the pursuing, egocentric Ahab here exchange
roles as centers, reinforcing their mysterious likeness. The crew
simultaneously contracts into a single instrument of Ahab's needs:

> They were one man, not thirty. For as the one ship that
> held them all; though it was put together of all contrasting
> things—oak, and maple, and pine wood; iron, and pitch,
> and hemp—yet all these ran into each other in the one
> concrete hull, which shot on its way, both balanced and
> directed by the long central keel; even so, all the indivi-
> dualities of the crew, this man's valor, that man's fear; guilt
> and guiltiness, all varieties were welded into oneness, and
> were all directed to the fatal goal which Ahab their one lord
> and keel did point to. (pp. 700–701)

Yet Ahab's inner struggle is not quite finished. In the second
day's chase the whale makes a labyrinth out of the numerous lines
trailed by the spears and harpoons embedded in its hump, drawing
the boats ineluctably to its center:

> But at last in his untraceable evolutions, the White Whale
> so crossed and recrossed, and in a thousand ways entangled
> the slack of the three lines now fast to him, that they
> foreshortened, and, of themselves, warped the devoted
> boats toward the planted irons in him. . . .
> Caught and twisted—corkscrewed in the mazes of the
> line, loose harpoons and lances, with all their bristling barbs
> and points, came flashing and dripping up to the chocks in
> the bows of Ahab's boat. (p. 703)

These mazes of line warping Ahab and his crew toward their prey
reify dynamically the manifold labyrinthine lines that have brought
the *Pequod* to this center: the Knossian patterns tattooed on
Queequeg's body and transferred to his coffin, the inscrutable patterns on the whale's brow that correspond to those on Ahab's
forehead, most notably the lines printed on Ahab's charts and traced
by his pencil, and the course through the four oceans of the world of
the *Pequod* herself. The energy of Ahab's pursuit is now transferred,
beyond his control, by the magnetic force of the whale in a deeply

ironic exchange of roles between hunter and prey. Although Ahab quick-wittedly averts disaster by cutting the entangling lines and rerigging his own, Moby Dick capsizes all the boats, and Ahab loses his ivory leg. Yet, rejecting one more plea from Starbuck to quit the chase, Ahab reaffirms the fatal direction of his quest: " 'Ahab is for ever Ahab, man. This whole act's immutably decreed. 'Twas rehearsed by thee and me a billion years before this ocean rolled. Fool! I am the Fates' lieutenant; I act under orders' " (p. 707).

In insisting that the present combat has ancient archetypal origins, Ahab imputes to Fate an eternal necessity that he must obey. This apparent change from his earlier insistence on the primacy of his own will suggests a new reluctance to insist on his personal responsibility for the quest. The shift is an attempt to endow the enterprise, as in the earlier covenants with the crew, with the efficacy of ritual and archetypal drama, as is his assertion, a few pages later, that " 'by the eternal Poles! these same Trades that so directly blow my good ship on; these Trades, or something like them—something so unchangeable, and full as strong, blow my keeled soul along!' " Ahab thus arrogates to his own journey the status of an Aeneas driven by fate, but the discovery that, during the night, he has overrun the whale, challenges his fatalistic assumptions. As Ahab orders course reversed, Starbuck exposes his captain's fallacy in logic: " 'Against the wind he now steers for the open jaw' " (p. 711). For the last time Starbuck tries to sway Ahab from his purpose:

"Starbuck!"

"Sir?"

"For the third time my soul's ship starts upon this voyage, Starbuck."

"Aye, sir, thou wilt have it so."

"Some ships sail from their ports, and afterwards are missing, Starbuck!"

"Truth, sir: saddest truth."

"Some men die at ebb tide, some at low water; some at the full of the flood;—and I now feel like a billow that's all one crested comb, Starbuck. I am old;—shake hands with me, man."

Their hands met; their eyes fastened; Starbuck's tears the glue.

"Oh, my captain, my captain!—noble heart—go not—

go not!—see, it's a brave man that weeps; how great the agony of the persuasion then!"

"Lower away!"—cried Ahab, tossing the mate's arm from him. "Stand by the crew!" (pp. 712–13)

All relentings now behind him, Ahab proceeds to "dart his fierce iron, and his far fiercer curse into the hated whale" (p. 718). His line snaps, and Moby Dick now turns his course toward the *Pequod* herself as the source of his torments and strikes her bow head-on. Once more Ahab buries a harpoon in the whale. Now the running line catches him by the neck and whips him off into the depths, exactly as it did Fedallah. So Fedallah's Delphic prophecy that only hemp could kill Ahab is fulfilled.

As the *Pequod* goes to the bottom, "concentric circles seized the lone boat itself, and all its crew, and each floating oar, and every lance-pole, and spinning, animate and inanimate, all round and round in one vortex, carried the smallest chip of the *Pequod* out of sight" (p. 722). "Animate and inanimate" are fused in the centripetal downward force of the whirlpool, as the last of a series of centers with its ineluctable point puts its final stop on Ahab's quest. The *Pequod* goes down, carrying at her mainmast the impotent symbols of Ahab's aspirations, with Tashtego still nailing new colors aloft and a skyhawk caught between the nail and the mast. So the labyrinthine flights of the predatory seabird and the vertiginal descent of the predatory *Pequod* come inextricably together in a climactic symbol.

In a brief coda marked off from the body of the tale by italics, Ishmael, the sole survivor by virtue of his distance from the whirlpool, brings *Moby-Dick* to a tranquil close:

> *Round and round, then, and ever contracting towards the button-like black bubble at the axis of that slowly wheeling circle, like another Ixion I did revolve. Till, gaining that vital centre, the black bubble upward burst; and now, liberated by reason of its cunning spring, and owing to its great buoyancy, rising with great force, the coffin life-buoy shot lengthwise up from the sea, fell over, and floated by my side. Buoyed up by that coffin, for almost one whole day and night, I floated on a soft and dirge-like main.* (p. 724)

Ishmael is rescued by the *Rachel.*

Here, as in his experience at the center of the enormous revolving pod of whales in "The Armada," Ishmael seems to exemplify the heroism of "the Divine Inert." Like other heroes, his involvement in the labyrinth draws him toward the vertiginal point of death and then, after the moment of vision, leads to his deliverance. The coffin of Queequeg, with its mystical mazelike design carved in the black wood, is the obvious symbolic focus of this theme, interfusing life and death, the way down and the way up, the peripheral and the central.

Clearly, Ishmael owes his survival to chance, but, as he concluded in "The Mat-Maker," chance and fate are not necessarily incompatible with free will. It seems fair to claim, then, that Ishmael's deliverance is also in recognition of the fact that he, of all the *Pequod's* crew, has achieved both a profound and comprehensive understanding of the voyage in all its implications and an accompanying assimilation of the dark, "savage" side of his personality into his consciousness. His rescue by Queequeg's coffin reminds us of the indispensable role his savage friend has played in this ordeal of individuation. If Ahab's drowning vortex represents the fatal egocentricity of the one on whom it is centered, the "vital centre" from which Ishmael's coffin-buoy emerges represents a wholly opposite kind of centering, with a saving awareness of the mystical complexities of reality as its coordinates. Preserved by the coffin-buoy and rescued by the bereaved *Rachel*, Ishmael alone has mastered the understanding that empowers him to tell the tale and to complete his voyage home.

If Ahab's quest is abortive because, in Newton Arvin's words, "he has long since ceased to be anything but an Ego, a noble Ego to be sure; a heroic one; but *that* rather than a Self,"[10] Ishmael emerges from his ordeal of initiation, encounters with threshold figures and, finally, with death, as the "unfolding sensibility" that Walter Bezanson sees as "the prime experience for the reader."[11] His rite of passage, beginning with the ivory gate to the bar of the Spouter Inn and concluding with his emergence from the vortex on his strange black vessel and rescue by the *Rachel* (still roaming the seas in search of her lost children), marks his transformation from an orphaned *isolato* into a reclaimed and individuated self.

8 Imperial Horror: Conrad's *Heart of Darkness*

> *The horror lies in wait to be discovered by anyone who is spiritually adventuresome. The* Erziehungsroman, *invented by Goethe and others on the assumption that beneath ironic undercuttings there were some solid truths that a hero could be educated to, turned into this even more ironic form when authors became convinced that the only final education for a mature man was to recognize the emptiness, the abyss. But there are still limits here: nothing undercuts the importance of the quest, of honesty in unmasking error and facing the truth, of courage in facing the horror. Though everything else may be ironized, the nobility of the quest is not.*
>
> Wayne Booth

Conrad despised *Moby-Dick*.[1] An experienced captain of merchant ships, he thought for a while of shipping on a whaling voyage, as Melville had done, but instead, with the impulsiveness of his Charlie Marlow or of Melville's Ishmael, took leave of the merchant marine for a voyage of unanticipated danger and unfathomable horror. *Heart of Darkness* follows very closely the story of his voyage up the Congo on the decrepit steamer *Roi des Belges* belonging to the Société anonyme pour le Commerce du Haut-Congo, an imperial enterprise of King Leopold II dedicated to a rapacious quest for ivory. Kurtz, like Ahab an insatiable monomaniac, manages to "strike through the mask" of the tantalizingly phenomenological and apprehend, at the moment of his death, the horror at the center of the heart of darkness. As he discovers, he is himself Ahab's "pasteboard mask"—in Marlow's description of another "pilgrim," a "papier-mâché Mephistopheles"[2]—but his final recognition is, ironically, a last-minute achievement of true self-affirmation. To the extent that his dying words are an indictment of his monstrous African career, Kurtz's moment of truth resembles Ahab's extraordinary confession to Starbuck of the desolation of his forty-year career as a whaler, a confession of utter alienation that nonetheless fails to deter him from his commitment to vengeance on Moby Dick.

In their concern with the destruction, for commercial purposes, of the largest animals that inhabit land and sea, *Heart of Darkness* and *Moby-Dick* seem to share a subject, but the resemblance is only superficial. Whereas Ishmael and his shipmates are immersed in sperm whales and their element, Marlow strives to keep his distance from the jungle and never sees an elephant. He is utterly indifferent to the ivory so rapaciously and ineffectually sought by "the faithless pilgrims," the treacherous, back-stabbing agents of the feckless imperial enterprise. The gun, it is assumed, has taken the heroism out of elephant hunting, just as the harpoon-gun was to turn whaling into just one more bloody industrial process. The mystery that fascinates Marlow does not lurk behind the elephant's majestic brow. Rather, it is "the fascination of the abomination" that lurks in the dark and enigmatic savagery of man released, in the jungle, from conventional inhibitions. Equally attracted and repelled by this savagery, Marlow preserves his fragile decency and threatened sanity by devoting himself to the "surface truth" of his manifold ordeals as captain of the tinpot steamer in his ultimate dedication to rescuing the extraordinary emissary of enlightenment, Kurtz. Kurtz is Marlow's white whale, and Marlow is mesmerized by this legendary figure of pan-European origins who appears uniquely to have preserved his ideals, his sanity, and his effectiveness as an ivory-hunter, immune alike to "the flabby devil" of the other agents and to the hot-blooded savagery of the cannibals.

Despite Conrad's dislike of *Moby-Dick*, his novel, like Melville's, marked a major life crisis, and their profound concern with similar crucial mythic themes suggests that Conrad may have been more influenced by *Moby-Dick* than he knew. On the other hand, theories of archetypal myths and the collective unconscious may support the idea that Conrad could shape his most powerful tale independent of Melville.

If the thematic and symbolic resemblances are close and if both books emphasize an unliterary, oral, narrative mode, they are utterly different in scope and structure. Devoid of the digressive, wide-ranging, episodic, and encyclopedic character of Melville's leviathan of a book, *Heart of Darkness* is condensed and concentrated. Where Melville explores his central themes in a leisurely and expansive way,

Conrad announces his at the outset and tracks them unswervingly to the very heart of the Congo. Marlow's riverine voyage leads him to a physical and metaphysical cul-de-sac. Only after he has captured Kurtz, only after Kurtz has made the final judgment on his experience in his dying exclamation, only after his delivery from the river's toils, can Marlow commit himself to the lie that will save the memory of Kurtz for his bereaved and devoted fiancée. The end of the story proposes the enigma that Marlow's "lie" is closer to the truth about Kurtz than the literal truth could be. We are left with a somberly ironic judgment, one that falls short of Ishmael's final revelation and deliverance from the vortex created by the sinking *Pequod*. Increasingly hemmed in by the jungle that crowds and jeopardizes his tinpot steamer, Marlow experiences a traumatic and equivocal rebirth. In contrast to the more and more confining and hazardous encroachments of the Congo's dark heart, the *Pequod's* voyage extends through four oceans, its course marked by Ahab's abandonment of all earthbound concerns. Perhaps, in their opposing centripetal and centrifugal movements, the two books are reciprocal, somewhat like descending and ascending gyres. However expansive or restrictive their narrative courses may be, both reach their climaxes in labyrinthine centers of a numinous experience.

Heart of Darkness may also be seen as an *Aeneid* in reverse. The ancient mother Aeneas seeks has become a primeval savagery that challenges and dissolves the fundamental values of Western civilization. Far from sparing the weak and humbling the proud, the predatory agents of the new imperialism destroy the helpless natives and plot endlessly the advancement of their own sordid ambitions. In contrast to the collective vision of Aeneas's Trojans, Conrad's faithless pilgrims are impelled only by their lust for ivory. Avaricious and inept, bewitched, as Marlow observes, within the rotten fence of the central station by the charm of ivory, they may remind us of Odysseus' comrades whom Circe transformed into swine. Like Circe's victims, Conrad's pilgrims have lost interest in returning home: in fact, they all seem to be without families or homes, and the closest relation to be found among them is that between the villainous manager of the central station and his equally contemptible uncle.

In their impotent invocations of ivory, Conrad's damned Dantean pilgrims are frozen in attitudes that seem to fulfill Virgil's darker implications about the grand imperial enterprise of Aeneas. As we have seen, Aeneas, in his final battles in the cause of *imperium sine fine*, at times abandons the restraints enjoined on him by his ghostly father, becomes another berserk Achilles, and acts out the final equivalent to Kurtz's cherished report to the Society for the Suppression of Savage Customs, "Exterminate the brutes!" Like Virgil, Conrad is deeply suspicious of the benevolent programs undertaken by the lightbearers who enter or leave the underworld by the ivory gates. It may be merely an odd coincidence that in the *Iliad*, the *Aeneid*, *Moby-Dick*, and *Heart of Darkness*, ivory is a symbol of the devastating illusions of the ego. Marlow's prototypical examples of "decent young Romans," making their way up the Thames in the time of Virgil's Augustus, confronting the savage Britons and impenetrable forests and longing for their civilized homes, sustained, perhaps, by the "surface truths" of their responsibilities and by the hope of promotion to a significant position in the imperial navy at Ravenna, suggest a quiet, resourceful heroism that titanic heroes like Achilles, Ahab, and Kurtz cannot accommodate themselves to. Their commitment to the Absolute seems inevitably to transform them, in their crises, into destroyers.

Marlow's trip up the (unnamed) Congo, a trip to the heart of darkness simultaneously centripetal and centrifugal, may be compared with Aeneas's voyage up the Tiber to the primitive but pristine and vital community of Evander. Pallanteum exemplifies a golden age of simplicity and integrity. To develop the Roman future and shape its institutions, Aeneas must get back to his lost cultural and racial roots. In contrast to this lovely hiatus in the violence of Aeneas's career, Marlow is threatened with an increasing involvement in an abominable and fascinating upriver passage that takes him away from his cultural roots, such as they are, and into a world that threatens his naive Western values and his seamanlike sense of duty. The collective values of the Roman ship of state are negated in the disintegrating egotism of the "pilgrims." Marlow's Roman instances are crucial paradigms of his own introduction to an experience for which there is no initiation:

> I was thinking of very old times, when the Romans first came here, nineteen hundred years ago—the other day. . . . Light came out of this river since—you say Knights? Yes; but it is like a running blaze on a plain, like a flash of lightning in the clouds. We live in the flicker—may it last as long as the old earth keeps rolling! But darkness

was here yesterday. Imagine the feelings of a commander of
a fine—what d'ye call 'em?—trireme in the Mediterranean,
ordered suddenly to the north; run overland across the
Gauls in a hurry; put in charge of one of these craft the
legionaries—a wonderful lot of handy men they must have
been, too—used to build, apparently by the hundred, in
a month or two, if we may believe what we read. Imagine
him here—the very end of the world, a sea the colour of
lead, a sky the colour of smoke, a kind of ship about as rigid
as a concertina—and going up this river with stores, or
orders, or what you like. Sand-banks, marshes, forests,
savages,—precious little to eat fit for a civilized man, nothing but Thames water to drink. No Falernian wine here, no
going ashore. Here and there a military camp lost in a
wilderness, like a needle in a bundle of hay—cold, fog,
tempests, disease, exile, and death,—death skulking in the
air, in the water, in the bush. They must have been dying
like flies here. Oh, yes—he did it. Did it very well, too, no
doubt, and without thinking much about it either, except
afterwards to brag of what he had gone through in his time,
perhaps. They were men enough to face the darkness. (p.
68)

Barred from going ashore, such an ex-commander of a trireme,
exposed to the privations and frustrations of a voyage through the
darkness, is sustained, Marlow suggests, only by "keeping his eye on
a chance of promotion to the fleet at Ravenna by and by, if he had
good friends in Rome and survived the awful climate." Thus Charlie
Marlow himself, in the tale he is about to tell us, unable to find
another berth at sea despite six years or so of duty in the eastern
oceans, engages the influence of his well-placed aunt in Brussels to
become skipper of a "tinpot" steamboat plying the serpentine river
into the heart of darkness.

The trireme commander may be man enough to face the darkness, but he passes through it without engaging it. By implication he
is isolated from any real encounters with whatever darkness and
savagery the banks of the prehistoric Thames conceal, so his voyage
falls short of the ultimate ordeal of actually entering the heart of
darkness, while his morale and moral and psychological stability are
sustained, the passage implies, by Roman discipline (with its concom-

itant discouragement of unnecessary reflection or speculation) and the prospect of moving up the corporate ladder. And so Marlow proposes a more extreme case:

> Or think of a decent young citizen in a toga—perhaps too much dice, you know—coming out here in the train of some prefect, or tax-gatherer, or trader even, to mend his fortunes. Land in a swamp, march through the woods, and in some inland post feel the savagery, the utter savagery, had closed round him,—all that mysterious life of the wilderness that stirs in the forest, in the jungles, in the hearts of wild men. There's no initiation either into such mysteries. He has to live in the midst of the incomprehensible, which is also detestable. And it has a fascination, too that goes to work upon him. The fascination of the abomination—you know, imagine the growing regrets, the longing to escape, the powerless disgust, the surrender, the hate. (p. 69)

This passage rewards close inspection. Consider, first of all, Marlow's tone. He is among old friends who have all, at one time or another, "followed the sea," although they have all now become landsmen: lawyers, directors of companies, accountants. The familiar, colloquial style, with traces of the dramatic monologue, as Marlow responds to actual or fancied objections or questions, the repeated invitation to his listeners to participate in imagining an episode cast in the subjunctive mood, the ordeal of "a decent young citizen in a toga," the idiom that suggests a consensus between the teller and his listeners, all combine to validate Marlow's inference about "the fascination of the abomination," and also, of course, to win the assent of us who are overhearing his words. If the Director of Companies, who "was our captain and our host," standing in the bows of the yawl checking the anchor and looking to seaward, "resembles a pilot, which to a seaman is trustworthiness personified," Marlow's style is vital to establishing his own credentials as a pilot/narrator.

The moment of Marlow's introduction of his tale and the atmosphere that surrounds that moment bear directly on the distinctive character of his adventure. Where "the yarns of seamen have a direct simplicity, the whole meaning of which lies within the shell of a cracked nut," for Marlow "the meaning of an episode was not inside like a kernel but outside, enveloping the tale which brought it out only as a glow brings out a haze, in the likeness of one of those misty haloes that sometimes are made visible by the spectral illumination of moonshine" (p. 68). The present moment, of course, is slack water at the top of the flood. There is no breeze, and the four companions are waiting for the ebb which will take the yawl *Nellie* down the river. The box of dominoes is open, but no one is ready to play, and so the architect is "toying architecturally with the bones." In this hiatus in the lives of four busy men there is a poise between the "benign immensity of unstained light" on the river and the Essex marshes to the east and "the gloom to the west, brooding over the upper reaches" in the smoky air of London, "becoming more sombre every minute, as if angered by the approach of the sun" (p. 66). The dying Turneresque glow of the sunlit haze over the immense city is clearly linked to Marlow's kind of story, where the meaning is outside the episode, enveloping it "as a glow brings out a haze." At this still point before the story begins, a balance is struck between the gloom that "broods" in the west and the promising light that plays over the east. The actual sunset is rendered in a portentous bit of Conradian virtuosity:

> And at last, in its curved and imperceptible fall, the sun sank low, and from glowing white changed to a dull red without rays and without heat, as if about to go out suddenly, stricken to death by the touch of that gloom brooding over a crowd of men. (p. 66)

In the "serenity" now "less brilliant but more profound" that surrounds the anchored vessel, an anonymous narrator (presumably one of the *Nellie's* company) is moved to celebrate the mercantile, military, and missionary services of "the old river, resting unruffled at the decline of day, after ages of good service done to the race that peopled its banks." In words reminiscent of Pope's apostrophe to the Thames at the end of "Windsor Forest" as a source of affluence and benign cultural influence, the narrator celebrates "the tranquil dignity of a waterway leading to the uttermost ends of the earth" (p. 66).

The reflections that follow are anything but profound. They resemble what one might find in any Victorian school history book infused with a proper Victorian respect for the manifest destiny of the British Empire, and the tone comes perilously close to that of Joyce's mock-Carlylean encomium on the polyphiloprogenitive Doady Purefoy:

We looked at the venerable stream not in the vivid flush of a short day that comes and departs for ever, but in the august light of abiding memories. And indeed nothing is easier for a man who has, as the phrase goes, "followed the sea" with reverence and affection, than to evoke the great spirit of the past upon the lower reaches of the Thames. The tidal current runs to and fro in its unceasing service, crowded with memories of men and ships it had borne to the rest of home or to the battles of the sea. It had known and served all the men of whom the nation is proud, from Sir Francis Drake to Sir John Franklin, knights all, titled and untitled—the great knights-errant of the sea. It had borne all the ships whose names are like jewels flashing in the night of time, from the *Golden Hind* returning with her round flanks full of treasure, to be visited by the Queen's Highness and thus pass out of the gigantic tale, to the *Erebus* and *Terror*, bound on other conquests—and that never returned. It had known the ships and the men. They had sailed from Deptford, from Greenwich, from Erith—the adventurers and the settlers; kings' ships and the ships of men on 'Change; captains, admirals, the dark interlopers of the Eastern trade, and the commissioned "generals" of East India fleets. Hunters for gold or pursuers of fame, they all had gone out on that stream, bearing the sword, and often the torch, messengers of the might within the land, bearers of a spark from the sacred fire. What greatness had not floated on the ebb of that river into the mystery of an unknown earth! . . . The dreams of men, the seed of commonwealths, the germs of empires. (pp. 66–67)

Finally, darkness falls on the *Nellie* and interrupts the apostrophe to British maritime glory. " 'And this also,' said Marlow suddenly, 'has been one of the dark places of the earth' " (p. 67).

Obviously the romantic paean we have just heard is an ironic overture to the tale we are now to hear from Marlow. Its indiscriminate celebration of the various imperial opportunities the Thames has had in a sequence of pathetic fallacies serves to comment ironically on the dark incongruities of Western enlightenment about which we are to learn. In *his* prelude, Marlow calls the imperial theme an exercise in brute force: "They grabbed what was to be got. . . . It was

just robbery with violence." What distinguishes rapine from civilization as a cause, he says, lamely, is "an idea at the back of it; not a
sentimental pretence but an idea; and an unselfish belief in the idea—
something you can set up, and bow down before, and offer sacrifice
to . . ." (pp. 69–70).

Conrad, in the early stages of his story, has set afloat a congeries
of suggestive and disturbing, even subversive, ideas: the official view
of the imperial theme, which seems to be mocked by the vague and
undiscriminating purple prose in which it is cast; the Wagnerian or
Turneresque sunset that obligingly cooperates with the breathless,
tideless Thames to provide both an overture to Marlow's tale and an
illustration of his narrative method, as he gropes for a distinction
between "rapine" and "civilization" in an idea, "something you can
set up, and bow down before, and offer sacrifice to."

The anonymous voice which has orchestrated the Turneresque
evening and the sentimental tribute to the history of the Thames
disappears until the end of the story, when Marlow again begins to
speak. If Marlow's awkward attempt to distinguish a worthwhile
imperial cause from mere "robbery with violence" does little to
illuminate the issue he is trying to define, that failure may indicate a
struggle with intrinsic limitations in the narrator's point of view and
idiom as he begins his account of an experience that challenges both
conventional morality and conventional narrative techniques. Moreover, the Marlow who begins the tale assumes, at times, the naiveté
of his younger self, who, with the heedlessness of youth, had
embarked on an adventure into the unknown.

And so Marlow's sensibility grows as he gropes his way through
the experiential and epistemological pitfalls of the account of his
extraordinary voyage, and the first step in his development as a
narrator is marked by the differences between the two cases of Roman
voyagers going up the prehistoric Thames. The first, a former
commander of a trireme, never goes ashore and merely views the
wilderness and its savages and the tiny trading stations from the
decks of his vessel. It is unhealthy, boring, nasty duty in an alien
climate, but he is sustained by reasonable hopes of getting home
again and of promotion to a highly agreeable post.

Marlow's second case comes much closer to the real issues, and
although it, too, is cast hypothetically, it is in every detail much
closer to Marlow's own experience: "Land in a swamp, march
through the woods, and in some inland post feel the savagery, the

utter savagery that had closed in around him—all the mysterious life of the wilderness that stirs in the forest, in the jungles, in the hearts of wild men" (p. 69). He goes on to say that "there's no initiation either into such mysteries," a stipulation that appears to set his ordeal apart from the ritual aspect of most of the other heroic adventures considered in this study.

The ordeal of Marlow in *Heart of Darkness* can have no initiation, principally because initiation is a social ritual founded on a shared belief in some cosmogonic experience. The initiation is essentially constructive and helps to preserve or restore the vital myth on which the community is founded. But for Marlow as well as for Kurtz, the ordeal in the dark heart of Africa is unintelligible and bears somewhat the same relation to an authentic rite of passage that the black mass does to the true mass. Throughout, it reverses or inverts the regenerative and integrating functions of ritual. Thus, Marlow's trip up the Congo to find Kurtz at the Central Station and to "rescue" him can be seen as an inversion of Aeneas's initiation in book 6 and his idyllic voyage up the Tiber in book 7 to visit the pristine community of Rome's distant ancestors. For threshold guardians like Charon and Cerberus we have the two black-clad knitters of black wool whom Marlow thinks of as Norns "guarding the door of Darkness" in a European capital, "a city that always makes me think of a whited sepulchre" (p. 73), its whiteness thus contrasting with that of Alba Longa. For the Sibyl who guides Aeneas into the illuminating darkness of the underworld we have Marlow's aunt, whose unsibylline enthusiasm has blinded her to the realities of the rapacious imperial enterprise and entranced her with what she regards as its "glorious idea" (p. 76). Where Aeneas sanctified his voyage with the ritual sacrifice of a white sow and her litter, Marlow's command of the river steamer is made possible by the death of his predecessor, Fresleven, in a sort of mock sacrifice, a quarrel with a native chief that "arose from a misunderstanding about some black hens" (p. 72). As we shall see, the nearer Marlow gets to his goal, the more insistent are the indications of disintegration and decay: the faithless, backbiting "pilgrims," the rotting hippo meat on which the cannibal crew depends for sustenance, the loss of his navigator, the increasingly acute sense of alienation and isolation in a milieu that is utterly incomprehensible to Europeans, even decent ones.

Finally, in the case of the traveler through an alien land who "has to live in the midst of the incomprehensible, which is also detestable," the phrase "the fascination of the abomination" is as close as nominal language can come to suggesting the symbolic experience at the core of *Heart of Darkness*. Oxymoronically it indicates the opposing drives deep down in the heart of man, savage or civilized, that fascinate the Karamazovs—*la nostalgie de la boue* and a lot more. Rudolf Otto's definition of the *mysterium tremendum et fascinans* illuminates and elaborates the conflicting experience of a mystical encounter with the supernatural that goes beyond Marlow's staunchly secular point of view:

> These two qualities, the daunting and the fascinating, now combine in a strange harmony of contrasts, and the resultant dual character of the numinous consciousness, to which the entire religious development bears witness, at any rate from the level of "daemonic dread" onwards, is at once the strangest and the most noteworthy phenomenon in the whole history of religion. The daemonic-divine object may appear to the mind an object of horror and dread, but at the same time it is not less something that allures with a potent charm, and the creature who trembled before it, utterly cowed and cast down, has always at the same time the impulse to turn to it, nay even to make it somehow his own. The "mystery" is for him not merely something to be wondered at but something that entrances him; and beside that in it which bewilders and confounds, he feels a something that captivates and transports him with a strange ravishment, rising often enough to the pitch of dizzy intoxication; it is the Dionysiac-element in the numen.[3]

In the rest of this chapter we shall explore the ways in which Marlow's paradigmatic young Roman in a toga, attracted and repelled by "the fascination of the abomination," acts as a surrogate figure for the adventures of Marlow himself and those of Kurtz in the heart of darkness. This investigation will reveal in what ways and to what extent Conrad's tale achieves an authentic mythic vision of a mystical encounter like that described by Otto.

Unlike Odysseus, Aeneas, Dante, or the Jesus of *Paradise Regain'd*, the object of Marlow's journey is ill defined at his setting out:

> In the street [after the interviews in the Company's offices]—I don't know why—a queer feeling came to me that I was an impostor. Odd thing that I, who used to clear out for

any part of the world at twenty-four hours' notice, with less
thought than most men give to the crossing of a street, had
a moment—I won't say of hesitation, but of startled pause,
before this commonplace affair. The best way I can explain
it to you is by saying that, for a second or two, I felt as
though, instead of going to the centre of a continent, I were
about to set off for the centre of the earth. (p. 60)

With the impetuousness and curiosity of youth, Marlow embarks on
an adventure that is, like Ishmael's, more a flight from the mundane
life on land than it is the pursuit of any recognizable destination. He
may think of himself as heading for the center of a continent, but the
tale will increasingly press the question as to whether the continent
he will explore has any center at all except in a purely geographic
sense. Even this modest goal seems problematical, as his misgivings
suggest to him that he is really "about to set off for the centre of the
earth." That, of course, is an essential experience of Homer's,
Virgil's, Dante's, and Milton's heroes, whose exalted company Charlie Marlow unwittingly joins, if only momentarily; his naiveté and
matter-of-fact self-ignorance will permit him, in the early stages of
his journey, only brief and hesitant intuitions about the deeper
implications of "this commonplace affair." His lack of purpose at the
outset of his adventures is an unheeding submission to chance that
resembles the aleatory passiveness of Byron's Don Juan or, more
closely, Melville's Ishmael. Unlike Juan, however, and like Ishmael,
Marlow has a great capacity for learning from and growing from
experience.

But Marlow is like both Juan and Ishmael and unlike his heroic
forebears in undertaking his journey without a guide. This is clearly a
requirement in a story about the experiences of a decent young
westerner testing himself against the ordeals of an incomprehensible
wilderness, but it is also a function of the fact that into this unknown
no possible guide could lead him. Instead of an Athena, a Sybil, a
Virgil, or a Holy Spirit, Marlow meets a succession of false guides
whose leadership he must reject as evil or inept. Furthermore, like
Juan and unlike the others, Marlow has no idea to guide him.
Rejecting "sentimental pretence," he nevertheless lacks, or at least
cannot find in the activities of the Company's agents, "an unselfish
belief in the idea—something you can set up, and bow down before,
and offer a sacrifice to."

Nor does anything he finds in his approach to Africa suggest that, even at the most pragmatic level, there is any controlling idea. A warship shells the jungle endlessly while its men die from malaria:

> Pop, would go one of the six-inch guns; a small flame would dart and vanish, a little white smoke would disappear, a tiny projectile would give a feeble screech—and nothing happened. Nothing could happen. There was a touch of insanity in the proceeding, a sense of lugubrious drollery in the sight; and it was not dissipated by somebody on board assuring me earnestly there was a camp of natives—he called them enemies!—hidden out of sight somewhere. (p. 62)

"*Nothing could happen.*" In the absence of any real idea, nothing can happen. There can be no acts, only activities, and Marlow witnesses a succession of scenes in a theater of the absurd in which the players repeatedly try to invest their futile activities or inactivities with meaning through the perversion of language. The natives allegedly encamped in the impenetrable jungle shelled by the French warship are "enemies." Their enslaved and dying counterparts in the Company's operations are "workers," whom Marlow finds when he steps "into the gloomy circle of some Inferno" (p. 81). A white man Marlow encounters on the trail explains that he is in charge of "upkeep of the trails," but the only sign Marlow can find of his performance is "a nigger with a bullet-hole in his forehead" (p. 86).

There is a corresponding discrepancy between the commercial and humanitarian goals of the Company and its actual performance. There is a rigid hierarchy in the managerial cadre, yet every official seems to be plotting against his fellows. The hierarchical structure, clearly essential to the effective functioning of any such enterprise, is mocked by one of Conrad's most brilliant touches, as the manager of the Central Station confounds disputes over precedence at meals: "when annoyed at meal-times by the constant quarrels of the white men about precedence, he ordered an immense round table to be made, for which a special house had to be built. This was the station's mess-room. Where he sat was the first place—the rest were nowhere" (p. 74). With "no genius for organizing, for initiative, or for order even," the manager acquires power from his capacity to "inspire uneasiness" (p. 73), a capacity reflected in his negation of the customary associations of the round table.

What Marlow witnesses in most of his encounters with the

officers of the Company is the systematic alienation of language and other signs from their conventional meanings. He turns his back on the station and concentrates all his energies on the practical task of raising and rehabilitating the steamer:

> In that way only it seemed to me I could keep my hold on the redeeming facts of life. Still, one must look about sometimes; and then I saw this station, these men strolling aimlessly about in the sunshine of the yard. I asked myself sometimes what it all meant. They wandered here and there with their absurd long staves in their hands, like a lot of faithless pilgrims, bewitched inside a rotten fence. The word "ivory" rang in the air, was whispered, was sighed. You would think they were praying to it. A taint of imbecile rapacity blew through it all, like a whiff from some corpse. (p. 89)

Marlow tries to interpret the imbecilic spectacle: "I asked myself sometimes what it all meant," but the reality eludes his assumption that there must be meaning here, in this culminating instance of nonmeaning. Coherence in every sense of the word—purpose, human associations toward shared ends, intelligibility, a discernible order—does not exist. The pilgrims believe in nothing but material self-advancement. Unlike Odysseus' men, seduced by the Lotus-eaters or bewitched by Circe into losing the paramount motive of the *Odyssey*, the memory of home, these characters have no home, no point of departure or return, and they have bewitched themselves, obsessed with a rapacious desire for ivory which they do nothing to acquire. Thus even the conventional goal of the enterprise is a mere phantasm, and the word *ivory* they constantly invoke no longer stands for anything but their self-induced rapacity. As a signifier shorn of its meaning, with no referential reality, the word hangs in the air, an impotent magical invocation. Without coherence, without meaning, without a goal, *nothing can happen*; indeed the plotting of the pilgrims prevents anything from happening. If nothing can happen and the activities of the members of the Company have no intelligible meaning, then it inevitably follows that language as they use it is no longer language, but an impotent or fraudulent fiction. Even the goods used to trade for ivory are valueless—"rubbishy cottons, beads, and brass-wire" (p. 83)—and of no imaginable benefit to the natives. When a grass hut full of this trash burns down, the whites arbitrarily beat up an African who happened to be nearby: "They said he had caused the fire in some way" (p. 90). This rough justice is expounded by one of the more colorfully idiotic "pilgrims": "What a row the brute makes. . . . Serve him right. Transgression—punishment—bang! Pitiless, pitiless. That's the only way. This will prevent all conflagrations for the future" (p. 93). Such abuse of power is a kind of insane magic, like a later episode in which the white men on the steamer spray the jungle with rifle fire and succeed only in obscuring the treacherous river with smoke, a telling emblem of the obfuscation of meaning in word and deed that characterizes everything they do.

Two things save Marlow's sanity in this cruel farce of incomprehensible unreality, outside which "the silent wilderness struck me as something great and invincible, like evil or truth, waiting patiently for the passing away of this fantastic invasion" (p. 89). One, as we have already noted, is the "surface truth" of repairing the tinpot steamer. In recovering it from the muddy rot of the riverbed and improvising repairs without the spare parts that are being held downriver, Marlow is creating an instrument with a limited but intelligible goal: to get to Kurtz. The final arrival of the essential rivets makes it possible to fasten the plates of the wrecked vessel. At the news of their coming Marlow and his fellow worker, a widowed boilermaker with six children at home, dance a jig in celebration on the deck of the steamer. Their festive, shared delight over something as mundane as rivets Marlow tries to dismiss with the commonsense remark, "I don't know why we behaved like lunatics" (p. 97), but their lunacy is utterly different from the imbecile rapacity of the pilgrims, with their invocation of "ivory." Rivets unite. Ivory disintegrates. Rivets are essential to the restoration of a ship, and the ship is essential to Marlow's growing interest in reaching and rescuing Kurtz, whom the backbiting and plotting officials of the Company are, for once, united in hating. Without the rivets, "nothing could happen." The rivets make significant action possible, and the unequivocal identification of the word and the object marks Marlow's recreation of linguistic coherence, while the operation of the vessel itself requires a cooperation that implies cultural revival. Rescued from sabotage and primeval slime, the tinpot steamer takes its place among a host of vessels of epic importance: Odysseus' raft; Aeneas's ships; and, more especially, Charon's leaky boat, Dante's figurative "little bark"; Juan's shipwrecked *Trinidada;* Melville's *Pequod;* the raft of Huck and Jim; and countless others.

Yet, however, honestly restored and skillfully navigated by Marlow, however admirable his conception of his mission to Kurtz, the steamer in *Heart of Darkness* is on a quest that is ineradicably ambiguous. Despite the integrity of its skipper and cannibal crew, it is a *Narrenschiff,* its European passengers bringing nothing but rapacity into the wilderness and learning nothing from it. Marlow, on the other hand, courageous, restrained, and ingenious, is alone capable of the ultimate journey, the mystical ordeal that he tries gropingly to suggest to his listeners early in the tale. Of his devotion to helping Kurtz he says:

> He was just a word for me. I did not see the man in the name any more than you do. Do you see him? Do you see the story? Do you see anything? It seems to me I am trying to tell you a dream—making a vain attempt, because no relation of a dream can convey the dream-sensation, that commingling of absurdity, surprise, and bewilderment in a tremor of struggling revolt, that notion of being captured by the incredible which is of the very essence of dreams. (pp. 94–95)

As we saw earlier, Marlow is handicapped in his rite of passage by the fact that there is no ritual to guide him in his encounter with the heart of darkness; that the ultimate experience is not an illumination but a dark vision of human degradation; that the light by which Kurtz leads him is extinct; that, as he said earlier of the young Roman, "There's no initiation either into such mysteries" (p. 69). His ordeal, then, is an ordeal of individuation without any sustaining or authenticating myth and without any ritual to endow it with a more than purely personal coherence. He exemplifies the plight of man in a secular society that has discarded the encounter with the numinous as unscientific nonsense.

In Marlow Conrad has devised a modern hero with all the strengths that decency, humanity, and technological acumen can provide. In the moral chaos he encounters among the rapacious hollow men who exemplify racist, imperialistic capitalism at its worst, Marlow is forced to survive by creating a standard of values that depends ultimately on his fidelity both to Kurtz and to what Kurtz represents. His attachment to Kurtz depends only in part on the latter's celebrated humanitarianism. It also depends on his contempt for Kurtz's enemies, the devotees of "the flabby devil." He overhears the manager of the Central Station conniving with his uncle:

> "The extraordinary series of delays is not my fault. I did my best." The fat man sighed. "Very sad." "And the pestiferous absurdity of his talk," continued the other; "he bothered me enough when he was here. 'Each station should be like a beacon on the road towards better things, a centre for trade, of course, but also for humanizing, improving, instructing.' Conceive you—that ass! And he wants to be manager! No, it's—" Here he got choked by excessive indignation, and I lifted my head the least bit. I was surprised to see how near they were—right under me. I could have spat upon their hats. They were looking on the ground, absorbed in thought. The manager was switching his leg with a slender twig: his sagacious relative lifted his head, "You have been well since you came out this time?" he asked. The other gave a start. "Who? I? Oh! Like a charm—like a charm. But the rest—oh, my goodness! All sick. They die so quick, too, that I haven't the time to send them out of the country—it's incredible!" "Hm. Just so," grunted the uncle. "Ah! my boy, trust to this—I say, trust to this." I saw him extend his short flipper of an arm for a gesture that took in the forest, the creek, the mud, the river—seemed to beckon with a dishonouring flourish before the sunlit face of the land a treacherous appeal to the lurking death, to the hidden evil, to the profound darkness of its heart. (pp. 101–02)

The manager's uncle is leader of the Eldorado Exploring Expedition, "reckless without hardihood, greedy without audacity, and cruel without courage" (p. 87). Like nearly all the other European traders in *Heart of Darkness* he is engaged in an enterprise that is a perversion or inversion of Aeneas's career. The dishonorable gesture of affection toward his nephew (like all the pilgrims, he is childless) is a malign parody of Aeneas's relation to Iulus, while his ghastly invocation of the death-dealing wilderness as something to "trust to" may remind us of Anchises' famous proclamation to his son of the imperial Roman ethos:

tu regere imperio populos, Romane, memento
(haec tibi erunt artes) pacique imponere morem,
parcere subiectis et debellare superbos.

Remember thou, O Roman, to rule the nations with thy
sway—these shall be thy arts—to crown peace with law,
to spare the humble and to tame in war the proud.

[6.851–53]

The voyage upriver to the Inner Station confronts Marlow with
increasingly inscrutable phenomena compared to which the banal evil
of the pilgrims is a relatively simple matter. Physically, the voyage is
a blind movement through an occult medium: "Imagine a blindfolded
man set to drive a van over a bad road" (pp. 103–04). As narrative,
the blindfolded voyage suggests the problems of telling a tale without
precedent:

> We were wanderers on a prehistoric earth, on an earth that
> wore the aspect of an unknown planet. We could have
> fancied ourselves the first of men taking possession of an
> accursed inheritance, to be subdued at the cost of profound
> anguish and of excessive toil. But suddenly, as we struggled
> round a bend, there would be a glimpse of rush walls, of
> peaked grass-roofs, a burst of yells, a whirl of black limbs, a
> mass of hands clapping, of feet stamping, of bodies swaying,
> of eyes rolling, under the droop of heavy and motionless
> foliage. The steamer toiled along slowly on the edge of a
> black and incomprehensible frenzy. The prehistoric man
> was cursing us, praying to us, welcoming us—who could
> tell? We were cut off from the comprehension of our
> surroundings; we glided past like phantoms, wondering and
> secretly appalled, as sane men would be before an enthusi-
> astic outbreak in a madhouse. We could not understand
> because we were too far and could not remember, because
> we were travelling in the night of first ages, of those ages
> that are gone, leaving hardly a sign—and no memories.
> (p. 105)

The white man's steamer makes it possible to penetrate "the night of
first ages" without comprehending it, and he stares at the contradictory and inscrutable behavior of the savages in bewilderment, without the intellectual equipment to understand what he sees; stares at

gestures—are they curses or prayers?—that his dualistic mentality can read only as mutually exclusive and blank contradictions. Marlow hints, nonetheless, that modern man has lost touch with a primitive power that might have helped him to understand the savages. So, unlike other epic voyagers, the nearer Marlow travels toward his goal, the more incomprehensible are his experiences.

Yet at times he has sympathetic intuitions, hints of a kinship with these savages:

> The earth seemed unearthly. We are accustomed to look upon the shackled form of a conquered monster, but there—there you could look at a thing monstrous and free. It was unearthly, and the men were—No, they were not inhuman. Well, you know, that was the worst of it—this suspicion of their not being inhuman. It would come slowly to one. They howled and leaped, and spun, and made horrid faces; but what thrilled you was just the thought of their humanity—like yours—the thought of your remote kinship with this wild and passionate uproar. Ugly. Yes, it was ugly enough; but if you were man enough you would admit to yourself that there was in you just the faintest trace of response to the terrible frankness of that noise, a dim suspicion of there being a meaning in it which you—you so remote from the night of first ages—could comprehend. And why not? The mind of man is capable of anything—because everything is in it, all the past as well as all the future. What was there after all? Joy, fear, sorrow, devotion, valour, rage—who can tell?—but truth—truth stripped of its cloak of time. (pp. 105–06)

Here Marlow, who is in no way bookish, seems to be groping toward an understanding of primitive archetypal experiences like those explored in *The Golden Bough* and a plethora of studies in comparative anthropology and mythology that appeared at the turn of the century, when *Heart of Darkness* was published. But both his testimony to the "truth" of savage feeling and his response to it are blocked by the contradictory truth that a man "must meet that truth with his own true stuff—with his own inborn strength. . . . I hear; I admit, but I have a voice too, and for good and evil mine is the speech that cannot be silenced" (p. 106). As Jacques Berthoud observes, "This *antithetical* conception of reality—in which the recognition of a basic

truth prompts the affirmation of a counter-truth—is at the centre of
Heart of Darkness."[4]

Marlow's antithesis is more complicated than he seems to recognize. The simple opposition between savage and civilized behavior is qualified by the extraordinary restraint shown by the steamer's cannibal crew. They are starving because the pilgrims have thrown their store of rotten hippo meat overboard:

> Why in the name of all the gnawing devils of hunger they
> didn't go for us—they were thirty to five—and have a good
> tuck-in for once, amazes me now when I think of it. They
> were big powerful men, with not much capacity to weigh
> the consequences, with courage, with strength, even yet,
> though their skins were no longer glossy and their muscles
> no longer hard. And I saw that something restraining, one
> of those human secrets that baffle probability, had come
> into play there. . . . Yes; I looked at them as you would on
> any human being, with a curiosity of their impulses, mo-
> tives, capacities, weaknesses, when brought to the test of an
> inexorable physical necessity. Restraint! What possible re-
> straint? Was it superstition, disgust, patience, fear—or
> some kind of primitive honour? No fear can stand up to
> hunger, no patience can wear it out, disgust simply does not
> exist where hunger is; and as to superstition, beliefs, and
> what you may call principles, they are less than chaff in a
> breeze. Don't you know the devilry of lingering starvation,
> its exasperating torment, its black thoughts, its sombre and
> brooding ferocity? Well, I do. It takes a man all his inborn
> strength to fight hunger properly. (pp. 112–13)

Marlow's puzzlement in confronting the restraint of the starving cannibals marks a significant stage in his inward journey into the heart of darkness. In earlier stages he could expose the discrepancy between words and reality, as he reflected on "enemies," "criminals," and all the other misnaming of a brutal, rapacious, and ineffectual enterprise. The civilized white man, he assumes, is alone capable of the "inborn strength" to combat the ultimate ordeal of starvation. Cannibals, so designated, are theoretically incapable of restraint. And yet most of the white men he encounters have no restraint, while the cannibals refrain inexplicably from exercising their prerogatives. What he implies is that cannibals have taboos fundamental to a system of values mocked by the degenerate whites. Remarks which Marlow overhears from the manager of the Inner Station make this clear:

> They approached again, just as the manager was saying, "No one, as far as I know, unless a species of wandering trader—a pestilential fellow, snapping ivory from the natives." Who was it they were talking about now? I gathered in snatches that this was some man supposed to be in Kurtz's district, and of whom the manager did not approve. "We will not be free from unfair competition till one of these fellows is hanged for an example," he said. "Certainly," grunted the other; "get him hanged! Why not? Anything—anything can be done in this country." (p. 91)

"Anything can be done in this country." And the white men do it indiscriminately, while, as Tony Tanner observes, "for the most part cannibalism is not indiscriminate and is usually highly ritualised in cases of extreme 'meat hunger.' "[5]

If, as the manager says, "anything can be done in this country," we confront, once again, the anomaly that where there are no rules and no shared purposes nothing can be done. The story of the Company has, therefore, no narrative line: its "bewitched" and "faithless" pilgrims are immobilized in an eternal present of impotent plotting. With no authentic needs or passions they are infinitely more savage than the hungry cannibals and the other passionate Africans with whom Marlow increasingly identifies. The role of Marlow, both as narrator and as voyager, is to define and pursue a goal in defiance of a world where nothing could happen. The voyage to rescue Kurtz, the reconstruction and navigation of the sabotaged boat, the supervision of the cannibal crew, are all part of the creation of a cosmos out of chaos and a rehabilitation of meaning and language.

Marlow's climactic meeting with Kurtz finally destroys the antithetical pattern that has governed *Heart of Darkness*. The self-proclaimed emissary of light, a champion of nineteenth-century European liberalism, has proved to be more brutal and rapacious than his repulsive fellow officials. For all the ideals he proclaimed, Kurtz, drawn into participation in "unspeakable" deeds and far more savage than the savages, allowed himself to be treated as a god.

At this point in the story Conrad introduces a curious surrogate narrator, the young "harlequin" Russian wandering in the wilderness, who has devotedly tended Kurtz in his illnesses, even though Kurtz threatened to kill him. Kurtz's murderous megalomania, unlimited rapacity, and unbridled egotism, the logical extension of the racist economic imperialism of the Company, do not bother this innocent in motley, and Marlow, for a while, is captivated by him:

> The glamour of youth enveloped his particoloured rags, his destitution, his loneliness, the essential desolation of his futile wanderings. For months—for years—his life hadn't been worth a day's purchase; and there he was gallantly, thoughtlessly alive, to all appearances indestructible solely by virtue of his few years and his unreflecting audacity. I was seduced into something like admiration—like envy. Glamour urged him on, glamour kept him unscathed. He surely wanted nothing from the wilderness but space to breathe in and to push on through. His need was to exist and to move onwards at the greatest possible risk, and with a maximum of privation. If the absolutely pure, uncalculating, unpractical spirit of adventure had ever ruled a human being, it ruled this bepatched youth. I almost envied him the possession of this modest and clear flame. It seemed to have consumed all thought of self so completely, that even while he was talking to you, you forgot that it was he—the man before your eyes—who had gone through these things. I did not envy him his devotion to Kurtz, though. He had not meditated over it. It came to him, and he accepted it with a sort of eager fatalism. I must say that to me it appeared about the most dangerous thing in every way he had come upon so far. (p. 129)

This young, cosmopolitan *naïf* exemplifies idealism and self-abnegation. Utterly without egotism, he surrenders himself unreflectingly to the mesmerizing power of Kurtz. He is a secular example of God's fool, and the privations he suffers in the wilderness cannot fail to remind us of Milton's hero in *Paradise Regain'd*, with the radical distinction, of course, that, if he is entirely unegocentric, he is also entirely lacking in a mature self. He serves in the story as an example of a youth of great potential deprived of the cultural and moral influences that might shape his life toward some significant goal. His uncritical devotion to Kurtz is Conrad's intimation of the process by which, in the absence of positive values, the idealistic and brave and innocent will submit themselves to the worst of leaders. The youth's devotion to Kurtz anticipates the mentality that made possible the rise of Hitler. "In a large historical perspective the evolutionary optimism of the mid-century can be seen as having weakened the two main lines of demarcation which had traditionally defined man's estate; there was the upper one which separated man from God and the angels; and there was the lower one which separated him from the animals."[6]

In the case of Kurtz, where secular idealism has usurped the place of religion and myth, the illusion of godlike power induces, in Jung's terms, inflation of the ego. Supposing that he is capable of anything, Kurtz's regression is inevitable. While Marlow decides to protect Kurtz's reputation, because he had judged himself, his own penetration of the heart of darkness leaves him and us wondering whether darkness has a heart or even a center. In his rite of passage Marlow has won through to a cautious, tentative decision to adhere to whatever standards of decency still have validity—above all, to self-restraint—and to avoid any further interrogations of darkness.

Ian Watt provides an illuminating commentary on Conrad's stance in relation to the dominant ideals of his period:

> From the traditional religious point of view this faith in man's self-propelled spiritual ascent was essentially heretical; nevertheless the idea that the world's salvation could be expected from a boundless increase in individual development had been supported by all the strongest new forces in nineteenth-century life: by the developing imperatives of Romantic individualism, with its Faustian ideal of absolute liberation from religious, social, and ethical norms in the pursuit of experience. . . .[7]

The climax of Marlow's rite of passage confronts him with a moral dilemma that encompasses most of the central issues of the tale. Back in Brussels he summons up the courage to call on Kurtz's fiancée and give her some of Kurtz's papers, including his report to the Society for the Suppression of Savage Customs, without, of course, its final prescription, "Exterminate all the brutes!" Moved partly by the bereaved young woman's passionate belief in Kurtz's noble purpose and her insatiable need to know something about his final moments, Marlow, who detests lies above all things, nevertheless forces himself to tell her that Kurtz's dying word was her name. Given his deep sympathetic need to spare her the horrible truth,

Marlow's lie is more than an act of humanity. In a world where, as he has discovered, truth is often darkly enigmatic and simple decency more a matter of luck than of moral fortitude, his lie about Kurtz is closer to truth than an unvarnished and literal account of Kurtz's degradation could be. In saving Kurtz's reputation, Marlow, aware of his own responses to "the fascination of the abomination," pays tribute to what he has come to see as Kurtz's final, heroic confrontation with the dark horror of his soul, the darkness into which his facile, secular idealism has been transformed by the alienating power of the utter savagery he encountered in the unknown heart of the Dark continent, a power that overwhelmed his defenses and took his own heart captive: "Both the diabolic love and the unearthly hate of the mysteries it had penetrated fought for the possession of that soul satiated with primitive emotions, avid of lying fame, of sham distinction, of all appearances of success and power" (p. 146).

Yet, as Kurtz dies, Marlow sees "on that *ivory* face the expression of sombre pride, of ruthless power, of craven terror—of an intense and hopeless despair" (p. 147) (my italics). Having abandoned in this final apocalyptic moment all his lying pretences, Marlow implies, Kurtz ultimately reconciles the opposing forces that have contended for his soul in his last, whispered exclamation, in which, after the most extreme discrepancies, language and reality are reunited. Although his "ivory face" at that moment may represent the equally hollow benign and malignant illusions that have destroyed him, these words express "some kind of belief" to which Marlow can respond:

> True, he had made that last stride, he had stepped over the edge, while I had been permitted to draw back my hesitating foot. And perhaps in this is the whole difference; perhaps all the wisdom, and all truth, and all sincerity, are just compressed into that inappreciable moment of time in which we step over the threshold of the invisible. (p. 149)

Recent studies have proposed ways in which *Heart of Darkness* traces mythic motifs like those in the *Aeneid* and the *Inferno*. While the correspondences are mostly conspicuous and undeniable, in *Heart of Darkness* they mark stages in a heroic ordeal that is utterly devoid of the integrating, overarching mythic and ritual structures that endow the journeys of Aeneas and Dante with cosmogonic value. Although such motifs as threshold guardians, sacrificial victims, descents to the center of the earth, infernal rivers, and the final passage from life to death and return are present in all three works, only in *Heart of Darkness* do they have a predominantly negative and ironic function. Ian Watt has given us a salutary warning against construing these parallels too systematically or too simply:

> Several critics have made the two knitters a primary basis for a large-scale symbolic interpretation . . . in which Marlow's whole journey becomes a version of the traditional descent into hell, such as that in the sixth book of Virgil's *Aeneid,* and in Dante's *Inferno.* This kind of critical interpretation assumes that the symbolic reference of the verbal sign must be closed rather than open, and that it arises, not from the natural and inherent associations of the object, but from a pre-established body of ideas, stories, or myths.[8]

While sharing in the archetype of the dark journey and extending the Virgilian ironies of Aeneas's emergence from the underworld through the ivory gates of illusion, the distinction of *Heart of Darkness* consists far more in Conrad's transformation of the Congo experience as an ironic version of the quest romance into a modern novel that commands our belief than on the skill with which he assimilates the wide range of motifs in his epic models. That the knitters of black wool are *not* Fates, the leaky steamer is *not* Charon's bark, Kurtz's intended is *not* a shade is as important to Conrad's secular symbolic mode as is the fact that they also have a tentative status as quasi-epic motifs.

The distinction is clear in the final image of Marlow, lean, yellow with old fevers, sitting cross-legged with his back to the *Nellie's* jigger and his hands in the lotus position, a figure who has no counterpart in the other works we have considered. Yet this oriental note, depicting Marlow as a meditating yogi, is an innovation of the utmost importance, because it marks his final detachment not only from the memory of Kurtz, now consigned to oblivion, but also from the banal and trivial preoccupations of the ordinary European. Although the response of the anonymous narrator to his shipmate's extraordinary tale, "We have lost the ebb," may seem as obtuse as his opening tribute to the imperial glories of British maritime enterprise, his concluding reflection that "the tranquil waterway of the Thames seemed to lead into the heart of an immense darkness" reverses his earlier facile optimism of the Thames as a bearer of light.

Conclusion

Yet, yet a moment, one dim Ray of Light
Indulge, dread Chaos and eternal Night!
Of darkness visible so much be lent,
As half to shew, half veil the deep Intent.
Ye Pow'rs! whose Mysteries restor'd I sing,
To whom Time bears me on his rapid wing,
Suspend a while your Force inertly strong,
Then take at once the Poet and the Song.

Pope, *Dunciad* IV

We have considered eight major works in the epic tradition from Homer to Conrad, a span of almost three millennia. Each of them has been an account of crucial moments in the quest for self-discovery. In that quest they range from unequivocal success to evident failure, and between the extremes we have found examples either equivocal or enigmatic. The first four works, in the classical or Christian tradition, have specifically invoked the structures and symbols of ancient myths. The last four avoid the explicit use of myth.

Except for Odysseus, all the heroes under consideration are what Melville calls *isolatoes:* they are without wives and families, and their parental relationships are tenuous at best. Venus is Aeneas's *mater abscondita;* his father, a virtual relic whose main role is to introduce his son to a vision of the new Rome that is to become Troy's *mater antiqua,* an empire in the founding of which he will have a purely instrumental role. Dante's initiatory passage through Hell is guided by a Virgil as incapable as Aeneas of realizing the ultimate vision. More solitary than any other hero, Jesus, at a key moment, reflects on the fact that after "four times ten days . . . Wand'ring this woody maze" he is hungry: "Where will this end?"

In the case of Odysseus, Aeneas, Dante, and Jesus, we know where it will end. In each case the controlling myth is familiar to us if not to the hero.

217

In Wordsworth, Byron, Melville, and Conrad, there is no controlling myth. "Where will this end?" is a question that engages the reader as pressingly as it does the heroes of the earlier epics. Wordsworth tries to make his physical and mental wanderings into a shaped quest reflecting the growth of the poet's mind. Byron systematically demolishes the promises of fulfillment and closure central to the epic mode. With a Ulyssean boldness condemned by Dante, Melville projects a titanic voyage encompassing the oceans of the world and simultaneously annihilating the epic motif of the return home; while Conrad, in his intense novella, makes even the goal of Marlow's voyage problematic.

Thus the first four works we have considered emphasize points of departure and crucial moments of deliverance or arrival, under the control of Greek, Roman, and Christian myths, while the remaining four begin with arbitrary points of departure and lack clearly defined conclusions.

This is not to say that Wordsworth, Byron, Melville, and Conrad are utterly disorientated in their narratives. Rather, they are recording quests that in many ways are more challenging than those of their predecessors, quests undertaken in milieus that lack the definition and orientation of traditional epic. There is no fate; no community to restore; no dynasty to establish, no soul to educate; no redeeming mission to divine. In narrative structure the later works tend to return to their beginnings, or at least to have less than epic impact on the world's business. Whatever vision is achieved tends to be purely personal and private.

More personal, private, and—one might add—more intimate. Homer, Virgil, Dante, and Milton address themselves to a public audience that shares their assumptions about reality, about the paramount importance of Troy, Rome, and the redeeming intervention of Christ. The reality of their narratives is authenticated by divinity. The ultimate spiritual or political worth of their ordeals is not to be questioned, and, if the hero sometimes falls short of the values established in his epic, his failure works in a negative way to affirm them. The heroic heirs of the great epic poets bear the burden of a drive for self-discovery without the aid of objective, authenticating tokens.

As Marlow declares of the plight of Roman colonists in prehistoric Britain, "There's no initiation." Rowing up the unknown Thames past chartless forests inhabited by savages, the civilized

Roman is topographically alienated and culturally isolated from his milieu. If he has to leave his trireme and go ashore he is utterly disoriented. No initiation means no mode of translating his bewildering impressions into anything approaching comprehension. He has no way of knowing what lies ahead in space or time. His assumptions about human behavior are useless in his encounters with savages whose customs and language in no way correspond to his own. Where Virgil, as the master of those who know, can translate the varied grotesquerie of the damned into language and values that Dante can understand as they penetrate a highly structured and rationalized Hell, Marlow, like Kurtz, must confront "the fascination of the abomination" with nothing to guide him but inadequate hypotheses and conjectures. For the "faithless pilgrims" who have been corrupted by greed there is but one index of value: ivory. Kurtz acquires it by force and has locked himself into the circle of the violent. The others, who lust after it ineffectually, are endlessly involved in fraud. Anchises' proclamation of Roman discipline and restraint, which seeks to subjugate the proud and spare the humble, has yielded to a brutal economic imperialism that Marlow characterizes as "mere robbery with violence." The political and cultural genius of Rome has been translated, under the King of the Belgians, into a pitiless, ineffectual despoliation. As we have seen, the unmitigated rapacity of the Company's agents inverts and annihilates linguistic conventions so that words and signs are divorced from normal meanings and values. The strain apparent in Marlow's sometimes hyperbolic attempts to communicate the incomprehensible is an index of his heroism, just as "rivets" marks his respect for "surface truths."

The corrupt metamorphosis of language in *Heart of Darkness,* which corresponds to the universal entropy of the jungle and the unrestrained human evil where "anything is possible," marks the ultimate degradation of epic language and epic conventions. A comparison with Odysseus' experience illuminates the distinction, as he moves from the language and behavior appropriate to a just war to an act of genocide that precipitates him into a monstrous milieu that repeatedly jeopardizes his habitual sense of self. Lost in a terror-filled waste of ocean, he is nearer the truth than he realizes when he identifies himself to the Cyclops as Nobody. The nadir of his alienation occurs when he finds himself on the island of the bewitching Circe, which Homer describes as "the navel of the sea." He is thus at the center of a circle the perimeter of which is unknown, and this point is his "heart of darkness," the center of his twelve adventures between Troy and Ithaca. To his fearful and despairing comrades he declares the impossibility of continuing the voyage until they have learned from the witch Circe where they are. Homeric scholars have ignored, as far as I can tell, the etymological link between *Kirke* and *kirkos* or *krikos*, meaning "circle." At this midpoint of his adventures Odysseus' alienation is emphasized by Circe's informing him that he must visit the land of the dead, consult the seer Tiresias, and return to Aegea. Only by traveling to the perimeter of the world can he escape her charmed circle and reorient himself in visiting the shades of his great forebears, from whom he learns about both his past and his future. The *nekuia*, then, is at once the initiatory ritual and turning point of this hero's journey, just as Virgil makes the descent to the underworld the central experience of Aeneas's voyage. Dante's encounter with the Angel of Peace in the central canto of the *Purgatorio* (17) seems to function in the same way, as does Jesus' summary dismissal of political and military power and wealth at the end of *Paradise Regain'd*, in a central and decisive rejection of Satan's strongest temptation:

> But to guide Nations in the way of truth
> By saving Doctrine, and from error lead
> To know, and knowing worship God aright,
> Is yet more Kingly; this attracts the Soul,
> Governs the inner man, the nobler part;
> That other o'er the body only reigns,
> And oft by force, which to a generous mind
> So reigning can be no sincere delight.
> Besides, to give a Kingdom hath been thought
> Greater and nobler done, and to lay down
> Far more magnanimous than to assume.
> Riches are needless then, both for themselves,
> And for thy reason why they should be sought,
> To gain a Scepter, oftest better miss't.

[2.473–86]

Perhaps it is reasonable to see in these four central, critical moments the hero's rejection of egotistical drives and submission to transpersonal values that authenticate the Self. "Christ," as Jung observes, "exemplifies the archetype of the self."[1]

The restoring of an initial state is an "eschatological" one ("the end looks to the beginning, and contrariwise"). This is exactly what happens in the individuation process, whether it take the form of a Christian transformation ("Except ye become as little children") . . . or a psychological process of development in which the original propensity to wholeness becomes a conscious happening.[2]

Jung's reference to Heraclitus supports Campbell's view, with which this study began—that epic "marks the dark interior passage from tragedy to comedy" in the ordeals through which the hero moves from ego to self.

Thus the *Odyssey, Aeneid, Inferno,* and *Paradise Regain'd* alike begin with an ending and end with a beginning. In each the narrative point of departure is defined by a destroyed city, a ruined culture, a hero ignorant of his true identity, whose mission is the ordeal of self-individuation in the service of cultural redemption. These four works, tracing the hero's passage from fallen Troy, corrupted Rome, and fallen Eden, imply from their beginning a redeemed Ithaka, the founding of Italy, the redemption of Rome, and the liberation of Jerusalem from the Roman yoke at the same time that their heroes discover themselves in the process of defining their redemptive public roles. Each work is also controlled and energized by a myth that expresses symbolically the reconciliation and mystical integration of opposing forces at the heart of the heroic ordeal, forces which the hero meets in the middle of his life journey when he begins to assume his private and public destiny.

Our four modern examples in this epic tradition all lack the prevailing myths that have authenticated the roles of previous culture heroes. While they, too, all start with fallen civilizations—the maelstrom of nineteenth-century London, the political and social corruption of Europe, an American port that is a mere base and market for the whaling industry, and a "whited sepulchre" (Brussels) that functions only as a base for rapacious capitalistic enterprises in Africa—no return or renewal of the culture is implied when the hero starts on his journey and turns his back on the city. His cultural exile carries no promise of cultural renewal; the best he can hope for is to achieve some degree of self-knowledge. Without myth he journeys through milieus that are inherently enigmatic, indefinable, full of contradiction. This experiential confusion is reflected in the structure and style of the books. Wordsworth's Miltonic style intensifies the reader's impression of *The Prelude's* fundamentally un-Miltonic nature, while Byron, often hilariously, exploits the total incapacity of his culture to sustain an epic vision. Like *The Prelude* and *Don Juan*, *Moby-Dick* and *Heart of Darkness* reveal a split between narrator and hero of which we find traces in the *Aeneid*. The absence of critical rites of passage in these later works, by which the traditional hero is initiated into the authenticating myths of his culture, inflicts upon him a fundamental confusion of identity that is marked by spasmodic alternations in point of view. His sense of his individuality is constantly jeopardized by the fluid milieu in which he acts. In response, he projects on the phenomenological a largely subjective reality, like Wordsworth; or, like Byron, alternates between sympathetic identification with and satirical rejection of his hero; or, like Ishmael, becomes for a long time the helpless instrument of the monomaniacal Ahab; or, like Marlow, is bewitched by the diabolical Kurtz. Meanwhile, the symmetries of epic form and style that have helped to authenticate the mythic reality behind the traditional epic have vanished. Wordsworth claims for his poem a structure that it plainly lacks, while Byron, having abandoned hope of closure or completeness in his interminable poem, was prevented by death from carrying it on indefinitely. In its leviathan expansiveness, *Moby-Dick* risks shapelessness, while Marlow's condensed, introspective, and sometimes incoherent attempt to render "the fascination of the abomination" threatens to become a purely private meditation on an almost incommunicable experience. Jung's comment on Christian individuation is germane:

> So far as I can see, no relevant objection could be raised from the Christian point of view against anyone accepting the task of individuation imposed on us by nature, and the recognition of our wholeness or completeness as a binding personal commitment. If he does this consciously and intentionally, he avoids all the unhappy consequences of repressed individuation. In other words, if he voluntarily takes the burden of completeness on himself, he need not find it "happening" to him against his will in a negative form. This is as much as to say that anyone who is destined to descend into a deep pit had better set about it with all the

necessary precautions rather than risk falling into the hole backwards.[3]

Heroes of traditional epic take various precautions when descending into the "deep pit" that is central to their ordeals. In visiting the dead, Odysseus is armed with vital information about the necessary sacrificial rituals; the Sibyl of Cumae informs Aeneas of the location and appropriate use of the golden bough; Virgil prepares Dante for the various stages of his infernal travels with information about the structure and meaning of stages in the vortex of Hell. So, too, Jesus performs a peripatetic meditation as he enters the desert:

> Thought following thought, and step by step led on,
> He enter'd now the bordering Desert wild,
> And with dark shades and rocks environ'd round,
> His holy meditations thus pursu'd.
>
> [1.192–95]

In contrast, our other heroes begin their journeys whimsically or unreflectingly, with little regard to purpose or goal. Wordsworth, led by a wandering cloud, simply turns his back on London. Don Juan's course is purely a matter of impulse or chance. Ishmael and Marlow are driven by centrifugal impulses to embark on voyages about which they make little effort to inform themselves. Ishmael casually sees the Fates "cajoling me into the delusion that it was a choice resulting from my own free will and discriminating judgment" (p. 29), while Marlow finds himself fascinated like a silly little bird by a snake as he gazes on a map of the Congo (p. 71). The vagrant impulses that drive these characters suggest that the modern hero is heedlessly venturesome. He is not a wayfarer but a wanderer; hence his journey will have a highly accidental, indeterminate character, and a more or less problematical ending. Chance stopped *Don Juan,* but it is hard to imagine a more negative final episode in the hero's career than his encounter with "her frolic Grace, Fitz-Fulke." In the ascent of Snowdon, Wordsworth employs every descriptive, poetic, and rhetorical device in his formidable repertoire to convince us that what is essentially a random experience is the thematic and structural conclusion of an integrated poem; but if we ask ourselves whether this grand visionary experience is essentially more comprehensive and final than some of the other great passages in *The Prelude,* the answer, I believe, must be no.

On the other hand, Melville and Conrad seem to have succeeded in the formidable task of creating fictions in the absence of organizing or integrating myths and a high degree of randomness that do succeed in winning through to ultimate and concluding visions. Within the symbolic context of *Moby-Dick*, which in a way creates its own implicit myth, Ishmael enacts and achieves a final experience of the numinous in a powerful reconciliation of opposites marked by the coffin-lifebuoy and his rescue by the child-bereft *Rachel*. While the end of *Heart of Darkness* does not develop the numinous vision of Melville's book, Marlow's final decision to misrepresent Kurtz's final words to his fiancée reconciles literal lie with essential truth, and the reconciliation is marked by Marlow's oriental appearance and Buddhist pose, which possibly symbolize his transcendence of occidental dualities.

❧

The great English-language writers of our century have rediscovered myth. It is impossible to imagine the work of Yeats, Eliot, Pound, or Joyce without their pervasive classical, oriental, or Christian archetypes. Oddly, however, myth seems to have disappeared from the work of post-modern authors, although structuralist critics such as Vladimir Propp and Claude Lévi-Straus have been absorbed with elaborate taxonomic analyses of myth. For Robert Scholes the Homeric myth as Joyce assimilates it is entropic: "Each chapter, in fact, is designed to run down when a certain temporal segment of a Dublin day has been covered. Whereupon the next Homeric parallel is activated to provide a diachronic scheme for the following chapter".[4]

While I would concede that most of the chapters of *Ulysses* display manifestations of experiential incompleteness, even that the principal characters find themselves repeatedly falling short of their romantic or heroic imaginings, I am persuaded that their personal sense of failure or frustration is linked, fundamentally, to their largely unrecognized success in working through the manifold and vagrant impressions of experience which beset them to moments of self-discovery that are truly Homeric. *Ulysses* transforms the lives of its main characters into epic roles of which they are largely unaware. The *Odyssey*, for Stephen, Buck, Blazes, Bloom, and Molly, is the unread text, is a controlling myth that ultimately shapes and authenticates their experiences. Of course, *Ulysses* is not a redaction of the *Odyssey*, but Homer's epic is a pervasive and vital imaginative presence in Joyce's fiction, just as the myth of Daedalus is the armature of Stephen's ordeal in *A Portrait of the Artist as a Young Man*. Myth, then, in Joyce, is a secret source of vision on its characters. But is this not so of Odysseus himself—or Telemachus— or Penelope? Homer's characters, like Joyce's, may have intimations of their roles as actors in heroic myths, but most of the time they are as unaware of the mythical and numinous influences on their lives as Joyce's are. Mythic visions, symbolic patterns that we can see as vital to their experiences, they perceive only dimly, infrequently, and obscurely. The *Odyssey*, to be sure, concludes with an elaborate and divine authentication of a complex resolution of issues that guarantees a renewed society. These visions, more or less imposed on Odysseus and accepted reluctantly by him, are dimly reflected in the microcosm of Joyce's Dublin by Bloom, Stephen, and Molly.

In modern literature myth has functioned as a source of self-discovery, especially in Eliot, Joyce, Pound, and Yeats. But the agonistic self-discoveries of their characters have been, in most ways, as obscure to them as the ordeals of their epic forebears. When Odysseus declares himself "sacker of cities" he betrays his ignorance of the role he must ultimately play. If we look for heroes in classical epic who see their identities established by authentications of their self-chosen heroic roles, we may go back to Achilles, the only major epic character to sustain consciously the clear-cut, private burden of a choice between modes of being.

Melville's characters function within subtle and complex mythological determinants or opportunities that they either fail to perceive or perceive wrongly. Dedication to the providential human enterprise saves Ishmael; rejection of it destroys Ahab and the rest of the *Pequod's* crew. Ultimately, the epic ordeal of individuation may be guided by the transpersonal, but in Melville as in Homer, the hero achieves self-discovery largely unaware of the numinous forces that are assisting him. The transcendental, universal status of myth is well described by Lévi-Strauss:

> A remark can be introduced at this point which will help to show the originality of myth in relation to other linguistic phenomena. Myth is the part of the language where the formula *traduttore, traditore* ["translator equals traitor"] reaches its lowest truth value. From that point of view it should be placed in the gamut of linguistic expressions at

the end opposite to that of poetry, in spite of all the claims
that have been made to prove the contrary. Poetry is a kind
of speech which cannot be translated except at the cost of
serious distortions; whereas the mythical value of the myth
is preserved even through the worst translation. Whatever
our ignorance of the language and the culture of the people
where it originates, a myth is still felt as a myth by any
reader anywhere in the world. Its substance does not lie in
its style, its original music, or in its syntax, but in the *story*
which it tells. Myth is language, functioning on an especially high level where meaning succeeds practically at
"taking off" from the linguistic ground on which it keeps on
rolling.[5]

Myth, then, seems in a sense to be extralinguistic to the extent that
its meaning is fundamentally independent of whatever language
happens to be employed in its telling. Furthermore, insofar as its
ultimate meaning is symbolic and irreducible to discursive language it
is a superlinguistic mode. An indication of this extra- or superlinguistic character is the traditional epic poet's anonymity as he yields his
personality and narrative function to the Muse, who alone has the
numinous vision to tell of things beyond the reach of mortal sight.
The epic poet's self-effacing and submissive stance is extremely
important in establishing the universal truth of a story ultimately
freed of any particular linguistic or cultural modes. The kind of
comparative mythology practiced so brilliantly by W. F. Jackson
Knight in *Cumaean Gates*, which reveals the universal occurrence of
cosmogonic mythical motifs where there can be no question of
cultural influence, as in the case of the labyrinths represented at
Cumae and at Malekula in the New Hebrides, is further evidence of
the unique status of this mode.

    With the decline of the Homeric tradition of anonymity, the
pristine and unique status of myth is increasingly threatened by the
author's assertion of his personal authorial function. We find this in
the rejected opening lines of the *Aeneid (Ille ego qui gracilis modula-
tus avena)* and in the intrusion into the narrative of authorial
comments, in contrast to Homer's consistently objective mode.
Virgil's innovations are reformed in *Paradise Lost* by Milton's undeviating dedication of his narrative to Urania or the Holy Spirit; while
Dante, despite the strong personal focus of his *Inferno*, defers to

Virgil and the Holy Spirit in somewhat the same way Homer does to the Muse. When Milton abandons the traditional epic conventions in *Paradise Regain'd*, it is not because he wishes to emphasize his role as poet—as a person he exists only in the first line ("I who erewhile the happy garden sung"), but rather because, in this epic of privation, he seeks a style that is both self-denying and austere and also appropriate to the radical simplicity of the essential truths of Christ's wilderness ordeal, governed by the myth of the Gospels. In somewhat the same way, the ordeal of Stephen in *A Portrait* is governed by the contending myths of institutionalized Catholicism, with its temptations to submit to corrupt values, and the Daedalian myth that helps to liberate him as a man and an artist. In apparent contrast to the linguistic economy of these works, *Ulysses*, in its limitless catalogue of information and experience and its pullulating linguistic versatility, may seem to subvert the implications of its adapted myth, but, in effect, stylistic and structural virtuosity serve rather to emphasize the power of myth to flourish in a medium apparently quite alien from that in which it first grew.

In this context the accessible and relatively coherent and conventional linguistic manner of *The Prelude* succeeds only intermittently in validating the implicit epic claims of the poem, because, as we have seen, it lacks social and cultural coherence and, most of all, because it lacks a controlling myth needed to objectify and give narrative continuity and vision to episodes that cannot transcend the mode of private and personal projections and reflections. It may not be an exaggeration to say that *The Prelude* has no story, and that therefore the growth of the hero's mind has no history. An extreme case of such alienation is Jay Gatz's self-transformation into the platonic idea of himself and the naive heroic myth he invents in his passion to win Daisy, although Gatsby has none of Wordsworth's deep powers of reflection.

In conclusion, it appears from this survey that the loss of myth in works cast in the major mode of epic is a disaster that reflects on our plight in the post-modern world of the twentieth century. Obviously the loss is not merely a literary phenomenon, but it helps to expose the sterile cultural chaos in which we try to live. From the viewpoint of cultural history it seems strange that the great writers of the past century, under the influence of comparative anthropologists and mythographers like Frazer, Murray, Harrison, and Hooke, should have rediscovered archetypal myth and revitalized the poetic

vision with it. Now, after Auden, Yeats, Eliot, Pound, and Joyce, we
seem to have been thrown back to a prevailing mode of lyrical or
autobiographical egotism. My argument moves toward Jung's idea
that "the primitive does not think *consciously*, but that thoughts
appear. The primitive cannot assert that he thinks; it is rather that
'something thinks in him.' "⁶ The "primitive," then, is in somewhat
the position of the Homeric poet in whom the Muse does the
"thinking." To continue Jung's observations:

> The primitive mentality does not *invent* myths, it *experi-
> ences* them. Myths are original revelations of the precon-
> scious psyche, involuntary statements about unconscious
> psychic happenings, and anything but allegories of physical
> processes. Such allegories would be an idle amusement for
> an unscientific intellect.⁷

Jung may be thinking here of the simplistic, reductive allegorism of a
Fulgentius, a Heraclitus, or a Natalis Comes, among those who were
dedicated to the task of reducing the irreducible myth to a simple and
self-evident moral exemplum. The early allegorists of Homer and
Virgil were bent on transforming their myths into mere instances of
virtuous or vicious behavior, in the process disintegrating the power
of the myth. To continue Jung's remarks,

> Myths, on the contrary, have a vital meaning. Not merely do
> they represent, they *are* the psychic life of the primitive
> tribe, which immediately falls to pieces and decays, like a
> man who has lost his soul. A tribe's mythology is its living
> religion, whose loss is always and everywhere, even among
> the civilized, a moral catastrophe. But religion is a vital link
> with psychic processes independent of and beyond con-
> sciousness, in the dark hinterland of the psyche.⁸

In conclusion, I would cite as the most subversive and perverse
recent practitioner of criticism and critical theory, in his systematic
subjugation of story to language, Jacques Lacan, for whom the
human initiation into experience is essentially verbal: "Un enfant se
cogne contre une table et l'on va vous dire que cette expérience lui
apprend le danger des tables. Eh bien, c'est faux. Quand l'enfant
heurte la table, ce n'est pas devant la table qu'il est placé, mais devant
un discours que lui fait immédiatement ses parents. De même pour
chacun de ses gestes. L'enfant est environné, submergé, noyé dans un

immense discours. . . . C'est dans le langage qu'il se développe. Le sujet est constitué par le langage, et non par le contraire."[9]

⤳

If we follow Lacan, the vital element of story in epic, not to mention other modes of fiction, is simply a matter of linguistic conditioning unrelated to any real experience. His perverse theory would give the headsman's final blow to the relation of *res* and *verbum*. As *Le Monde* comments,

> À la suite de Freud qui a montré qu'il y a «*des maladies qui parlent*» et qui nous a fait entendre la vérité de ce qu'elles disent, Lacan va montrer comment le langage perturbé qui fonctionne en dehors du sujet conscient place le sujet en dehors de lui-même; l'homme n'est plus au centre du lui-même dans le discours organisé et clair du conscient; il est dans le discours tout aussi indéchiffrable de l'inconscient; d'où la formule de Lacan: «Je pense où je ne suis pas; je suis où je ne pense pas.»[10]

Pope's pedant in the *Dunciad* puts such a position more elegantly:

> "Since Man from Beast by words is known,
> Words are Man's province, Words we teach alone. . . .
> Plac'd at the door of Learning youth to guide,
> We never suffer it to stand too wide.
> To ask, to guess, to know, as they commence,
> As fancy opens the quick springs of Sense,
> We ply the Memory, we load the brain,
> Bind rebel Wit, and double chain on chain,
> Confine the thought to exercise the breath;
> And keep them in the pale of Words till death."
>
> (IV. 149-160)

It is hard for me to imagine a more perverse conception of language and reality to end this study. If Lacan's school is to influence our approach to literature and experience, our plight is even more alarming than I have sometimes found it in this arbitrary exchange of the established roles of story (or experience) and language.

Notes

Introduction

1. Frank Lentricchia, *After the New Criticism* (Chicago, University of Chicago Press, 1980) pp. 324-25.
2. Joseph Campbell, *The Hero with a Thousand Faces* (Princeton: Princeton University Press, 1968), p. 29.
3. Quoted in ibid.

Chapter 1

1. Homer, *The Iliad*, trans. Robert Fitzgerald (Garden City, N.Y.: Doubleday, 1974), p. 51. This text is used throughout the chapter.
2. Homer, *The Odyssey*, trans. Robert Fitzgerald (Garden City, N.Y.: Doubleday, 1963), p. 3. This text is used throughout the chapter.
3. Frank Budgen, *James Joyce and the Making of "Ulysses"* (Bloomington: University of Indiana Press, 1960), p. 64.
4. Carl G. Jung, *The Collected Works of C. G. Jung*, vol. 9, pt. 2, *Aion: Researches into the Phenomenology of the Self*, Bollingen Series, no. 20 (Princeton: Bollingen, 1968), p. 21.
5. Hugo Grotius, *de Jure Bellis et Pacis* (The Hague, 1624).
6. Douglas Frame, *The Myth of Return in Early Greek Epic* (New Haven: Yale University Press, 1978).
7. James Hillman, "Senex and Puer," *Puer Papers* (Irving, Texas: Spring Publications, 1979).
8. Personal correspondence to author on his essay "The *Odyssey* and the Western World," *Sewanee Review* (1954).
9. *Aeneid* 6.851–53. The Latin text used throughout this book is from Loeb edition, prepared and translated by H. Rushton Fairclough (Cambridge, Mass.: Loeb Classical Library, 1937). All translations are based on this version.

Chapter 2

1. George deForest Lord, *Heroic Mockery: Variations of Epic Themes from Homer to Joyce* (Newark: University of Delaware Press, 1977), pp. 49–53.
2. Michael Putnam, *The Poetry of the "Aeneid"* (Cambridge, Mass.: Harvard University Press, 1965), pp. 87–88.
3. W. F. Jackson Knight, "Cumaean Gates," in *Virgil: Epic and Anthropology* (New York: Barnes & Noble, 1967), pp. 24–41.
4. David Riesman with Reuel Denney and Nathan Glazer, *The Lonely Crowd: A Study of the Changing American Character* (New Haven: Yale University Press, 1950).

5. Putnam, The *Poetry of the "Aeneid,"* p. 134.

6. E. R. Dodds, *The Greeks and the Irrational* (Berkeley: University of California Press, 1951), pp. 13–14.

Chapter 3

1. Erich Auerbach, *Dante: Poet of the Secular World*, trans. Ralph Mannheim (Chicago: University of Chicago Press, 1961), p. 110.

2. Dante Alighieri, *The Inferno*, trans. and ann. John Sinclair (London: Oxford University Press, 1971), 34.21. This text and translation are used throughout the chapter.

3. Francis Ferguson, *Dante's Drama of the Mind* (Princeton: Princeton University Press, 1953), p. 49.

4. John Demaray, *The Invention of Dante's "Commedia"* (New Haven: Yale University Press, 1974), p. 94.

5. Thomas Bergin, *A Diversity of Dante* (New Brunswick, N.J.: Rutgers University Press, 1969), p. 56.

6. Demaray, *The Invention of Dante's "Commedia,"* pp. 104–05.

7. Ibid.

8. Ibid., p. 110.

9. Ibid.

10. Auerbach, *Dante*, p. 142.

11. John Freccero, "Dante's Prologue Scene," *Dante Studies* 84 (1966): 1-25 passim.

12. Among four versions of the line in Chaucer, its employment by the lecherous May in connection with her feelings for young Damyan in *The Merchant's Tale* (line 1986) shows Chaucer's full awareness of its ironic potential.

13. W. H. Auden, "Musée des Beaux Arts".

14. Sinclair, *The Inferno*, p. 118.

15. Ibid., p. 191.

16. Northrop Frye, *Anatomy of Criticism: Four Essays* (Princeton: Princeton University Press, 1957), p. 147.

17. Sinclair, *The Inferno*, p. 191.

18. René Girard, *To Double Business Bound: Essays in Literature, Mimesis, and Anthropology* (Baltimore: Johns Hopkins University Press, 1978), p. 1.

19. Ibid.

20. Ibid., p. 2.

21. Ibid.

22. Ibid., p. 3.

23. Ibid.

24. Ibid., p. 4.

25. Ibid.

26. Ibid., p. 5.

Chapter 4

1. Joseph Campbell, *The Hero with a Thousand Faces* (Princeton: Princeton University Press, 1968), p. 30.

2. Ibid., p. 38.
3. John Milton, *Paradise Regain'd, the Minor Poems, and Samson Agonistes,* ed. Merritt Y. Hughes (New York: Odyssey Press, 1937), 1.217–20. This text of *Paradise Regain'd* is used throughout the chapter.
4. The omission of the *I* suggests that either God or Satan is repressing the full identity of the great *I am,* thus complicating Jesus' problems of self-discovery.
5. Campbell, *Hero,* pp. 77-78.

Chapter 5

1. John Freccero, *Dante: A Collection of Critical Essays* (Englewood Cliffs, N.J.: Prentice-Hall, 1965), p. 5.
2. William Wordsworth, *The Prelude,* ed. Ernest de Selincourt (1805; reprint ed., London: Oxford University Press, 1933), 1. 1–25. This edition is used throughout the book.
3. Geoffrey Hartman, *Wordsworth's Poetry, 1787–1814* (New Haven: Yale University Press, 1964), pp. 228–29.
4. Rudolph Otto, *The Idea of the Holy: An Inquiry into the Non-Technical Factor in the Idea of the Divine and Its Relation to the Rational,* trans. John W. Harvey (London: Oxford University Press, 1950), p. 31.
5. John Hodgson, *Wordsworth's Philosophical Poetry* (Lincoln: University of Nebraska Press, 1980), p. 120.
6. Hartman, *Wordsworth's Poetry,* p. 235.
7. Hodgson, *Wordsworth's Philosophical Poetry,* p. 136.
8. Ibid., pp. 113–14.
9. Ibid., pp. 114–15.
10. Ibid., p. 116.
11. Ibid., p. 120.

Chapter 6

1. George Gordon, Lord Byron, *Don Juan,* ed. Leslie A. Marchand (Boston: Houghton Mifflin, 1958), pp. iv–v. This text is used throughout the chapter, and is cited by canto and stanza.
2. George Ridenour, *The Style of "Don Juan"* (New Haven: Yale University Press, 1961).
3. Ibid., p. 47.
4. Ibid., p. 69.
5. Ibid., p. 92.
6. Michael Cooke, *The Blind Man Traces the Circle: On the Patterns and Philosophy of Byron's Poetry* (New Haven: Yale University Press, 1969), p. 141.
7. Michael Cooke, *Acts of Inclusion: Studies Bearing on an Elementary Theory of Romanticism* (New Haven: Yale University Press, 1979), p. 220.
8. Ibid.
9. Ridenour, *The Style of "Don Juan,"* p. 112.
10. Ibid., p. 110.

11. M. C. Richards, *Centering in Pottery, Poetry, and the Person* (Middletown, Conn.: Wesleyan University Press, 1969).

Chapter 7

1. Herman Melville, *Moby-Dick; or, the Whale,* ed. Charles Feidelson, Jr. (Indianapolis: Bobbs-Merrill, 1964), p. 38. This text is used throughout the chapter.
2. W. H. Auden, "Musée des Beaux Arts."
3. Feidelson, *Moby-Dick,* p. 215n.
4. Edward F. Edinger, *Melville's "Moby-Dick": A Jungian Commentary* (Norfolk, Conn.: New Directions, 1971), p. 59.
5. Ibid., p. 61.
6. Ibid., p. 26.
7. Ibid., p. 28.
8. Ibid., p. 129.
9. Ibid. p. 84.
10. Newton Arvin, *Herman Melville* (New York: Sloane, 1953), p. 47
11. Walter Bezanson, ed., *Clarel* (N.Y.: Hendricks House, 1960).

Chapter 8

1. In a letter to Sir Humphrey Milford written in 1907, Conrad said, "Lately I have had in my hand *Moby Dick.* It struck me as a rather silly rhapsody with whaling for a subject and not a single sincere line in the 3 volumes of it." Quoted from Frederick R. Karl, *Joseph Conrad: The Three Lives. A Biography* (New York: Farrar, Straus and Giroux, 1979), p. 615.
2. Joseph Conrad, *Heart of Darkness and The Secret Sharer* (New York: Signet, 1950), p. 93. This text is used throughout the chapter.
3. Rudolph Otto, *The Idea of the Holy: An Enquiry into the Non-Rational Factor in the Idea of the Divine and Its Relation to the Rational,* trans. John W. Harvey (London: Oxford University Press, 1957), p. 311.
4. Jacques Berthoud, *Joseph Conrad: The Major Phase* (Cambridge: Cambridge University Press, 1978), p. 53.
5. "Eating and Narrative in Conrad," in *Joseph Conrad: A Commemoration,* ed. Norman Sherry (London: Macmillan, 1976), p. 31.
6. Ian Watt, *Conrad in the Nineteenth Century* (Berkeley: University of California Press, 1979), p. 163.
7. Ibid.
8. Ibid., pp. 190-91.

Conclusion

1. C. G. Jung, *Aion: Researches into the Phenomenology of the Self,* Bollingen Series 20 (Princeton: Princeton University Press, 1968) vol. 9 part 2, p. 35.
2. Ibid., p. 169.
3. Ibid., p. 70.
4. Robert Scholes, "*Ulysses.* A Structuralist Perspective." In *Ulysses:*

Fifty Years, ed. Thomas F. Staley (Bloomington: Indiana University Press, 1974), pp. 161-71.

5. Claude Lévi-Strauss, *Structural Anthropology* (New York & London: Basic Books, 1963), p. 210.

5. C. G. Jung, *The Archetypes and the Collective Unconscious*, Bollingen Series 20 (Princeton: Princeton University Press, 1959), vol 9. part 1, p. 153.

7. Ibid., p. 154.

8. Ibid., p. 154.

9. *Le Monde*, May, 1980.

10. Ibid.

Bibliography

Primary Texts

Alighieri, Dante. *The Inferno*. Translated and annotated by John Sinclair. New York: Oxford University Press, 1971.

Conrad, Joseph. *Heart of Darkness and the Secret Sharer*. New York: Signet, 1950.

Gordon, George, Lord Byron. *Don Juan*. Edited by Leslie A. Marchand. Boston: Houghton Mifflin, 1958.

Homer. *The Odyssey*. Edited by W. B. Stanford. 2 vols. London: Macmillan, 1948.

Homer. *The Odyssey*. Translated by Robert Fitzgerald. Garden City: Doubleday, 1974.

Melville, Herman. *Clarel*. Edited by Walter Bezanson. New York: Hendricks House, 1960.

Melville, Herman. *Moby-Dick; or, The Whale*. Edited by Charles Feidelson, Jr. Indianapolis: Bobbs-Merrill, 1964.

Milton, John. *Paradise Regain'd, the Minor Poems, and Samson Agonistes*. Edited by Merritt Y. Hughes. New York: Odyssey Press, 1937.

Virgil. *The Aeneid*. Translated by H. Rushton Fairclough. London: William Heinemann and Cambridge, Mass: Loeb Classical Library, 1937.

Wordsworth, William. *The Prelude*. Edited by Ernest de Selincourt. London, 1805. Reprint. Oxford University Press, 1933.

Secondary Texts

Abrams, M. H. *The Mirror and the Lamp*. New York: Oxford University Press, 1953.

Abrams, M. H. "Structure and Style in the Center Romantic Lyric," in *From Sensibility to Romanticism: Essays Presented to Frederick A. Pottle*, edited by Frederick W. Hilles and Harold Bloom. New York: Oxford University Press, 1965, pp. 527-60.

Almeida, Hermione de. *Byron and Joyce through Homer: "Don Juan" and "Ulysses"* London: Macmillan, 1981.

Arvin, Newton. *Herman Melville.* New York: Sloane, 1953.

Auerbach, Eric. *Dante: Poet of the Secular World.* Translated by Ralph Mannheim. Chicago: University of Chicago Press, 1961.

Baird, James R. *Ishmael: A Study of the Symbolic Mode in Primitivism.* Baltimore: Johns Hopkins University Press, 1956.

Baird, James R. *"Puer Aeternus:* The Figure of Innocence in Melville." *Spring,* 1979, pp. 205-223.

Bergin, Thomas. *A Diversity of Dante.* New Brunswick: Rutgers University Press, 1969.

Berthoud, Jacques. *Joseph Conrad: The Major Phase.* Cambridge: Cambridge University Press, 1978.

Booth, Wayne C. *A Rhetoric of Irony.* Chicago: University of Chicago Press, 1974.

Bowra, C. M. *Heroic Poetry.* London: Macmillan, 1961.

Boyd, Elizabeth French. *Byron's "Don Juan": A Critical Study.* New York: Humanities Press, 1958.

Brandeis, Irma. *The Ladder of Vision: A Study of Dante's "Comedy."* Garden City, N. Y.: Doubleday, 1962.

Brodhead, Richard H. *Hawthorne, Melville, and the Novel.* Chicago: University of Chicago Press, 1973.

Campbell, Joseph. *The Hero with a Thousand Faces.* Princeton: Princeton University Press, 1968.

Campbell, Joseph. *The Masks of God: Occidental Mythology.* New York: Viking Press, 1970.

Cassirer, Ernst. *The Philosophy of Symbolic Forms.* Translated by Ralph Manheim. New Haven: Yale University Press, 1957.

Chase, Richard. *Herman Melville, A Critical Study.* New York: Macmillan, 1949.

Commager, Steele, ed. *Virgil: A Collection of Critical Essays.* Englewood Cliffs, N. J.: Prentice-Hall, 1966.

Conrad, Joseph. *Congo Diary and Other Uncollected Pieces.* Garden City, N. Y.: Doubleday, 1978.

Conti, Natale. *Mythologiae, sive explicationes fabularum, Libri Decem.* Lyons, 1653.

Cooke, Michael G. *Acts of Inclusion: Studies Bearing on an Elementary Theory of Romanticism.* New Haven: Yale University Press, 1979.

Cooke, Michael G. *The Blind Man Traces the Circle: On the Patterns and Philosophy of Byron's Poetry.* New Haven: Yale University Press, 1979.

Cruttwell, R. W. *Virgil's Aeneid at Work.* Oxford: Basil Blackwell, 1946.

Demaray, John. *The Invention of Dante's "Commedia."* New Haven: Yale University Press, 1974.

Dodds, E. R. *The Greeks and the Irrational.* Berkeley: University of California Press, 1951.

Edinger, Edward F. *Ego and Archetype: Individuation and the Religious Function of the Psyche.* New York: G. P. Putnam's Sons for the C. G. Jung Foundation for Analytical Psychology, 1972.

Edinger, Edward F. *Melville's "Moby-Dick": A Jungian Commentary.* Norfolk, Conn.: New Directions, 1971.

Eliade, Mircea. *A History of Religious Ideas.* Vol.1, *From the Stone Age to the Eleusinian Mysteries.* Translated by Willard R. Trask. Chicago: University of Chicago Press, 1978.

Eliot, T. S. "Virgil and the Christian World," in *On Poets and Poetry.* New York: Farrar, Straus and Co., 1957.

Feidelson, Charles, Jr. *Symbolism and American Literature.* Chicago: University of Chicago Press, 1953.

Ferguson, Francis. *Dante's Drama of the Mind.* Princeton: Princeton University Press, 1953.

Finley, M. I. *The World of Odysseus.* Rev. ed. New York: Viking Press, 1978.

Frame, Douglas. *The Myth of Return in Early Greek Epic.* New Haven: Yale University Press, 1978.

Freccero, John, ed. *Dante: A Collection of Critical Essays.* Englewood Cliffs, N. J.: Prentice-Hall, 1965.

Freccero, John. "Dante's Prologue Scene." *Dante Studies.* 84, 1-25.

Freud, Sigmund. *The Ego and the Id.* Standard Edition, Vol. XIX. London: Hogarth Press, 1961.

Frye, Northrop. *Anatomy of Criticism: Four Essays.* Princeton: Princeton University Press, 1957.

Girard, René. *To Double Business Bound: Essays in Literature, Mimesis and Anthropology.* Baltimore: John Hopkins University Press, 1978.

Girard, René. *Violence and the Sacred.* Translated by Patrick Gregory. Baltimore: Johns Hopkins University Press, 1977.

Greene, Thomas. *The Descent from Heaven: A Study in Epic Continuity.* New Haven: Yale University Press, 1963.

Geretti, James. *The Limits of Metaphor: A Study of Melville, Conrad and Faulkner.* Ithaca: Cornell University Press, 1967.

Hartman, Geoffrey. *Wordsworth's Poetry, 1787-1814.* New Haven: Yale University Press, 1964.

Havelock, Eric A. *The Greek Concept of Justice from its Shadow in Homer to its Substance in Plato.* Cambridge, Mass., Harvard University Press, 1978.

Havens, Raymond Dexter. *The Mind of a Poet: A Study of Wordsworth's Thought,* 2 vols., Baltimore: Johns Hopkins University Press, 1941.

Hillman, James. "Puer Wounds and Ulysses' Scar." *Puer Papers.* Irving, Texas: *Spring Publications,* 1979, 100-128.

Hinks, Roger. *Myth and Allegory in Ancient Art.* London: Warburg Institute, 1939.

Hodgson, John. *Wordsworth's Philosophical Poetry.* Lincoln: University of Nebraska Press, 1980.

Johnson, W. R. *Darkness Visible: A Study of Vergil's Aeneid.* Berkeley: University of California Press, 1976.

Jung, Carl G. *Aion: Researches into the Phenomeonology of the Self. The Collected Works of C. G. Jung.* Bollingen Series, vol. 9, pt. 2, no. 20. Princeton: Princeton University Press, 1968.

Jung, Carl G. *The Archetypes and the Collective Unconscious. The Collected Works of C. G. Jung.* Bollingen Series, vol. 9, pt. 1, no. 20. Princeton: Princeton University Press, 1959.

Jung, Carl G. *Mysterium Coinunctionis,* 2nd ed. Translated by R. F. C. Hull. *The Collected Works of C. G. Jung.* Bollingen Series, vol. 14, no. 20. Princeton: Princeton University Press, 1970.

Karl, Frederick R. *Joseph Conrad: The Three Lives. A Biography.* New York: Farrar, Straus and Giroux, 1979.

Kerényi, Carl, *Dionysus: Archetypal Image of Indestructible Life.* Translated by Ralph Manheim. *Archetypal Images in Greek Religion.* vol. 2. Princeton: Princeton University Press, 1976.

Kerényi, Carl. *The Heroes of the Greeks.* Translated by H. J. Rose. London: Thames and Hudson, 1978.

Kerényi, Carl. *Zeus and Hera, Archetypal Image of Father, Husband and Wife. Archetypal Images in Greek Religion.* vol. 5. Princeton: Princeton University Press, 1975.

Kirk, G. S. *Homer and the Epic.* Cambridge University Press, 1965.

Kirk, G. S. *Myth: Its Meaning and Functions in Ancient and Other Cultures.* Cambridge, England: Cambridge University Press and Berkeley: University of California Press, 1970.

Knight, W. F. Jackson. *Many-Minded Homer.* London: Allen and Unwin, 1968.

Knight, W. F. Jackson. *Roman Vergil.* London: Faber and Faber, 1944.

Knight, W. F. Jackson. *Vergil: Epic and Anthropology.* New York: Barnes and Noble, 1967.

Lentricchia, Frank. *After the New Criticism.* Chicago: University of Chicago Press, 1980.

Lévi-Strauss, Claude. *La Pensée sauvage.* Paris: Plon, 1962.

Lévi-Strauss, Claude. *Structural Anthropology.* New York and London: Basic Books, 1963.

Levy, G. R. *The Gate of Horn.* London: Faber and Faber, 1948.

Lewalski, Barbara K. *Milton's Brief Epic: The Genre, Meaning, and Art of "Paradise Regained."* London: Methuen, 1966; Providence: Brown University Press, 1967.

Lord, George deForest. *Heroic Mockery: Variations on Epic Themes from Homer to Joyce.* Newark, Del.: University of Delaware Press, 1977.

Lord, George deForest. *Homeric Renaissance: The "Odyssey" of George Chapman.* London: Chatto and Windus and New Haven: Yale University Press, 1956; Hamden, Conn.: Archon, 1972.

Martz, Louis. *The Paradise Within.* New Haven: Yale University Press, 1964.

Marx, Leo. *The Machine in the Garden: Technology and the Pastoral Ideal in America.* New York: Oxford University Press, 1964.

Matthiessen, F. O. *American Renaissance: Art and Expression in the Age of Emerson and Whitman.* London and New York: Oxford University Press, 1941.

Mazzotta, Giuseppe. *Dante, Poet of the Desert: History and Allegory in the "Divine Comedy."* Princeton: Princeton University Press, 1979.

Merton, Thomas. *Zen and the Birds of Appetite.* Norfolk, Conn.: New Directions, 1968.

Moore, Tom. "Artemis and the Puer," *Puer Papers.* Edited by James Hillman, *Spring,* 1979, 169-204.

Neumann, Erich. *Amor and Psyche*. New York: Pantheon, 1956.

Neumann, Erich. *The Origins and History of Consciousness*. New York: Pantheon, 1954.

Onorato, Richard J. *The Character of the Poet: Wordsworth in "The Prelude."* Princeton: Princeton University Press, 1971.

Otis, Brooks. *Virgil: A Study in Civilized Poetry*. Oxford: Clarendon Press, 1963.

Otto, Rudolph. *The Idea of the Holy: An Inquiry into the Non-Technical Factor in the Idea of the Divine and Its Relation to the Rational*. Translated by John W. Harvey. London: Oxford University Press, 1950.

Otto, Walter. *Dionysus: Myth and Cult*. Translated by Robert B. Palmer. Bloomington: Indiana University Press, 1976.

Pope, Elizabeth, M. *"Paradise Regained": The Tradition and the Poem*. Baltimore: Johns Hopkins University Press, 1947.

Pöschl, Victor. *The Art of Vergil: Image and Symbol in the "Aeneid."* Translated by Gerda Seligson. Ann Arbor: University of Michigan Press, 1962.

Putnam, M. C. J. *The Poetry of the Aeneid*. Cambridge: Harvard University Press, 1965.

Quinn, Kenneth. *Virgil's "Aeneid": A Critical Description*. Ann Arbor: University of Michigan Press, 1968.

Richards, M. C. *Centering in Pottery, Poetry and the Person*. Middletown: Wesleyan University Press, 1969.

Ricks, Christopher. *Milton's Grand Style*. Oxford: Oxford University Press, 1963.

Ridenour, George. *The Style of "Don Juan."* New Haven: Yale University Press, 1960; Hamden, Conn., Archon, 1969.

Riesman, David. *The Lonely Crowd: A Study of the Changing American Character*. New Haven: Yale University Press, 1950.

Roscher, W. H. *Ausführliches Lexikon der Griechischen und Römischen Mythologie*. Leipzig/Stuttgart: Teubner; Hildesheim: Olms, 1965.

Sealts, Merton M. Jr. *Melville's Reading*. Madison: University of Wisconsin Press, 1966.

Seltzer, Leon F. *The Vision of Melville and Conrad: A Comparative Study*. Athens: Ohio University Press, 1970.

Sherry, Norman, ed. *Joseph Conrad: A Commemoration*. London: Macmillan, 1976.

Snell, Bruno. *The Discovery of Mind*. Translated by T. G. Rosenmeyer. New York: Harper Torchbook, 1963.

Sprott, S. Ernest. *Milton's Art of Prosody*. Oxford: Oxford University Press, 1963.

Stanford, W. B., and Luce, J. V. *Quest for Ulysses*. London: Phaidon, 1977.

Stanford, W. B. *The Ulysses Theme*. Oxford: Oxford University Press, 1968.

Stein, Arnold. *Heroic Knowledge*. Minneapolis: University of Minnesota Press, 1957, Hamden, Conn., Archon, 1965.

Taylor, C. H. Jr. *Essays on the "Odyssey."* Bloomington: Indiana University Press, 1963.

Thompson, Lawrence. *Melville's Quarrel with God*. Princeton: Princeton University Press, 1952.

Thorburn, David. *Conrad's Romanticism*. New Haven: Yale University Press, 1974.

Vickery, John B. *The Literary Impact of the Golden Bough*. Princeton: Princeton University Press, 1973.

Vlachos, Georges L. *Les Sociétés politiques Homériques*. Paris, Presses Universitaires de France, 1974.

Vogler, Thomas. *Preludes to Vision: The Epic Venture in Blake, Keats, Wordsworth, and Hart Crane*. Berkeley: University of California Press, 1971.

Watt, Ian. *Conrad in the Nineteenth Century*. Berkeley: University of California Press, 1979.

West, Paul, ed. *Byron: A Collection of Critical Essays*. Englewood Cliffs, N. J.: Prentice-Hall, 1963.

Wind, Edgar. *Pagan Mysteries in the Renaissance*, 2nd edition. London: Faber & Faber, 1968.

Woodhouse, A. S. P. "Theme and Pattern in *Paradise Regained*." *University of Toronto Quarterly*, 25, 1956.

Zoellner, Robert. *The Salt-sea Mastodon: A Reading of Moby-Dick*. Berkeley: University of California Press, 1973.

Index